THE DOUBLE BASS BOOK
© 2021 by Jonas Lohse

First published in Germany 2018

Jonas Lohse Verlag, Nauheimer Str. 12, D-61169 Friedberg
WWW.LOHSE-VERLAG.DE
Cover photo: Fotostudio Rapuzzi per cortesia del MuSa, Salò, Italy
Layout: Jonas Lohse
English Translation: Martin and Maria Wind (WWW.MARTINWIND.COM)
Printed by Graspo Cz, a.s., Pod Šternberkem 324, CZ-76302 Zlín
ISBN 978-3-9822602-1-1

Bibliografische Information der Deutschen Nationalbibliothek: Die Deutsche National-bibliothek verzeichnet diese Publikation in der Deutschen Nationalbibliografie; detaillierte bibliografische Daten sind im Internet über http://dnb.d-nb.de abrufbar.

Jonas Lohse

The Double Bass Book

English translation by Martin and Maria Wind

Foreword by Martin Wind

Martin Wind is a bassist/ composer with a broad stylistic musical back- ground. Born in Flensburg, Germany, he earned a diploma as an orchestra musician at the music con- servatory in Cologne. After winning the third prize at the 1995 Thelonious Monk Bass Competition and the Cognac Hennessy/Blue Note Jazz Search in 1996, he moved to New York City, where he has since worked with a large variety of world renown artists in the fields of jazz, Brazilian music, pop, and film music.

I believe it was sometime in 2019 that I received an intriguing inquiry from Jonas Lohse, a multi-talented jazz bassist, set-up specialist, bass shop owner, publisher, author from Frankfurt, Germany. He was looking for somebody to translate his marvelous textbook *Das Kontrabass-Buch* for a first English edition. I soon realized that the person he was looking for was me! I've been bilingual since moving to New York City in 1996 and have always been interested in our instrument's history, the making of them, as well as the biographies of important orchestra players, soloists, and jazz bassists.

Working on this book turned out to be a gift in so many ways: it helped me keep my sanity by giving me something meaningful to work on during those long COVID lockdown times, and allowed my wife Maria and I to share in a professional engagement (she proofread and corrected my work); in the process I also got to improve my vocabulary and grammar, but most importantly, I LEARNED SO MUCH!

Here are a few fun facts that you will be able to discover over the next 200 + pages: did you know that Domenico Dragonetti traveled to Bonn, Germany from London at the age of 83 years to participate in a performance of Beethoven's 5th Symphony as the principal of 13 bassists, or that Giovanni Bottesini conducted the world premiere of Verdi's "Aida" in Cairo, Egypt in 1871? How about the fact that German makers dominated the global market for simple, inexpensive string instruments for over two centuries, before manufacturers from Japan, Korea and China took the lead in the 1970s? Or that at the beginning of the 19th century a ¾ orchestra bass was being offered in the Sears, Roebuck & Co catalogue for $ 22.85?

I hope that you will enjoy this excursion into the world of the double bass as much as I have! I have gained a much deeper understanding of the craftsmanship that goes into making and setting up instruments. I'm more aware of major technological inventions and the scientific conditions that allow us to experience sound. But most of all, I learned to appreciate even more the wonderful community of bassists that have helped lead the way and elevate our instrument to unknown heights. Now fasten your seatbelts and enjoy the ride!

Martin Wind
Teaneck, New Jersey, June 2021

photo: Olff Appold

Foreword by Rufus Reid

Mr. Jonas Lohse has gathered an incredibly detailed information about the beginnings and development of our beloved instrument, the double bass. He has made this 240 page book extremely interesting and accessible to learn of the origins and the history of the double bass by utilizing detailed graphics, illustrations, and beautiful photographs throughout the book. The information gathered here is very engaging from the novice to the most astute professional luthier.

There is information about how the bridges are constructed and used. There are beautiful portraits of the various significant styles of beautiful instruments from around the world. There are fingerboard charts, glossaries, and illustrations with the various sizes and measurements used to construct the instrument. There is also a section that discusses and illustrates the origins of the bass guitar. There is also unique information never discussed in other books about the various types of music, both European classical, Jazz, and music from around the globe performed on the double bass.

Mr. Lohse's *The Double Bass Book* is a fantastic and most impressive labor of love with articulate precision. It will be a beautiful addition to any library. Thank you.

Rufus Reid
Jazz Bassist/Composer

Rufus Reid and his Josef Reiger bass (made ca. 1805 at Mittenwald/Germany)

photo: John Abbott

Table of contents

The history of the Double Bass at a glance

Bassist Slam Stewart, 1948

At the centre of Renaissance music (15th and 16th centuries) is polyphonic vocal music. The most common domestic instrument of this period was the lute, and organs were used in churches. In addition to the further development of the musical instruments of the Middle Ages, many new instrument families are emerging in modern Europe: woodwind, brass and string instruments are now being built in staggered vocal registers (soprano/discant, alto, tenor and bass) in the style of the vocal quartet.

First stringed instruments in bass or contra-bass register can be found in the family of the viols. Gambas originated at the end of the 15th century and were popular in the Renaissance and the Baroque era. They typically have five or six strings, are fretted and are tuned in fourths or thirds and fourths. They were made in different sizes and registers: treble, alto, tenor, bass and contra bass. A viola da gamba in bass register will be also referred to as the violone, and places at the disposal of the bridge instrument to the double bass.

While double bass making in Germany was based on the gamba, and double basses were made with sloping shoulders, flat backs and blunt corners, in Italy the round back and pointed corners also adopted typical characteristics of the newly formed violin family.

6-string viola da gamba, 1563 by Hanns Vogel, Nuremberg/Germany

▶ **Andrea Amati**
luthier, Cremona/Italy
*1505 †1577
Progenitor of violin making in Cremona. Amati belongs to the first generation of violin makers who used the basic shapes and sizes that are still used today for their violins, violas and cellos.

1500

Ottaviano dei Petrucci (*1466 †1539), Italian letterpress printer and music publisher from Venice. In 1498, he invented the printing of music by moving metal types. His collection of masses, the „Harmonice Musices Odhecaton A" (1501), was the first polyphonic music to be printed.

1550

painting by
Evaristo Baschenis
(*1617 †1677)

▶ **Gasparo (Bertolotti) da Salò**
luthier, Brescia/Italy
*1542 †1609

▶ **Giovanni Paolo Maggini**
luthier, Brescia/Italy
*1580 †1632

▶ **Nicolo Amati**
luthier, Cremona/Italy
*1596 †1684

The invention of gut strings wound
with metal wire made it possible to
produce strings in thinner diameters
and thus to improve the playability of
the low stringed instruments.

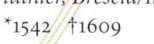

1600

▶ **Venturo Linarol**
luthier, Venice, Padua/Italy
Violone da Gamba, 1585,
tuned E-A-D-G-C-F

"Gross Contra-Bass-Geig"
with five strings, mentioned by
Michael Praetorius in "Syntagma
Musicum" 1619

1650

The music of the 17th and early 18th century, the Baroque, is characterized by the basso continuo and monody (solo voice or solo instrumental voice with accompaniment). While instrumental music was previously strictly coupled to singing, it emancipated itself in the Baroque. Innovations in instrument making, the printing of notation and composition commissions from the aristocracy and bourgeoisie gave impulses to music. New genres such as opera and the instrumental concerto are created, and forms such as the fugue, suite, cantata and oratorio emerge.

painting by british artist
Peter Lely (*1618 †1680)

1661 – in a document
signed by Nicolo Amati
on the purchase of an
instrument, the term
"contrabasso" is used
for the first time to distinguish it from "viola
da gamba" (Cremona
City Archive)

► **Matthias Klotz**
luthier, Mittenwald/Germany
*1653 †1743
In 1684 Matthias Klotz returned from Italy
to Mittenwald and founded the violin
making tradition in his home town.

► **Matteo Gofriller**
luthier, Venice/Italy
*1670 †1742

► **Carlo Giuseppe Testore**
luthier, Milano/Italy
worked aprox. 1685–1735

► **Antonio Stradivari**
luthier, Cremona/Italy
*1644 †1737
Considered the most important and influential violin maker. However, any double
basses from his workshop are unknown.

1663 – first use of double basses
in a symphony orchestra (Paris)

1700

first mention of violin makers in
Markneukirchen (Germany) and
Mirecourt (France)

1700 – first use of double basses
in the Italian opera

The epoch of the Classicism is divided into the Pre-Classical (ca. 1730—1770) and Viennese Classicism (ca. 1770—1830). In the early classical period, instead of the polyphonic interweaving of independent voices, the melody becomes the distinctive carrier of expression. The linear compositional technique is replaced by a vertical one (formation of harmony instead of counterpoint). In the Viennese Classical period (ca. 1780—1830) the strict polyphony of the Baroque is finally broken up; the compositions have simpler harmonies but are rich in contrasts: they make increased use of extreme changes in tempo and dynamics and surprising sound effects.

▶ **Carl Ludwig Bachmann**
luthier, Berlin/Germany
*1743 †1809
Bachmann applied for a patent for the double bass machine heads in 1778.

▶ **Johannes Matthias Sperger**
double bassist and composer
*1750 †1812

▶ **August Carl Ditters von Dittersdorf**
Violinist and composer of double bass concertos
*1739 †1799

▶ **Domenico Dragonetti**
double bassist
*1763 †1846

▶ **Giovanni Baptisti Ceruti**
luthier, Cremona/Italy
*1756 †1817

1808 – G. Andreoli teaches the four-string double bass for the first time at the Milan Conservatory.

▶ **Johann Joseph Stadelmann**
luthier, Vienna/Austria
*1720 †1781

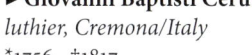
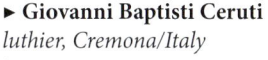

▶ **Vincenzo Panormo**
italian luthier, worked from 1790 to †1813 in London/England

▶ **François Xavier Tourte**
bow maker, Paris/France
*1747 †1835
Tourte developed the basic form of today's bow and is considered the "Stradivarius of the bow".

In the time of Viennese Classicism, the Viennese tuning F-A-D-F#-A was predominant in Germany and Austria. Mozart, Haydn, Dittersdorf and Sperger wrote their bass parts in this tuning.

1800

1750

In the music of the Romantic period (19th to early 20th century) the classical forms were dissolved and the traditional harmonies were expanded. Characteristic is also the emphasis on emotional expression and the combination of music with extra-musical, often literary themes (programme music). In the 19th century, orchestral instrumentation was repeatedly expanded and varied to enable new sound effects (e.g. octobass).

1881 – Double bassist and luthier Carl Otho from Leipzig/Germany applies for a patent for the five-string double bass in C-E-A-D-G.

Fingerboard extensions for the E-string are launched in 1885 by Karl Pittrich (Hofkapelle Dresden), and in 1897 Max Poike and Ludwig Glaesel jr. (Markneukirchen/Germany)

► **Giovanni Bottesini**
double bassist, conductor and composer
*1821 †1889
Bottesini played a three-string, as was popular at the time for the solo bass.

► **Alexander H. Pöllmann**
luthier, Saxony
(today: Mittenwald, Germany)
Foundation of workshop in 1888

► **Bernhard Fendt**
luthier, London/England
*1755 †1832

► **Charles Nicolas Eugène Gand**
luthier, Paris/France
*1825 †1892

► **Joseph Rubner**
luthier, Markneukirchen/ Germany
Foundation of workshop in the late 19th century

► **Ernest Auguste Bernandel**
luthier, Mirecourt/France
*1826 †1899

► **Jean Baptiste Vuillaume**
luthier, Mirecourt + Paris/France
*1798 †1875
most important violin maker of his time; made double basses as well as four octobasses

► **Franz Simandl**
double bassist, Czech/Austria
*1840 †1912
Author of the Simandl method, which is still in use today

► **William Tarr**
luthier, Manchester/England
*1808 †1891

Baß-Bogen.

Butler- oder Leipziger Muster.

Deutsches Muster.

Bottesini- oder franz. Muster.

Dragonetti- oder engl. Muster.

► **John Frederick Lott**
luthier, London/England
*1775 †1853

Until at the beginning of the 20th century the German and the French bow became established, a variety of bow models were common.

► **Abraham Prescott**
luthier, New Hampshire/U.S.A.
The first American violin maker; starts making bass in 1819

1858 – The Bavarian state founds a violin making school in Mittenwald

The tuning E-A-D-G becomes the standard tuning

1850

► **Serge Alexandrovich Koussevitzky**
double bassist, conductor and composer;
Russia/U.S.A.
*1874 †1951
Probably the first double bass player
who was recorded

► **Charles Quenoil**
luthier Paris/France
*1878 †1955

► **Emanuel Wilfer**
luthier, Bohemia (today:
Bubenreuth/Germany)
Foundation of workshop
in 1905

► **George Murphy "Pops" Foster**
Jazz double bassist
*1892 †1969

► **Gary Karr**
double bassist, U.S.A.
*1941
founder of the International
Society of Bassists (1967)

The first pickups and amplifiers
for double bass become available

1945 – the instrument makers based in
Egerland/Bohemia are expelled from their
homeland after the Second World War
and resettle in Mittenwald (Bavaria),
Nauheim (Hesse) and for the most part
around Erlangen/Bubenreuth (Franconia)

1946 – Jazz guitarist George van Eps
applies for a patent for the height-
adjustable double bass bridge.

► **Jimmy Blanton**
Jazz double bassist
*1918 †1942
The father of
modern Jazz bass

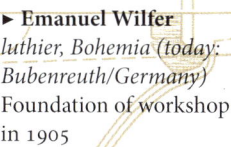

1901 – Augustus Stroh launches his
"Stroh Bass" with metal
resonator instead of acoustic body

1942 – Bob Haggart releases the
first method for jazz double bass.

1900

1936 – Rickenbacker launches an
Electric Upright Bass and amp

1950

Steel strings are becoming
increasingly popular and
are more and more replacing
gut strings

NACH DER MVSIC GEIGEN WIR DREI ·
GANTZ KVNSTLICH VND ARTLICH DABEI

The history of the double bass

400 years of low notes –
The history of the Double Bass

The names "double bass" and "contrabass" refer to the instrument's range and use in the contra octave. Other terms for the instrument are "string bass" (to distinguish it from brass bass instruments such as tubas), "upright bass" or simply "bass".

The first double bass instruments already existed in the 16th century—but the question of how old the double bass (as we know it today) actually is cannot be answered that easily. Historical sources, especially illustrations, are often imprecise and do not reliably document important details. Historical instruments are rarely preserved in their original condition and therefore only provide conditional information. Above all, the very definition of the double bass is not quite simple.

While the violin and cello have remained largely unchanged in form, size and tuning since the mid-16th century, the development of the double bass continued well into the 20th century. Only in the middle of the 18th century did the double bass join its already long-established string family members, the violin and cello, as a regular orchestral instrument. And to this day, different preferences and schools exist throughout the world: five-string or four-string with fingerboard extension, German or French bow, orchestra tuning, solo tuning, fifth tuning—not to mention different fingering methods.

Historical string instruments, second volume of "Syntagma musicum" by Michael Prätorius, 1619

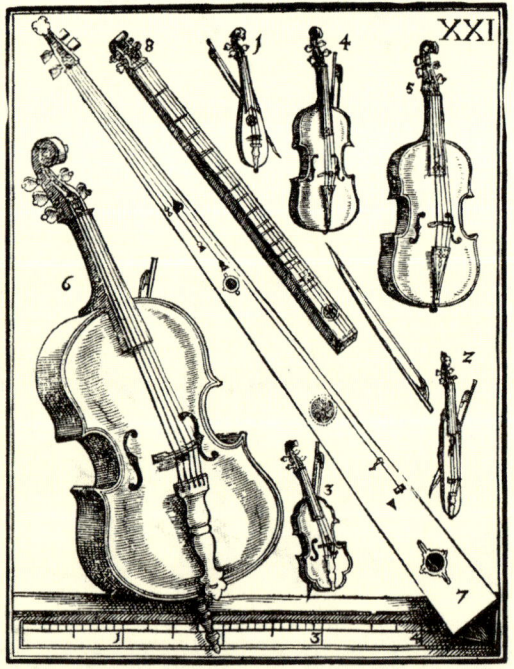

1. 2. 3. Violn de Gamba. 4. Viol Baſtarda. 5. Italianiſche. Lyra de bracio

1. 2. Kleine Poſchen / Geigen ein Octav höher. 3. Diſcant-Geig ein Quart höher.
4. Rechte Diſcant-Geig. 5. Tenor-Geig. 6 Baſ-Geig de bracio. 7. Trumſcheidt.
8. Scheidtholtt.

Despite, or maybe as a result of these variations and different approaches, the degree of organization of double bass players is broad in scope. It manifests itself in the existence of the *International Society of Bassists (ISB)*, the *European Society of Bassists*, annual international conferences (conventions), competitions and other meetings of the bass scene.

With its string length exceeding one meter, the double bass is the largest and deepest-sounding member of the violin instrument family. Considering its origin, it occupies a special position. The first precursors of today's double bass can be found in the viola da gamba family (viols) towards the end of the 16th century. So genealogically, it belongs to the viola da gamba family, but also contains numerous characteristics of the viola da braccio.

As both are bowed string instruments, violas da gamba and violins appear to be quite similar at first glance, but differ in decisive characteristics. Gambas are held between the knees for playing, which led to them also being called knee violins. They usually had frets of gut strings tied around the neck and fingerboard. Gambas existed in a multitude of variations, differing in tuning, scale and number of strings. In general, however, they were equipped with six strings tuned in fourths. Over the centuries they were replaced by the violin, viola and cello, and today are merely of historical significance. Some construction characteristics of

6-string bass viol by Ventura Linarol, with frets and 72 cm string length

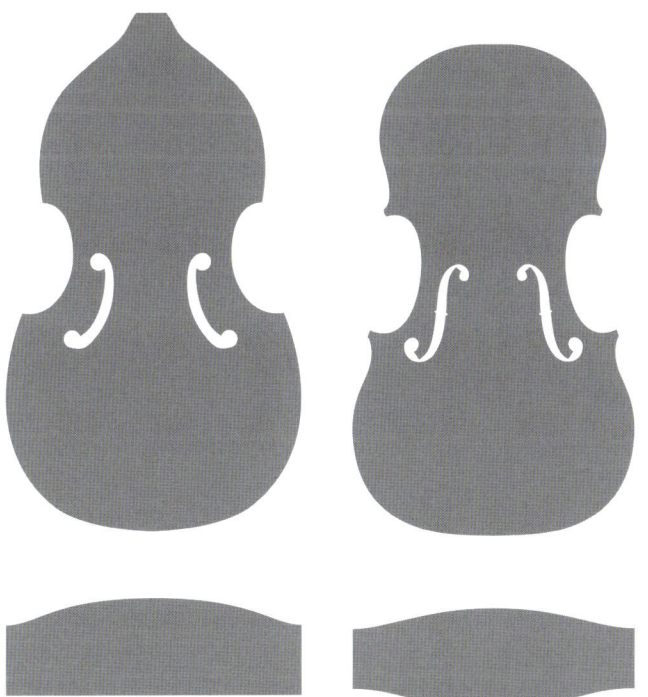

Gamba (Viola-da-gamba family) and Violins (viola-da-braccio family) in a schematic overview (front and cross section): typical for viols are sloping shoulders, blunt corners in the middle bout and the flat back.

the viol have been preserved in the design of the double bass to this day: the sloping shoulders, the canted flat back, the tuning in fourths, and the German style bow held from below. In addition to gamba-shaped instruments, Italian makers started building basses that imitated the contours of a violin at around 1600. They did not have flat backs but carved ones, and the typical violin-like pointed ribs in the middle bout.

Another milestone in the development of the double bass was the introduction of wound gut strings in 1650. This new manufacturing method made smaller string diameters possible, which resulted in improved playability. The instruments no longer had to be of such monstrous sizes in order to achieve the desired range in depth.

Double bass by Gasparo da Salò, around 1570. The instrument is now on display at the museum of the city of Salò.

Several early double bass instruments from the workshop of the Venetian instrument maker Ventura Linarol (*1540 †1604) have been preserved. This 6-string viol from the Germanisches National-museum in Nuremberg dates from 1604 and has a string length of 73 cm. A Linarol bass with a 107.5 cm scale dated 1585 is now exhibited at the Kunsthistorisches Museum in Vienna.

photos: Photostudio Rapuzzi per cortesia del MuSa; Günther Kühnel/Germanisches Nationalmuseum Nürnberg

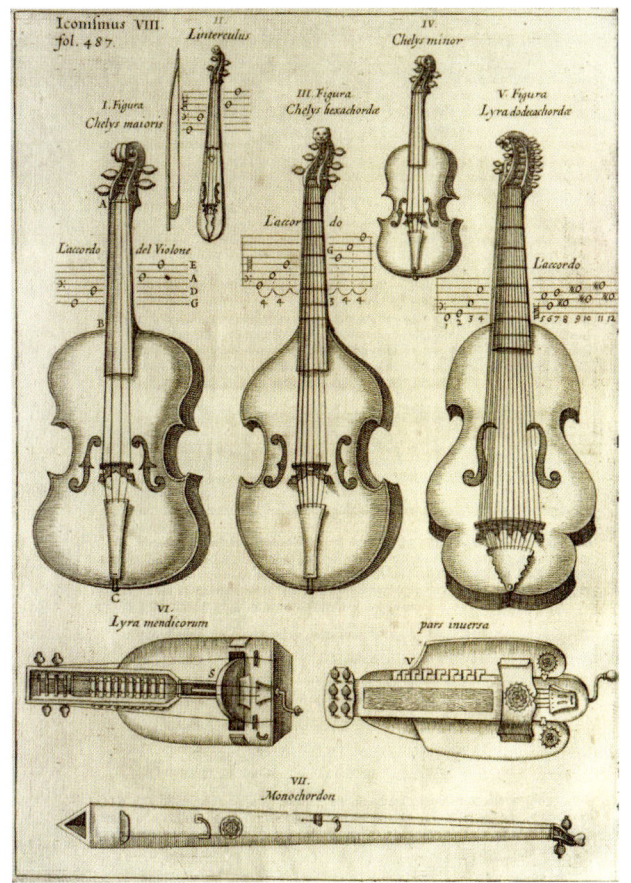

"Musurgia universalis" (Rome 1650), the baroque encyclopedia of the music of the Jesuit priest Athanasius Kircher, who taught in Rome, is one of the main music-historical sources of the 17th century. The forms and tunings of these string instruments varied significantly at that time.

This 6-string viola da gamba by Nuremberg violin maker Hanns Vogel is one of the oldest preserved double bass instruments. It dates from the year 1563.
The resonating string length is 94 cm, which corresponds to today's ½ sized bass. The constrictions in the upper and lower bout give the instrument its distinctive shape.

Michel Corrette: Method pour Apprendre a Jouer de la Contre-basse, Paris 1781. The instrument pictured has a gamba form and is fretted, but already has the forth tuning.

"The double bass, or violone as it is called in Italy, is an octave lower than the cello. (...) The body and finger-board are almost twice as large as the cello, as are the strings. (...) The double bass is usually tuned with four strings in fourths Sol (G), Re (D), La (A), Mi (E), which corresponds to the inversion of the viola; there are also musicians who use five strings or only three. But four strings are the most common. (...) Those who already play the cello soon learned to play the double bass."

De l'étenduë de la Contre basse a 4 Cordes

L'étenduë de la contre basse montée à 4 cordes est de 13 Sons Naturel sans demancher.

Quand on ne veut point demancher pour faire le Re, d'en haut B, on le fait sur la 2ᵉ corde a vuide C et le Re, d'en bas D, ne pouvant pas se faire sur la 4ᵉ corde on le transporte aussi sur la 2ᵉ corde C, a l'egard de l'ut d'en bas E qui n'est pas faisable non plus sur la 4ᵉ corde on le prend sur la 3ᵉ corde F.

Tunings

While frets disappeared completely as early as 1800, it took until the 1920s for the four-stringed double bass with today's usual tuning E-A-D-G, the so-called orchestral tuning, to fully assert itself. It was first mentioned by B. Bismantova in 1694.

Until the beginning of the 20th century, many basses had only three strings, and several older basses that have survived to this day have been converted from three to four strings. In addition to orchestra tuning, solo tuning (F♯-B-E-A) is also common today. This scordatura (retuning) appears a whole tone higher than orchestral tuning. Introduced by virtuoso Giovanni Bottisini it has become standard in the solo literature of classical music since the middle of the 19th century. With it, the double bass becomes a transposing instrument in D: the voice is notated in C, but it sounds a whole tone higher.

Numerous works from the Viennese Classical period have been passed down, originally written for five-stringed, fretted double bass in third-quarter tuning, the so-called Viennese tuning (F-A-D-F♯-A, or four-stringed A-D-F♯-A). Among others, Carl Ditters von Dittersdorf, Johann Matthias Sperger, Johann Baptist Vanhal, Michael Haydn and Wolfgang Amadeus Mozart wrote solo concertos and chamber music for double bass during this period. The sound ideal was based on an open, resonant sound with frequent use of empty strings and harmonics—for which this open triad tuning was ideally suited. However, this approach only works in certain keys—others are difficult or practically impossible to play. Due to this limited range of application, Viennese tuning today is only significant for historical performance practice.

The "Freerange Xtender" from Hipshot is mounted to the tailpiece and allows you to tune the string down by a preset interval using a lever.

The advantage of the fingerboard extension and the contra- and C-mechanism is that it can be mounted on almost any four-stringed double bass to extend the lower range.

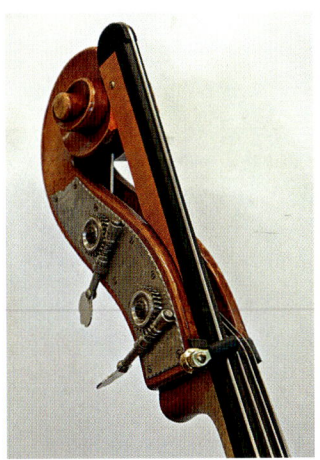

In order to extend the range, basses might be equipped with five strings—a low string tuned to C or B or (more rarely) a high C string. Due to the higher string tension and the greater mass of the bridge, the response and sound of the instrument often suffers. In addition, the strings are closer together, which makes playing more difficult for both the left and right hand. These disadvantages resulted in the appearance of fingerboard extensions around 1890. German instrument makers Karl Pittrich (Dresden), G. A. Buschmann and Max Poike (Berlin) were the first ones to develop a design that increased the vibrating string length by extending the string beyond the upper saddle to the scroll. This resulted in the extension of the tonal range down to a low C, while the tone E was now being played at the level of the saddle. Some of these extensions are additionally equipped with a mechanism for temporarily holding a particular note. While fingerboard extensions are very common in the U.S.A. and England, five-string basses are still preferred in German orchestras today.

Some bassists revived the tuning in fifths (C-G-D-A) for the double bass in the middle of the 20th century. One advantage of fifths tuning is the larger range, which makes fingerboard extensions or solo tuning unnecessary. The American jazz bassist Red Mitchell was one of the first to explore this tuning option. He experimented with a cello tuned in fourths and noticed that the sound worsened compared to the fifths tuning. He applied his observation to the double bass, tuned it in fifths and was so enthusiastic about the open, resonant sound of the instrument that he immediately changed his technique. In addition, the new tuning gave him access to the contra C without the use of a fifth string or any complicated mechanics.

Contrebasse .

Portrait of a double bass player, Paris 1782

Several notations have become established for marking the octave spaces (see page 60). The Scientific Pitch Notation, which is also often used in music software, has become generally accepted: from Co in the sub-contra octave range, which is just audible at 16.35 Hz, a line is added upwards from the lower octave to the upper octave (C1, C2). In German Helmholtz Notation, the notes of the lower octaves are designated by capital letters (C), those of the higher octaves by small letters (c); for each higher or lower octave a dash is added (,C/c").

The double bass player, composer and conductor Gustav Laska (*1847 †1928) was not really enthusiastic about the five string:

"As for five-stringed basses, I am a determined opponent of them. The gentlemen who prefer them, almost all of them bandleaders, only think of the low notes that the four-stringed bass lacks, but not of the immense difficulties associated with playing the five-stringed bass. I yet have to find the double bass player who prefers to play the five stringed monster. The condemned always complain about the wide fingerboard and the necessary stretching of the left hand in order to get a good and tight grip of the C string. How exhausting and tiring that is, ordinary mortals don't know anything about it! Aditionally, the three middle strings, D, A and E, cannot be struck powerfully out of caution not to strike the neighbouring strings. All passages on the 'thick neck' are difficult to execute."

Among classical musicians, Joël Quarrington, the principal bassist of the Toronto Symphony, was one of the first to switch to fifths tuning. He writes about his experiences with it: "The physics are different when you tune in fifths because you are in the same groove as the rest of the string section. The bass in fourths is impossible to tune—if you make the fourths perfect, your low strings will be too flat and of course will not relate to the open strings of the other instruments, just because it's turned upside down."

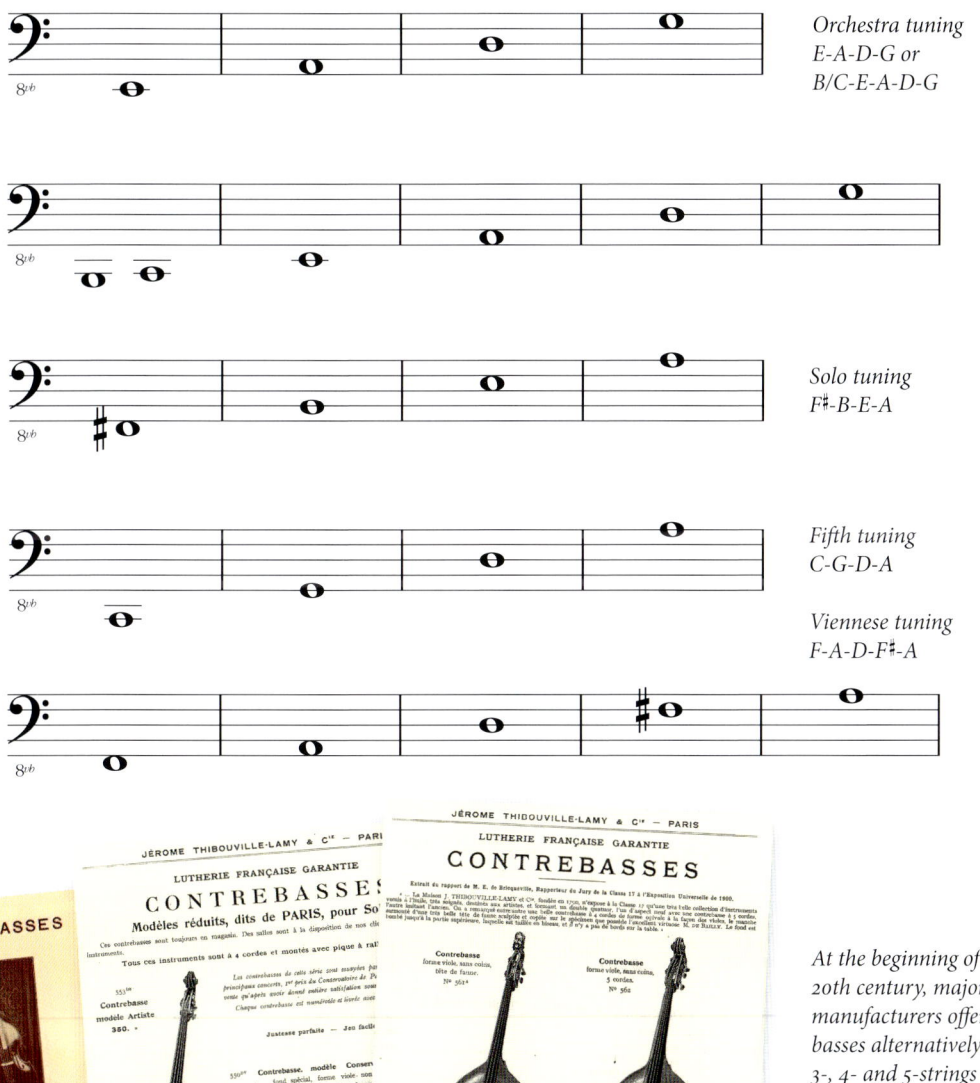

Orchestra tuning
E-A-D-G or
B/C-E-A-D-G

Solo tuning
F♯-B-E-A

Fifth tuning
C-G-D-A

Viennese tuning
F-A-D-F♯-A

At the beginning of the 20th century, major manufacturers offered basses alternatively as 3-, 4- and 5-strings (fig.: Jerôme Thibouville-Lamy and Laberte-Humbert, Mirecourt/France; 1912)

Shapes

Compared to other string instruments, the double bass has the greatest variety of forms. Although many bass builders do copy proven designs of old masters, sizes and proportions are less standardized than for violins or cellos.

To this day, both the violin and viola da gamba forms have been preserved as the most common corpus forms. In addition, there are variations such as the Busetto form, or more rarely, the pear or guitar form. After the Second World War some German manufacturers produced basses with a cutaway in order to make the higher register more accessible, as with jazz guitars. Regardless of the body shape, basses either have the flat back coming from the viola da gamba or the curved back typical for the violin. Both have advantages and disadvantages, which is why neither type has been able to establish itself as the standard. But while differences in body shape tend to be a matter of taste, curved versus flat backs affect stability,

manufacturing effort and sound. A curved back is more stable than a flat one simply because of the curvature. Therefore, flat backs are additionally reinforced with three or four transverse beams, in some cases also with X-shaped crossed beams. In manual production, a carved back is much more time-consuming and material-intensive than a flat one. From the same amount of wood that is needed for a carved back, several flat bottoms can be produced in less time. In industrial production, however, the round back has advantages: since it is routed by machine and does not require reinforcement by bracing, most factory basses (and almost all plywood basses) have round backs.

Due to their static properties, round backs are less sensitive to humidity. Flat backs are said to have specific sound properties: their sound is commonly characterized as more focused, more direct and richer in overtones, while round backs are considered rounder and fuller in sound.

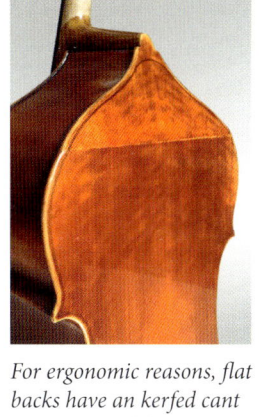

For ergonomic reasons, flat backs have an kerfed cant in the back table.

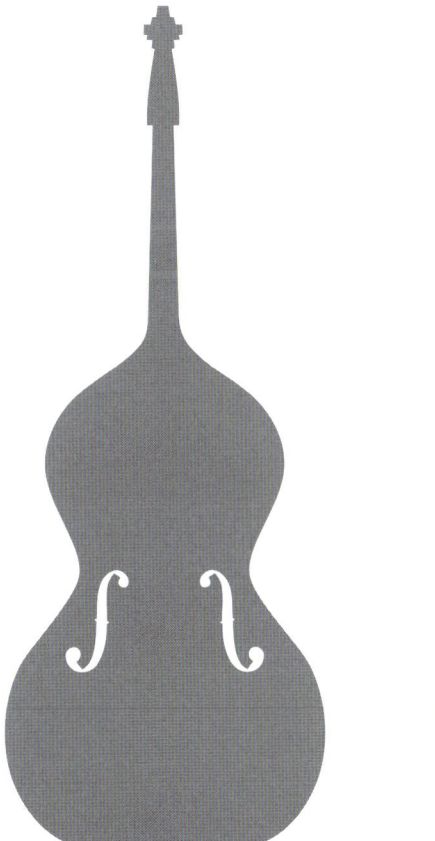

From left to right: gamba form, violin form, busetto, guitar or pear shape, gamba with cutaway (1950s).

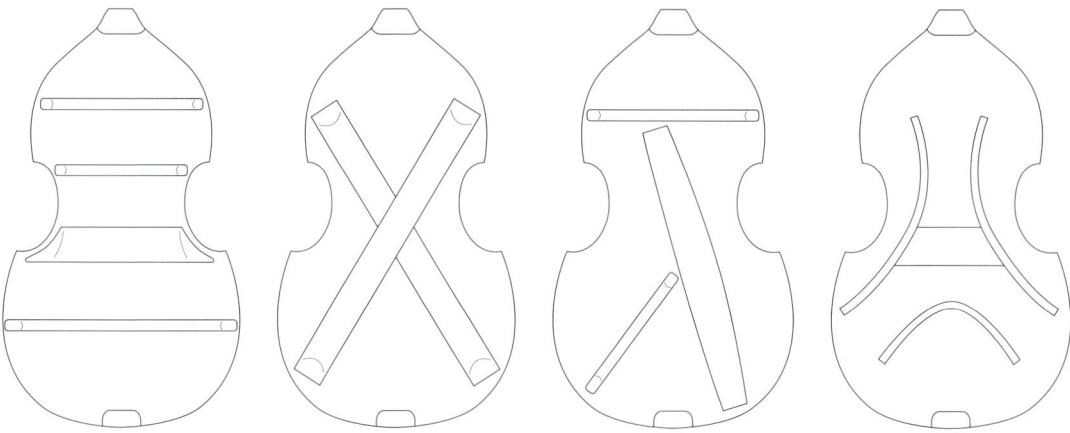

In contrast to the swelled back, flat backs need glued-on bars for reinforcement. Several parallel beams of spruce wood are common (Fig. left), but they can cause the back to sink in in the long term. Flat backs with X- or cross bars (middle left) or asymmetrical beams are less susceptible to sinking in. The figure on the right shows an innovative bracing by Australian luthier Matthew Tucker, made of curved, laminated spruce.

An elaborate decoration that is inlaid into the back is called a "flower".

In contrast to violins, violas and cellos, double basses only have a few uniformed, standardized measures due to their different shapes and proportions. Dimensions are generally expressed in fractions such as ⁴⁄₄, ⅞, ¾, ⅝, and ½. Depending on the manufacturer and model, however, these sizes vary. Today, ¾ basses with a vibrating string length (scale) of 104 cm to 106 cm are the most common. Scales with 110 cm or more are difficult to play and have become unpopular. Meanwhile many new ⁴⁄₄ basses are designed with more comfortable scales of less than 110 cm, and differ in width and length from the body of a ¾ model. Such large basses with a ¾ scale are often referred to as an intermediate size ⅞. Small ½, ¼ and ⅛ basses with scales of about 96 cm, 90 cm or 78 cm are usually built as student instruments and are not used in orchestras.

In addition to size and scale, the neck-body joint is an important feature of a bass. If the middle finger of the left hand, opposite the thumb "snapped in" at the neck heel, grasps a D on the G-string, one speaks of a D-neck; if that note is an E-flat, it is determined as an E-flat neck.

In 1903, violin maker Otto Roth (*1876 †1954) from Markneukirchen built a double bass with monstrous dimensions: total length 4.20 m, body 2.10 m, weight 70 kg. The bridge measured 34 cm, the tailpiece 70 cm. Due to its size, it could only be moved out of the workshop through the window. The bass was commissioned by the Chicago Opera Orchestra—but it is unknown whether it was ever used there. It is possible that the bass in the photo on the following page, taken in the U.S.A., is this "monster bass" by Otto Roth.

BIGGEST VIOLIN   5750-12

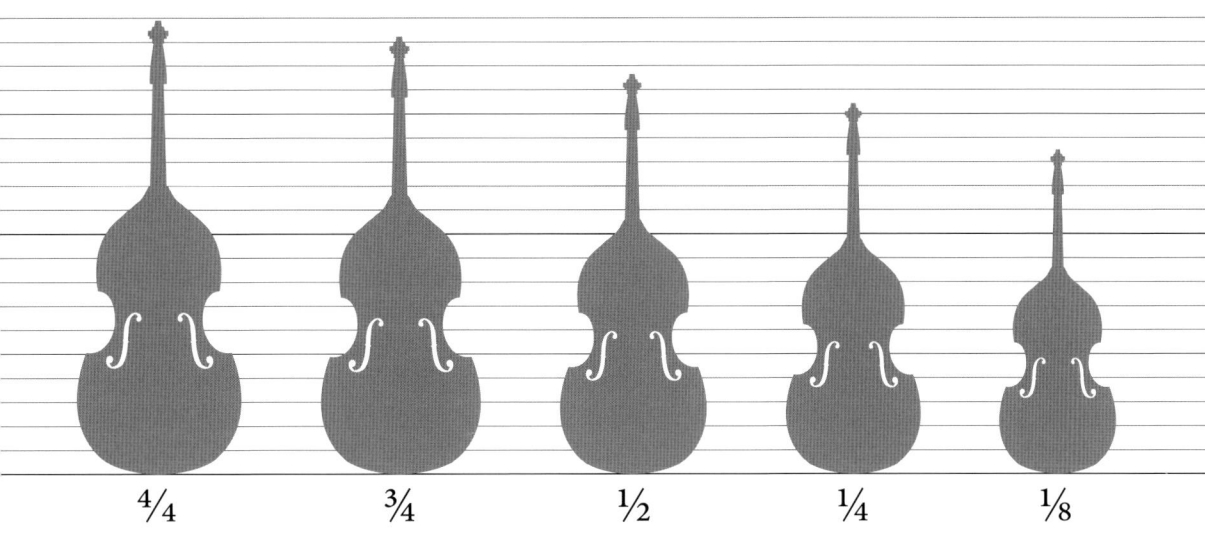

The vibrating string length between nut and bridge is called the scale of a bass. Depending on the manufacturer and model, there may be considerable deviations—the values given in the table are therefore approximate. The length of the body corresponds to approximately 105 % of the string length for all sizes.

Double bass sizes in comparison: half a double bass (½) is not half the size of a full size instrument (4/4).

size	vibraing string length	total length	body length	width (lower bout)
4/4	109 cm	190 cm	116 cm	70 cm
7/8	107 cm	190 cm	116 cm	70 cm
3/4	105 cm	182 cm	111 cm	68 cm
½	96 cm	168 cm	102 cm	60 cm
¼	90 cm	156 cm	95 cm	55 cm
⅛	78 cm	136 cm	62 cm	49 cm

In contrast to oversized basses, small basses have experienced a real boom in recent years. ¹⁄₁₆ basses (also called ¹⁄₁₀; scale 69–74 cm) or even ¹⁄₃₂ basses (60 cm) are used to teach elementary school students. These sizes correspond approximately to those of ¼ or ¾ cellos.

Bow sizes (German bow)

size	stick	total length	hair length
4/4	72 cm	77.5 cm	58 cm
3/4	69 cm	74.5 cm	55 cm
½	66 cm	70.5 cm	52 cm
¼	63 cm	67.5 cm	49 cm
⅛	60 cm	64.5 cm	46 cm

photo: David Angelovich

33

With a size of about three and a half meters and a weight of about 100 kg, the octobass cannot be played like a double bass. Instead of tapping the notes with the fingers, it is operated with seven lateral folding levers. With a tuning of C2–G2–C1, the octobass covers not only the 16' octave from contra-G down to contra-C, but also the 32' octave below in the sub-contra range.

The violin maker J. B. Vuillaume built three instruments: one was sold to London in 1851 and was later destroyed in a fire. A second can be seen today in the Cité de la musique in Paris (Fig. right), and a third was sold to St. Petersburg and is exhibited today in the archive of the Musikverein Wien (Austria). But the octobass remained a curiosity. Even though some composers took it into account in their works, handling and transportation were probably too complicated.

A replica of the octobass can also be seen in the Musical Instrument Museum in Phoenix, Arizona/U.S.A. Another instrument is owned by the Montreal Symphony Orchestra/ Canada (Fig. left). The German luthier Wolfgang Staab built several copies as well.

Tonewoods

The quality of woods used for the double bass—spruce for the top, maple for the sides, back and neck—is determined by both optical and physical (acoustic) properties. A spruce top should be fine-ringed, straight-grained and preferably free of knotholes and other irregularities—something that even the layman can see with the naked eye. However, in order to judge the elasticity and speed of sound and thus the tonal properties of the resonating wood, the instrument maker needs experience.

spruce

A distinction is made between plain and flamed maple qualities. Flames are transverse stripes caused by wavy grain. The varnish amplifies this pattern, resulting in three dimensional effects under varying incidences of light. In addition to maple, walnut and ash may also have flames. Only about 3 percent of maple trees are affected by this anomaly. The difference cannot be detected on the living tree. Due to its rarity, flamed maple wood is more expensive than the plain kind.

Besides the typically used spruce and maple there are other less frequently used woods. Fir, cedar and pinemay are used for the top, as well, while poplar and ash for the sides and back. Beech wood, willow, walnut, cherry and pear are more rarely used woods. For necks, beech wood is used as an alternative to maple, and for fingerboards, rosewood or fruit woods are used instead of ebony. Unlike in guitar making, no exotic wood woods aside from ebony are being used for the production of the double bass. It is crucial that the wood (no matter which kind) has been dried naturally for many years, before being used. This is the only way to avoid cracks as consequential damage to the instrument.

flamed maple

Double basses are usually categorized into two groups, based on their wood processing: veneered and carved basses. The arched top of a carved bass is worked out of the full wooden block, which is extremely labor and material intensive; with simpler solid instruments it can also be pressed into the arched form.

Basses made of multilayered, veneered wood are also called plywood basses. The tops and backs are formed by machine pressing, and therefore mostly industrially produced. Veneered basses are not only cheaper, but also more rigid. While carved basses are constantly prone to cracks, e.g. caused by careless handling or weather influences, the multilayer glued plywood is largely insensitive to these types of damages. Although their average sound quality may be generally good, but a certain classical sound ideal can only be achieved through carved construction. In most cases the sound of carved basses is richer in overtones, while plywood basses sound somewhat mellower. The price and quality of so-called hybrid basses is in between the two main categories. They usually have a solid top, but the back and sides are made of veneered wood.

For this bass, a three-layer plywood was used for the top.

Plywood basses became increasingly popular in the U.S.A. from the 1930s onwards. They were perfect for the numerous touring dance orchestras and big bands, and many well-known bassists played and promoted these rigid but comparatively simple instruments. While most instruments were still imported from Europe (mainly from Germany and today's Czech Republic), domestic manufacturers began to supply the American market around this time. In addition to Kay Musical Instruments, companies such as King and Epiphone produced plywood basses in large quantities.

The beginning of the 20th century saw the first attempts of using alternative building materials, such as metal sheets. German and American makers built aluminum-made basses in the 1920s and 1930s, that were intended for military and school orchestras. In the 1960s, fiberglass basses entered the market and were robust, but also very heavy. Today, fiberglass is more commonly used for trunks and cases rather than for instruments.

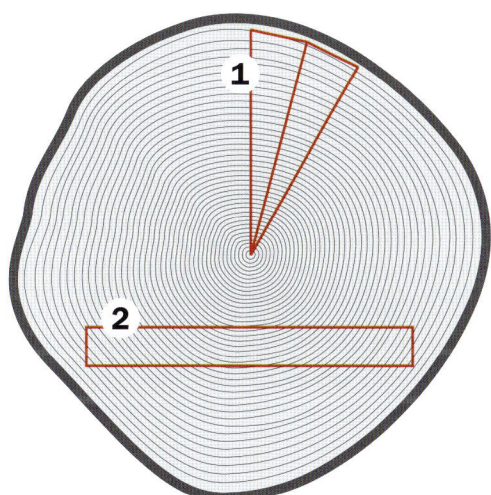

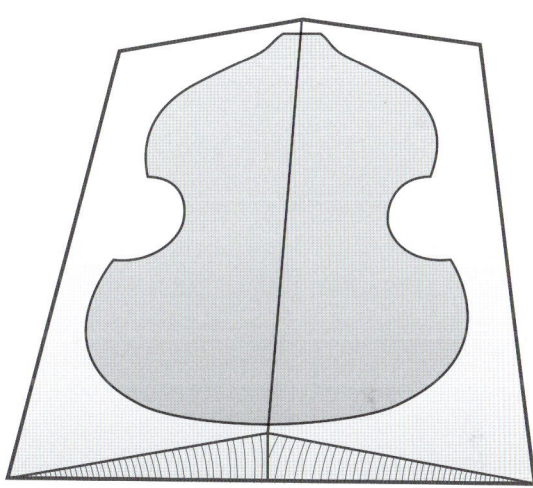

At the sawmill, a wooden log can be cut and processed in different ways into boards. For the top and back of a bass, the log is sawn or split into segments comparable to cutting a cake (quarter, rift or radially sawn, 1). The incision is made exactly parallel to the medullary rays, in order to lower the risk of cracks and distortions. Then, two adjacent segments get joined to form a book-matched image of the grain.

Boards with predominantly horizontal annual rings are called slab sawn (2) and are found less frequently in stringed instruments: they warp more easily. The annual rings appear in curved and wavy lines.

In handcrafted bass making, the arching is worked out of the solid wood with chisels, planes and scrapers. The bass maker can adjust to the specific characteristics of the wood.

Today, CNC machines are often used in workshops to roughly prepare and shape the tops and backs.

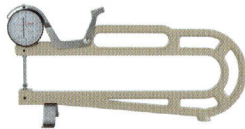

The thickness of a top or back is not uniform. In the area of the bridge (the "chest"), the top is thicker than at the edge. Drill hole markings guide the wood removal to the desired thickness. A thickness gauge offers additional control (fig. left).

Finally the surface is smoothed with the scraper. This results in the year rings becoming more visible, and the varnishing process makes the contrast even more intense.

The bass bar runs lengthwise under the top—it reinforces the top and distributes the vibrations. It is glued into the finished top. With old Bohemian basses you often find the integral (not glued in) bass bar shown here: when the top was carved, the maker simply worked around the bassbar.

After commercially and acoustically unsuccessful experiments with aluminium and fiberglass plastics, carbon material has successfully established itself as a wood alternative. In addition to complete instruments, carbon tailpieces, endpins, fingerboards and bridges are now commonly available. Carbon bows, in particular, have become an indispensable part of the market, as they offer an attractive price/performance ratio.

Carbon is generally known for its low weight and considerable strength, but also for its high manufacturing costs. It is mainly used in aerospace technology, but also in high-quality sports equipment such as tennis rackets, fishing rods and bicycle parts. Today, the term carbon is mostly used as a fashionable colloquial abbreviation for carbon fibre reinforced plastic (technical abbreviation: CFK). Like glass fibre reinforced plastic (GRP), CFRP is a composite material: the carbon fibres are embedded in epoxy or polyester resins (matrix). The resins stabilize and support the fibres by transferring and distributing the forces when under pressure. Although carbon fibers are highly resistant to tractive forces (six times stronger than steel), they break easily when subjected to compressive forces.

For the production of carbon parts, a negative mould is required in which the carbon fibre mats are inserted. Since acting forces have the potential to impact randomly, the mats are laminated on top of each other in varying directions. Enriched with the resin, the component is then cured under pressure and heat.

Many carbon components have a typical shiny black surface. This is the result of a mat, that is applied as a last, decorative layer. However, some parts are simply conventionally painted—therefore, this look says little about the quality of the carbon material. Today, some carbon bows are provided with pernambuco veneer for optical reasons, making them hardly distinguishable from classical wooden bows.

The American company Conn produced not only brass instruments, but also double basses made of aluminium. Other manufacturers were AlCoA (Aluminum Company of America) and G. A. Pfretzschner from Markneukirchen/Germany.

The renowned bassmaker Otto Rubner from Markneukirchen/Germany also offered an aluminium bass (1920s).

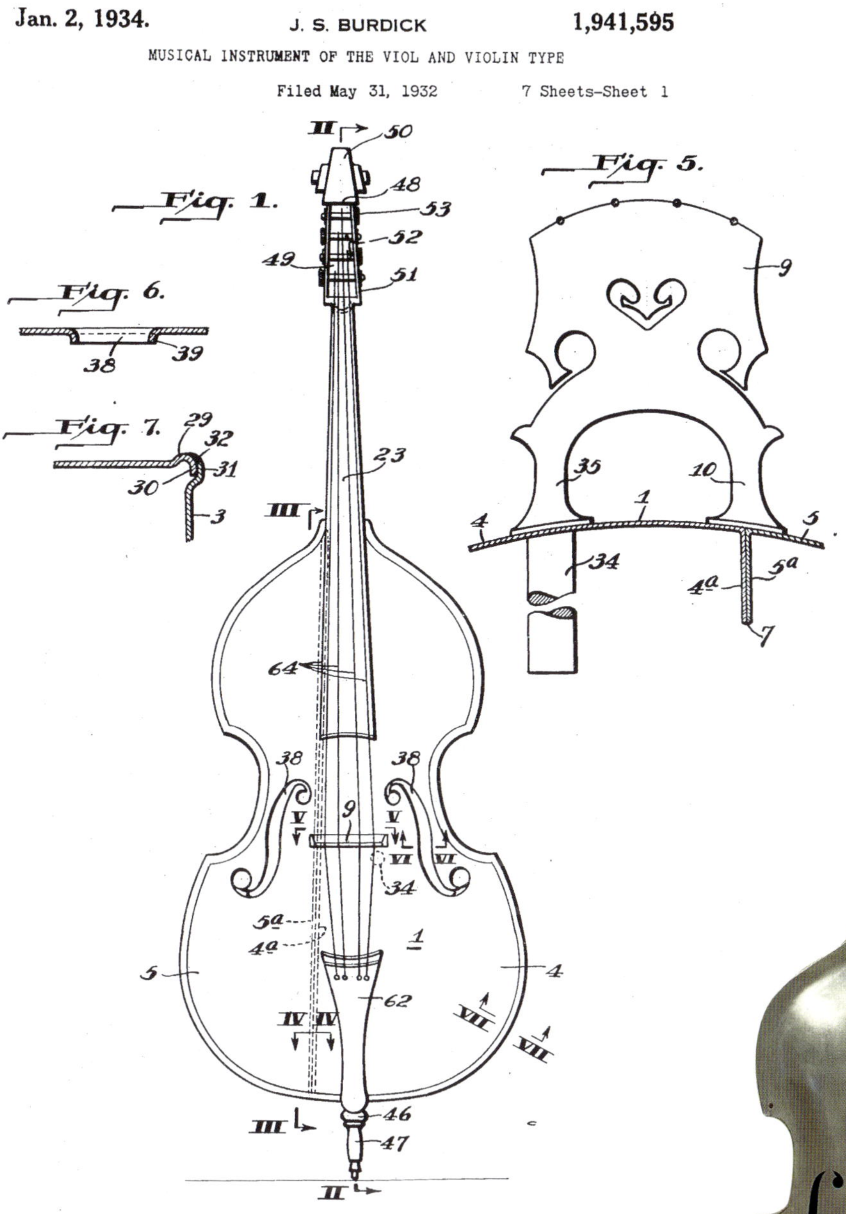

Jan. 2, 1934.   J. S. BURDICK   1,941,595

MUSICAL INSTRUMENT OF THE VIOL AND VIOLIN TYPE

Filed May 31, 1932   7 Sheets—Sheet 1

Fig. 1.

Fig. 6.

Fig. 7.

Fig. 5.

In 1934, J. S. Burdick had his aluminium string instruments patented in the U.S.A. The body and neck were made of sheet metal, while parts such as the bridge, tailpiece and soundpost were still made of wood. As can be seen in the drawing, the bass bar also consisted of a completely continuous fold made of sheet aluminum.
The photo shows a bass with maple neck; the wooden bass bar got attached by means of screws from the front.

Carbon therefore offers some convenient advantages for instrument making: It is insensitive to weather influences, has low weight and very good acoustic properties. Compared to wood, however, it is more difficult to work with, therefore carbon is now only used in the field of bow making. Just as with the production of pernambuco bows, knowledge of the material's properties and craftsmanship are crucial for the making of a good carbon fiber bow.

Ron Carter endorsing a fiberglass bass (1964)

left: the dry carbon fabrics are placed in a mould. The neck is then assembled from two such halves and filled with a casting compound.
middle: a back consists of several layers – like a traditional maple back, the chest area is stronger.
right: the synthetic resin is sucked into the dry carbon fabric of the back and top (vacuum infusion).

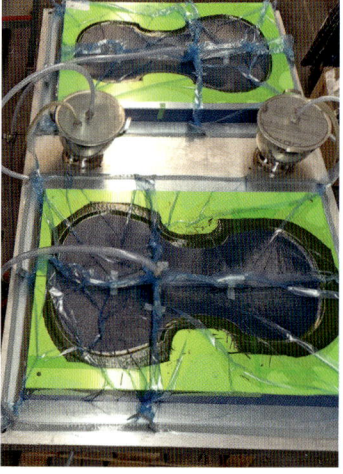

photos: Carbon-Klang, WingsAndMore GmbH & Co. KG

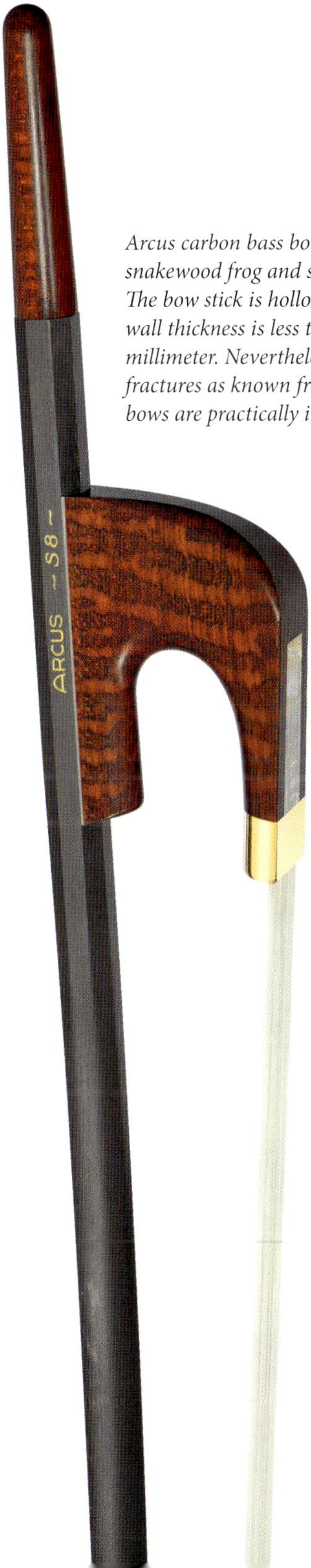

Arcus carbon bass bow with snakewood frog and screw. The bow stick is hollow, the wall thickness is less than one millimeter. Nevertheless, fatigue fractures as known from wooden bows are practically impossible.

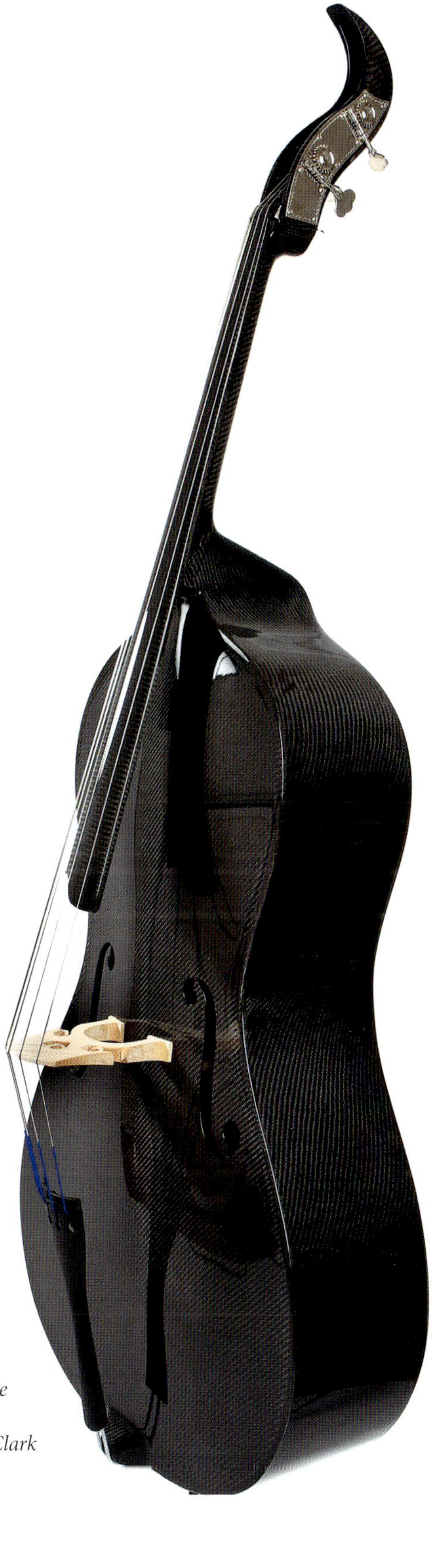

A double bass made almost entirely of carbon by Luis & Clark

photos: Arcus Bows, Luis & Clark

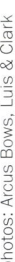

Bows

Early bows consisted of a bow stick bent outwards, at the ends of which the horsehair was simply hung or knotted. In the 16th century, the hair was clamped in mortises (holes cut out in the stick) with small wooden blocks. However, since the horse hair changes its length depending on humidity and temperature, the bow's tension was inconsistent. Therefore the player needed to adjust the tension with his right hand, while holding and guiding the bow in the common underhand grip.

In order to increase the distance between hair and stick at the lower end of the bow, a block was attached—the frog. Unlike in today's bows, the frog of early clip-in (or slot-notch) bows was only held by the horse hair and secured from slipping by a notch. The clip-in frog allowed for rough adjustment of the bow tension, but particularly with larger string instruments such as the double bass it was difficult to execute.

The crémaillière bow made it possible to regulate the tension mechanically in the 17th century. The frog was fixed with a wire loop to a toothed rack (French: "crémaillière"), which was carved into the upper edge of the bow stick. This mechanism was replaced in the 18th century by the principle of the bow screw, which is still being used today. This invention made fine tuning of the bow tension finally possible, enabling the musician to find the ideal compromise between quick response and balance.

Early baroque bows were made of yew wood, while snakewood and ironwood were used for particularly high-quality bows. In the second half of the 18th century, bows with an inwardly bent stick became more and more popular. This change made it possible to tighten the hair even more, since the ends of the bow stick could not move inwards even under increasing pressure. From around 1800 on, the trained watchmaker François Tourte had a lasting impact on bow making, and his models are still being used today. He was one of the first to use tropical pernambuco wood, which is still the preferred material for high-quality wooden bows.

Karl Friedrich Abel with Gamba; painting by Thomas Gainsborough, 1765. Interesting detail: The tension of the bow hairs was regulated with the fingers of the bow hand while playing.

German and French bow

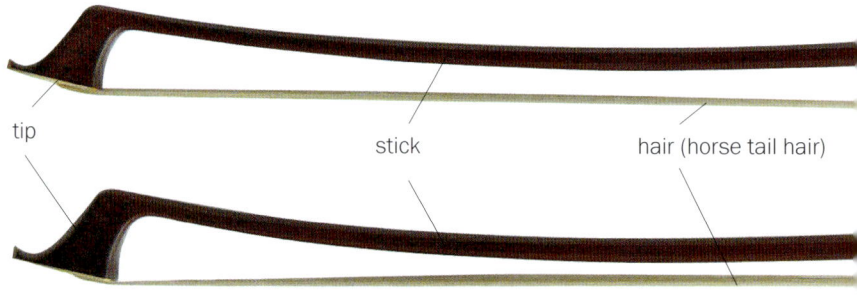

tip

stick

hair (horse tail hair)

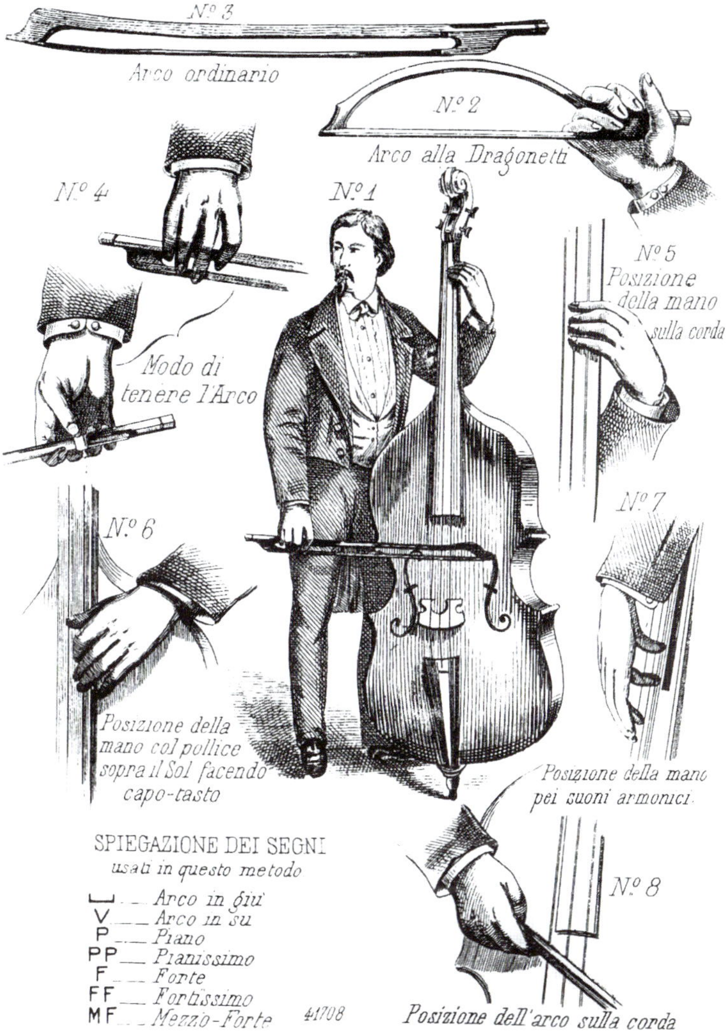

The French bow held in the upper grip goes back to the virtuoso Giovanni Bottesini.

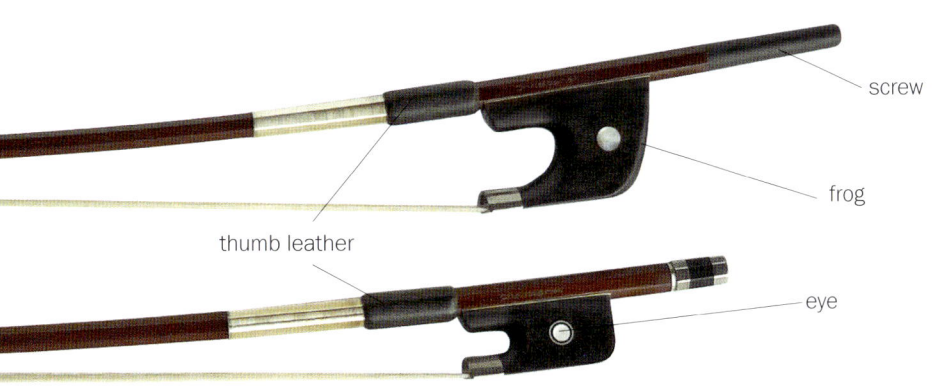

The great double bass virtuoso Dragonetti (*1763 †1846) played with bows that seemed archaic even during his lifetime since they had not adopted any of the technical innovations of the 18th and 19th centuries. Dragonetti played short, powerful bows with an extremely concave (outwardly bent) stick and no hair tensioning device. This bow particularly favoured the rapid and rhythmical staccato figurations typical of Dragonetti's playing. Saxon instrument makers took up the construction of the Dragonetti bow and combined it with the adjustable frog, as well as the concave (inwardly bent) bow bar introduced by François Tourte. This modernized Dragonetti bow finally led to a model that today is known as the "German Bow".

bow models
17th and 18th century

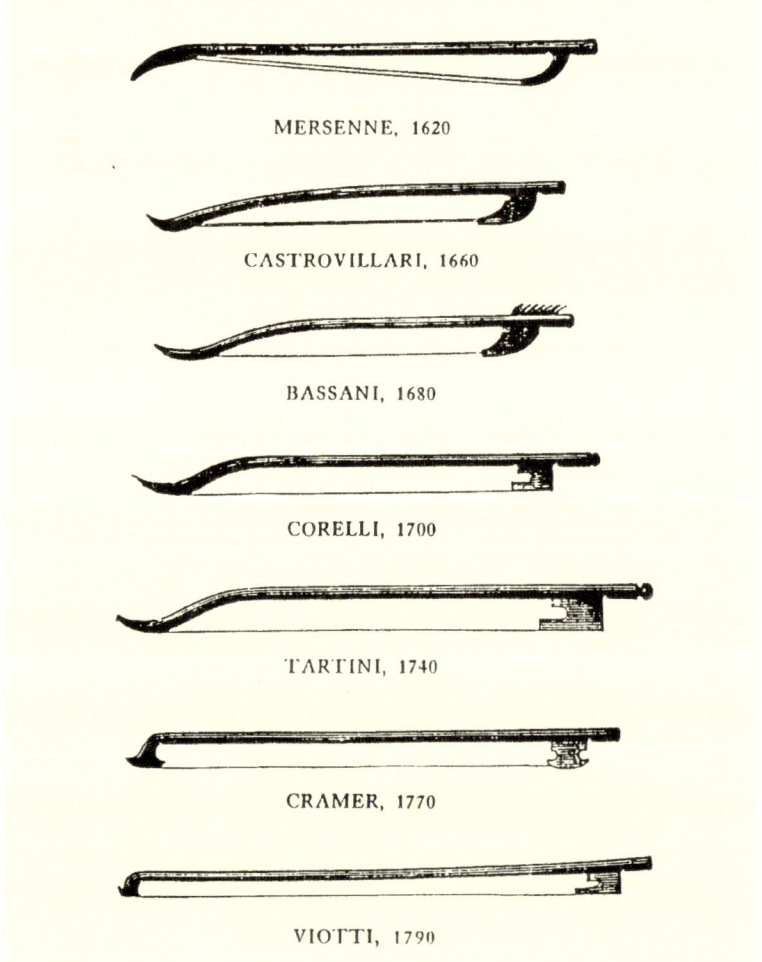

MERSENNE, 1620

CASTROVILLARI, 1660

BASSANI, 1680

CORELLI, 1700

TARTINI, 1740

CRAMER, 1770

VIOTTI, 1790

In contrast to Dragonetti, Giovanni Bottesini (*1821 †1889) played a double bass bow, which is comparable to the cello bow in construction and playing position. Today this type of bow is known as the "French bow". It was better suited than the somewhat ancient Dragonetti bow for the execution of characteristic elements of Bottisini's style: the fast runs, rich ornamentations and high register passages.

Today, both German and French bows can be found in the orchestras—albeit with regional preferences. In German-speaking countries, the German bow is predominant, while in France and the U.S.A. the French bow dominates.

bow models
early 20th century
(Schuster, Saxony)

Dragonetti with the
typical bow

"The most ideal one can imagine."—The double bass bows by H. R. Pfretzschner are in great demand today. H. R. Pfretzschner worked for several years with J. B. Vuillaume in Paris—at that time the first address in bow making. In 1875 he returned to Markneukirchen to take over his father's workshop. He is regarded as a pioneer of French bow making in Germany.

Among the outstanding German bow makers is also Franz-Albert Nürnberger jr. (here around 1915 with his sons Philipp Paul and Carl Albert in his workshop).

In modern bow making, pernambuco wood is the most commonly used wood for the stick. It belongs to the family of brazil woods (botanical name "caesalpinia echinata"), of which there are about 125 species. About 20 of those species are used in bow making. Originally, they were mainly felled in the province of Pernambuco—hence the name. The colouring of the pernambuco wood core ranges from light orange to brown tones, and to a deep reddish brown. Color, weight and overall quality differed between the individual species, with the original location having a great influence, too. For inexpensive school bows, a wood commonly referred to as Masaranduba is being used, as well. Closely related to pernambuco wood, this material has a grey-brown color, while being somewhat softer and lighter.

Brazilwoods have been regularly brought from South America to Europe since the 14th century for use in textile dyeing. However, the originally abundant supplies were decimated to such an extent that pernambuco wood was already an endangered species at the time of the introduction of synthetic aniline dyes around 1840. Since 2007, unprocessed pernambuco wood has been protected by the international CITES II ("Convention on International Trade in Endangered Species of Wild Fauna and Flora") agreement, which strongly regulates and restricts export and trade.

*double bass bow,
19th century*

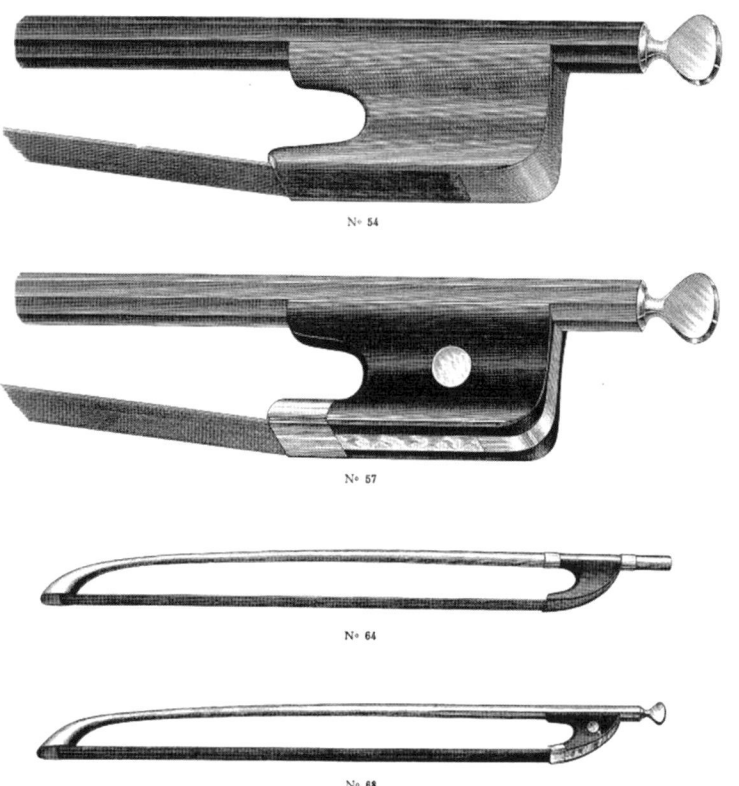

N° 54

N° 57

N° 64

N° 68

Double bass bows in the catalogue of bow maker Bazin, Mirecourt 1901

The workshop of the bowmaker Bazin, Mirecourt 1893.
Note the number of still very young assistants.
At that time quite common, today this would be considered child labor.

A common feature of string instruments is the scroll at the end of the pegbox. Depending on the violin or bass maker and the period, the scroll varies. Typical for the Viennese double bass is the jagged profile of the pegbox (Fig. right: Stadelmann).

In addition to the classic scroll, the upper end of the pegbox has always been decorated with figurative carvings. The lion's head (fig. left) is the most common. The contemporary Canadian bass maker Mario Lamarre chose elephant or dragon heads for his basses and took up these motifs for his fingerboard extensions.

Until the shape of the ƒ hole became established, sound holes came in a variety of shapes.

Electric Upright Bass (EUB)

With the appearance of electrically amplified instruments in the 1920s and 1930s, the first electric upright basses (or EUB) were built. These basses have a smaller, reduced solid body, usually made of wood; this makes them less sensitive to feedback and easier to transport. This is not a new idea, since in past centuries the so-called "muted" string instruments, without a resonating hollow body, were used for practicing purposes. However, electronic sound reproduction opened up new possibilities for instrument makers and musicians alike. The sound quality of electric double basses initially left a lot to be desired, since it took several decades for pickups and bass amplifiers to mature. Today, there is a large number of manufacturers on the market, that offer these instruments either as customized orders, or in small series.

While some consider it merely a conveniently transportable alternative to the "real" bass, musicians like Eberhard Weber or David Friesen decided to exclusively play the electric double bass, as they regarded it as a new, independent instrument. Constructional approaches can differ dramatically: while some electric double basses are designed to imitate the sound and feel of an acoustic double bass (and in some cases get quite close to it), others go in the opposite direction by detaching themselves from the acoustic model.

German jazz bassist Eberhard Weber switched from acoustic double bass to electric upright bass in 1972.

The "Stroh String Bass" was a blend of double bass and gramophone and was made in England at the beginning of the 20th century. It may be considered a precursor of the EUB.
"It is in every way as good as, if not better than, the Tuba or Sousaphone, and there is no question that it will become increasingly popular in the near future."

Zorko
*introduces a
startling new
breakthrough in
bass design*

"To me the ZORKO bass has a lot of
excellent features that should be of great
interest to every bass player. Just thinking offhand, I'd say the thing I really
enjoy about it is the volume control
which allows practicing late at night or
in hotel rooms on the road. But I guess
some of the other things about a Zorko
are more important; like the adjustable
neck for raising or lowering action, the
double bridges for amplifying gut
strings, the beautiful fibre-glass finish
which is not subject to climatic changes
and it's non-breakable . . . and believe
me, the sound is a gas. Oh, yeh, the
Zorko also has a full bass scale and can
be bowed. All in all, it's full of extra
features that have been needed on a
bass, and I dig it.
                                    Red Mitchell

Zorko Incorporated

Music 1961

*One of the first EUB was
introduced in 1936 by guitar
manufacturer Rickenbacker
(pictured left). The Zorko company released an EUB with a
fiberglass body in 1961 (pictured
above). Shortly thereafter,
Ampeg purchased the rights,
improved the pickup and started
offering the instrument as the
"Ampeg Baby Bass". Due to its
dry and percussive sound it is
still popular among Latin and
Salsa bassists.*

The Eminence Electric Upright Bass was launched in the 1990s. It has an acoustic body with bass bar and soundpost. It is equipped with a passive piezo pickup and is also available with a detachable neck, resulting in a very compact traveling size.

Like his brother Red, Whitey Mitchell was a jazz bassist and endorser for the Ampeg Baby Bass. Although Whitey played with such famous musicians as Herbie Mann, Gene Krupa, André Previn and Benny Goodman, he always stood in the shadow of his even more successful older brother, Red. Apparently he took it with a sense of humor: on his business card he introduced himself with the words "YES! I am Red Mitchell's brother". After having ended his carreer as a bassist, Whitey Mitchell became successful as a writer and producer for film, theatre and TV series.

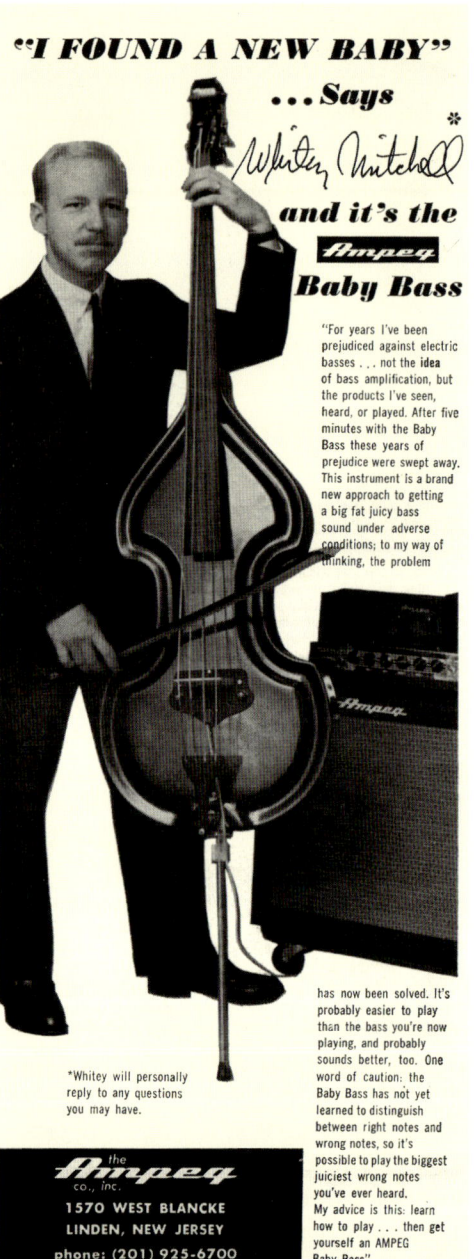

The Framus Triumph bass
was produced from 1953 to
1980. Jimmy Bond, bassist
with George Shearing, was
an endorser: "The Framus
Triumph unveils an exciting
new world to the modern
player. The first Electric
double bass with full resonant tone beauty, it affords
developmental opportunities
heretofore unexplored."

The Framus Triumph had a
magnetic pickup; and as a
result, the bass could only be
used with the then new steel
strings. The string action
was individually adjusted
by means of height-adjustable saddles, similar to an
electric bass.

The Futurama (or Resonet)
Electric Bass was distributed by the British company
Selmer in the 1950s. The
design was based on the
Framus Triumph. The
manufacturer was the Czech
company Drevokov/CSHN,
which made furniture and
electric guitars.

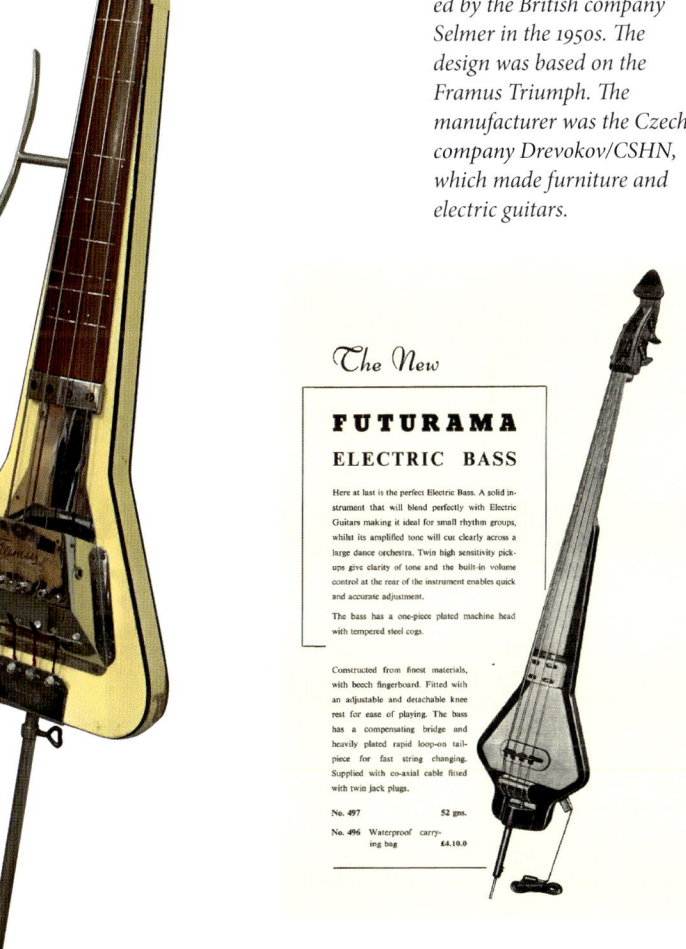

A double bass bag made of robust Cordura fabric, leather reinforcements, numerous handles and compartments for accessories

With transport wheels such as the Bass Buggie, a double bass can be transported without straining the back

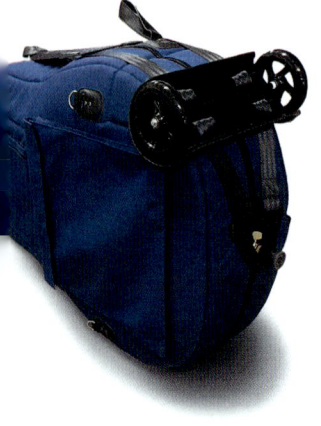

On the road with the double bass

"Why didn't you learn the flute?!"—bass players hear this supposedly funny comment a lot from pedestrians when walking around town with their instruments. Fortunately, a bass is not as heavy as it is bulky, since it is largely filled with air. Nevertheless, it is not easy to transport, because even well protected, it remains sensitive to bumps, hits and falls. Therefore, a well padded soft case is part of the basic equipment of a double bass.

Double bass bags are available in large numbers on the market. Most importantly, they should have a sturdy, high-quality zip fastener and plenty of handles to guarantee safe carrying and loading. A shoulder strap is also indispensable. Some bags are backpack-ready—but the disadvantage of this design is that the bass usually ends up hitting your calves or preventing you from passing through doors due to the additional height above your head. Colorful bags have the advantage of not heating up to the extent than black bags do.

If the bass is transported over longer distances on foot, it is advisable to use wheels to relieve your back. The simplest version is a single wheel that is inserted into the endpin socket (the endpin must be removable for this). An air-filled tire is recommended, as it has better suspension effect than solid rubber.

Easier to steer than a unicycle is the two-wheeled Bass Buggie, which is attached to the side of the body. It fits all bass sizes and is simply strapped on with a belt. Another big advantage of the Bass Buggie is that the bass doesn't roll away as easily as with a unicycle, freeing up one hand to unlock a door, press a traffic light button or answer your mobile phone.

Hardcases or flightcases make transportation safer, but also more bulky. They are therefore not preferable for daily use. Flight cases can barely be handled by a single person and do not fit in most cars, even those that can easily accommodate a bass in a regular gig bag. As a result, they are mainly used for concert tours and air travel. Since excess air travel luggage fees are calculated by weight, most cases are made of carbon fiber.

Unfortunately, travelling by plane with a musical instrument has become increasingly difficult in recent years. Uniform international regulations on the handling of instruments do not exist—every airline seems to follow their own protocol. Some airlines allow at least smaller instruments to be placed in the overhead compartment, or a separate seat may be booked for them. The double bass is usually only allowed to be transported as cargo baggage. In spite of stable flight cases, damages to our treasures occur routinely due to careless handling of the ground staff at airports all over the world. In addition there seems to be a frequent disconnect between agreements and promises during the booking process, versus the actual reality when dealing with airline representatives on site upon departure.

Only rarely do double bassists travel so light-heartedly by train as members of the Munich Philharmonic in this photo. It was taken in 2017 for advertising purposes, as Deutsche Bahn (German railway system) sponsors the orchestra as their *mobility partner*. "We are very pleased to have won the internationally renowned Munich Philharmonic Orchestra as a partner for our corporation, as it demonstrates to our customers how relaxed, harmonious and inexpensive traveling by train can be, especially for groups," says the company's marketing director. When specifically asked about the transportation of the double bass, the company admitted that, in contrast to their advertising, only the musicians travel by train, while the instruments are transported by truck to the performance venue. Although it is not generally forbidden to take a double bass (or harp) with you when travelling by train in Germany, musicians are usually at the mercy of the train commander on duty.

Double basses with removable necks have experienced a real boom in recent years, mainly due to the increasing issues with air travel. What's already detached can't be broken off—without a neck the risk of damage is minimized considerably. In addition, you can save money by only checking in the body as luggage and taking the heavy neck into the cabin as your carry-on.

A double bass made by the Christopher brand with removable neck. The joint is designed as a dovetail and is secured with a screw.

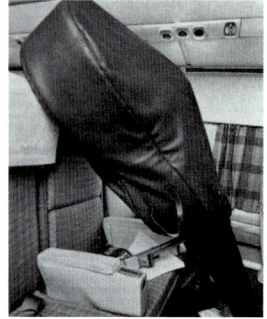

The idea of a removable neck is not that new. Even in the days of the stagecoach, traveling with the double bass was dangerous. Normally the neck heel is firmly glued into the neck block. For a double bass with a removable neck, various solutions for the neck-body connection are available. The simplest one is a screw that goes through the neck heel into a thread in the neck block. A little more complex and stable are dovetail joints, where the neck is pushed into the body from the front, and secured by a no-load carrying screw.

Some removable neck systems additionally allow the string height to be adjusted, making an adjustable bridge (otherwise very useful when traveling in different climatic conditions) unnecessary.

The problem of a collapsing soundpost is solved in many different ways. On basses by French maker Patrick Charton, a small dowel through the bottom fixes the soundpost. Other basses allow the soundpost to be set up without any tools through an opening in the frame that is large enough to reach through with your hand. Less invasive are the light foam pads that are glued into the Christopher RN and hold the soundpost reversibly.

When double basses were still allowed to fly in the main cabin … in his method book "The Evolving Bassist", published in 1984, Rufus Reid shows how best to stow the bass in a narrow plane: upside down.

The cover of this LP by the Bill Evans Trio (recorded 1968 in Copenhagen) shows bassist Eddie Gomez with his bass boarding an airplane. Taking the bass along as "hand luggage" was still possible back then.

This custom-made suitcase (it wasn't really a "flight case" back then) served Domenico Dragonetti for the transport of his beloved Gasparo da Salò. Today the case and the instrument are in the possession of St. Mark's Cathedral in Venice.

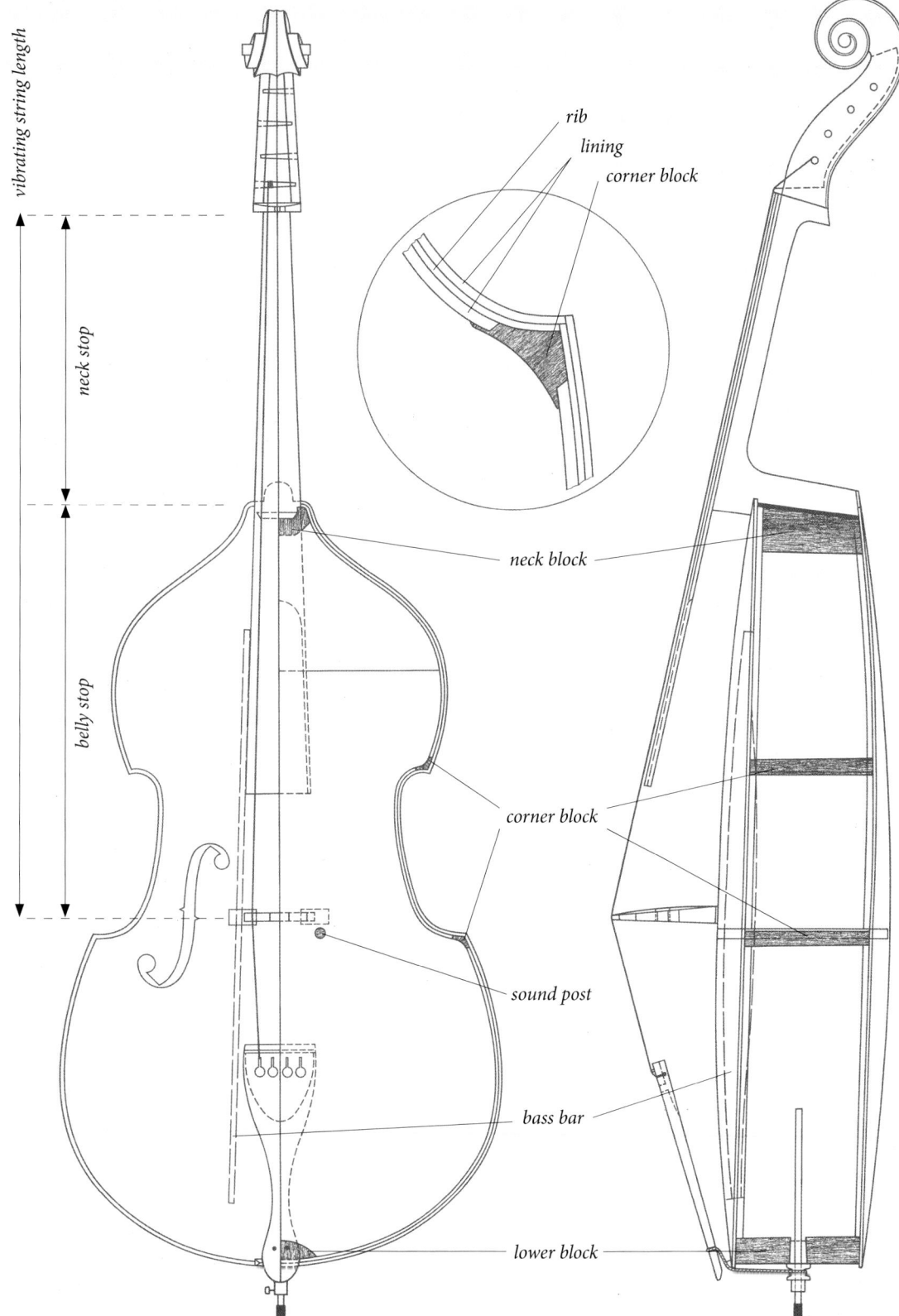

vibrating string length

neck stop

belly stop

rib

lining

corner block

neck block

corner block

sound post

bass bar

lower block

The double bass and its parts (in four languages)

	English	German	French	Italian
	arch	die Wölbung	la voûte	la bombatura
①	back	der Boden	le fond	il fondo
	bassbar	der Bassbalken	la barre d'harmonie	la catena
	block	der Klotz	le tasseau	il tassello
	body	der Korpus	le corps	la cassa armonica, la cassa
	body length	die Korpuslänge	la longueur de corps	la lunghezza della cassa
②	bridge	der Steg	le chevalet	il ponticello
	ebony wood	das Ebenholz	le bois d'ébène	il legno di ebano
③	endpin	der Stachel	la pique	il puntale
④	f-hole	das f-Loch	l'ouïe	fori armonici, effe
⑤	fingerboard	das Griffbrett	la touche	la tastiera
⑥	lower bout	der Unterbug	la largeur du bas	la zona inferiore
	maple wood	das Ahornholz	le bois d'érable	il legno di acero
⑦	middle (C-) bout	der Mittelbug	la largeur aux C	la zona della C
⑧	neck	der Hals	le manche	il manico
⑨	neck heel	der Halsfuß	le talon	il tacco
⑩	notch of soundhole/f-hole	die f-Kerbe	le cran de l'ouïe	le tacche delle ff
⑪	nut	der Obersattel	le sillet de tête	il capotasto
⑫	pegbox	der Wirbelkasten	le chevillier	la cavigliera
⑬	purfling	die Einlage, die Ader	les filets	i filetti
	rib	die Zarge	l'éclisse	la fascia
⑭	saddle	der Untersattel	le sillet du bas	il capo-cordiera
⑮	scroll	die Schnecke	la volute	il riccio
	soundpost	der Stimmstock	l'âme	l'anima
	spruce wood	das Fichtenholz	le bois d'épicéa	il legno di abete
	string length	die Mensur	la longueur de corde vibrante	il diapason
⑯	string	die Saite	la corde	la corda
⑰	tailgut	die Hängelsaite	l'attache cordier	il reggi-cordiera
⑱	tailpiece	der Saitenhalter	le cordier	la cordiera
⑲	top, belly	die Decke	la table	la tavola armonica
⑳	tuning machine	die Mechanik	la clé	la meccanica
	upper block	der Oberklotz	le tasseau du haut	il tassello superiore
㉑	upper bout	der Oberbug	la largeur du haut	la zona superiore
	varnish	der Lack	le vernis	la vernice

German Bow
Deutscher Bogen
l'archet allemand
l'archetto tedesco

French Bow
Französischer Bogen
l'archet français
l'archetto francesco

Range of the double bass, position of the notes on the piano keyboard

		Scientific Pitch Notation (SPN)	Helmholtz Pitch Notation (German)	frequency in Hz	octave range
	1	A_0	„A	27.50	sub-contra octave
	2	$A\sharp_0 / B\flat_0$	„Ais / „B	29.14	
	3	B_0	„H	30.87	
	4	C_1 (double pedal C)	‚C (Kontra-C)	32.70	contra octave
	5	$C\sharp_1 / D\flat_1$	‚Cis / ‚Des	34.65	
	6	D_1	‚D	36.71	
	7	$D\sharp_1 / E\flat_1$	‚Dis / ‚Es	38.89	
	8	E_1	‚E	41.20	
	9	F_1	‚F	43.65	
	10	$F\sharp_1 / G\flat_1$	‚Fis / ‚Ges	46.25	
	11	G_1	‚G	49.00	
	12	$G\sharp_1 / A\flat_1$	‚Gis / ‚As	51.91	
	13	A_1	‚A	55.00	
	14	$A\sharp_1 / B\flat_1$	‚Ais / ‚B	58.27	
	15	B_1	‚H	61.74	
	16	C_2 (low or pedal C)	C (großes C)	65.41	great octave
	17	$C\sharp_2 / D\flat_2$	Cis / Des	69.30	
	18	D_2	D	73.42	
	19	$D\sharp_2 / E\flat_2$	Dis / Es	77.78	
	20	E_2	E	82.41	
	21	F_2	F	87.31	
	22	$F\sharp_2 / G\flat_2$	Fis / Ges	92.50	
	23	G_2	G	98.00	
	24	$G\sharp_2 / A\flat_2$	Gis / As	103.83	
	25	A_2	A	110.00	
	26	$A\sharp_2 / B\flat_2$	Ais / B	116.54	
	27	B_2	H	123.47	
	28	C_3 (bass C)	c (kleines c)	130.81	small octave
	29	$C\sharp_3 / D\flat_3$	cis / des	138.59	
	30	D_3	d	146.83	
	31	$D\sharp_3 / E\flat_3$	dis / es	155.56	
	32	E_3	e	164.81	
	33	F_3	f	174.61	
	34	$F\sharp_3 / G\flat_3$	fis / ges	185.00	
	35	G_3	g	196.00	
	36	$G\sharp_3 / A\flat_3$	gis / as	207.65	
	37	A_3	a	220.00	
	38	$A\sharp_3 / B\flat_3$	ais / b	233.08	
	39	B_3	h	246.94	
	40	C_4 (middle C)	c' (eingestrichenes c)	261.63	1-line octave
	41	$C\sharp_4 / D\flat_4$	cis' / des'	277.18	
	42	D_4	d'	293.67	
	43	$D\sharp_4 / E\flat_4$	dis' / es'	311.13	
	44	E_4	e'	329.63	
	45	F_4	f'	349.23	
	46	$F\sharp_4 / G\flat_4$	fis' / ges'	369.99	
	47	G_4	g'	392.00	
	48	$G\sharp_4 / A\flat_4$	gis' / as'	415.31	
	49	A_4 (concert pitch)	a' (Kammerton)	440.00	
	50	$A\sharp_4 / B\flat_4$	ais' / b'	466.16	
	51	B_4	h'	493.88	
	52	C_5 (treble C)	c" (zweigestrichenes c)	523.25	2-line octave
	53	$C\sharp_5 / D\flat_5$	cis" / des"	554.37	
	54	D_5	d"	587.33	

Lutherie

Luthier Johann Reiter in his workshop at Mittenwald/Germany

Craft and industrial stringed instrument making

The idea of a master violin maker crafting an instrument from start to finish according to handed-down traditions, who manufactures all the parts of an instrument himself and assembles them to form a whole is an ideal image. Today, only very few violins, cellos and double basses are made with the same craftsmanship as in the heyday of violin making; the majority of instruments are manufactured industrially, based on a division of labor. However, industrial mass production began much earlier than is commonly known among collectors of vintage instruments. As early as the 18th century, stringed instruments were mass-produced through division of labour. Therefore its is just as incorrect to assume that every old instrument naturally is an individually manufactured one, or even a master instrument, as it is to regard all new ones as machine-made factory products.

Factory made violins from Germany

Until Asian manufacturers from Japan, Korea and China took over the lead in the 1970s, German manufacturers dominated the market for simple, inexpensive instruments for over two centuries. In addition to violins from Mirecourt (Vosges/France), there were mainly products from Mittenwald (Bavaria), Markneukirchen (Saxony), Schönbach (Bohemia, today called Luby/Czech Republic) and later, after the Second World War, also from new instrument making centres in Bubenreuth in Franconia/Germany and Nauheim in Hesse/Germany that satisfied the worldwide demand for plain, affordable instruments. Therefore, Germany has a long tradition in

Usually the instruments were crafted by hand even in the so-called violin "factories"—therefore the term "manufacture" is quite appropriate.

both the production of handmade musical instruments at the highest level, as well as the industrial production of "factory violins".

It all began in the second half of the 18th century, when a number of dealers or dealer families specialized in the distribution of instruments, which until then had mostly been handled by travelling dealers or peddlers. Most violin makers had neither the time nor the infrastructure to take care of sales themselves and to set up distribution structures. These violin wholesalers and exporters (the best known companies are Neuner & Hornsteiner and J. A. Baader & Co from Mittenwald, both founded in 1810) collected instruments from various violin makers and sold them all over the world.

In the centres of the violin making, monuments and museums have been erected in order to reflect the importance of the instrument making trade for the region.

GERMANY

Markneukirchen

Bubenreuth   Luby (Schönbach)

CZECH REPUBLIC

Mirecourt

FRANCE   Mittenwald

Cremona

ITALY

This list of independent trades of the Schönbach instrument makers from 1907 shows a strong division of labour:
Top maker
Back maker
Rib maker
Body maker
Bassbar carver
Neck carver
Bridge carver
Peg turner
Ebony fingerboard carver
Case maker
String maker
Bowmaker
Component producer
Varnisher

Cello and double bass making at the workshop of Laberte-Humbert Frères, Mirecourt

A small number of instruments were signed by their actual makers, with most (if any) baring the names of the wholesalers or imitated labels with the sonorous names of old masters.

Little by little wholesalers changed their business model from only buying finished instruments to including supplying parts and raw materials and reorganizing the production process to multiple specialized laborers: These included body makers, neck makers, scroll carvers, peg turners, stringer makers and varnishers who performed their tasks at home. Wholesalers built sawmills and established their own workshops. As a result, large quantities could be produced at reasonable prices to satisfy the demand for simple and cheap instruments. The products, their quantities and prices were determined by wholesalers. The strong division of labour and the export business fundamentally changed the way violin makers worked: the formerly independent craftsman became a home business operator who was just as dependent on the wholesaler, as the homeworker was on the factory owner.

Germany as a developing country

In the early 19th century, the German economy was generally regarded as backward. In addition to agricultural products, Germany mainly exported products such as embroidery, cuckoo clocks and musical instruments—i.e. handicraft products that could be produced cheaply because of low wages. Other industrially manufactured products such as machines and metal goods often did not meet the quality standards demanded abroad, because of lack of technical knowledge and capital to purchase the manufacturing equipment. The reputation of German industrial products was therefore initially miserable: even a German judge characerized the exhibits of his home country at the 1876 World Exhibition in Philadelphia as "cheap and

bad". In order to improve sales, many German manufacturers began to copy and plagiarize British, French and American quality products. For example, German made blades and cutting edges were given stamps like "Sheffield made". Great Britain reacted by implementing the "Merchandise Marks Act" of 1862, which obliged manufacturers to mark all imported articles with the country of origin in order to protect domestic products. From then on, "Made in Germany" was emblazoned on many everyday objects worldwide. At the same time, however, the quality of German products steadily improved: experts were poached from the more highly developed industrial countries, and production techniques were studied and adopted. Contrary to the British government's intentions, "Made in Germany" was soon perceived by consumers as a mark of reliable quality.

Manufacturers from the Saxon Vogtland around Markneukrichen and Klingenthal were among the global leaders at the end of the 19th and early 20th century.

The workshop of Karl Höfner, Schönbach (Egerland).
After the expulsion as a result of the 2nd World War, Höfner resettled in Baiers-dorf near Bubenreuth.

Advertisements from „Der Kontrabass – Mitteilungsblatt des Bundes der Kontrabassisten"; Merseburg/Germany 1929

Quality as competitive advantage

In 1858 a violin making school was founded in Mittenwald to enhance the qualification of Bavarian violin makers who had been trailing the national competition, especially from Saxony and West Bohemia areas. Many Mittenwald violin makers acquired new knowledge abroad, such as Ludwig Neuner from the wholesale company Neuner & Hornsteiner. He worked for several years with J. B. Vuillaume in Paris, the most important violin maker of his time. During his stay there Neuner studied many classical models of Italian masters and brought his experiences back with him to Mittenwald. Thus, artisan violin making—the individual production of instruments in master workshops—gradually became more important again.

The Vogtland region of Saxony and West Bohemia was Germany's other leading instrument making center. Here, almost all other orchestral instruments and harmonicas were made, in addition to string and plucked instruments. Instruments from the region around Markneukirchen in Saxony had a world market share of 80 percent at the beginning of the 20th century. The main market at that time was America, which even maintained a consulate in Markneukirchen until 1916. In 1904, the Klingenthal engineer William Thau invented a copy routing machine for the mechanical production of backs and tops, resulting in a high degree of automation. The two towns of Markneukirchen (Vogtland) and Schönbach (West Bohemia) are only 10 km apart, but were separated by the German-Czech border. For a long time the workers from Schönbach mainly supplied parts, while the more profitable trade and export of finished instruments were executed by the export companies in Markneukirchen. It was not until Schönbach was connected to the railway network that export companies were able to establish themselves there as well. A census by the local Chamber of

Copy milling machine of the Schönbach production co-operative. At the beginning of the 20th century, newly developed copy milling machines were used for the first time in Markneukirchen and Schönbach to produce violin tops and backs.
(Fig. from the commemorative publication "600 years of Schönbach", 1921)

...OUTFIT... No. 12R318 OUR HIGHEST GRADE ARTIST OUTFIT WONDERFUL ...VALUE...

BY SPECIAL ARRANGEMENT with the celebrated violin maker, Louis Lowendall, of Berlin, Germany, we have been able to procure a limited number of his high grade instruments for this special outfit. His violins are sought after by the greatest players in the world, as they possess all the qualifications of a fine violin. Anyone desiring to purchase an instrument could do no better than to order one of these outfits.

IN MAKING UP THIS OUTFIT we have endeavored to include a combination of instrument and equipment such as has never been offered by any concern in the world and which cannot be duplicated by any music dealer at anything like the price at which we offer it. The outfit includes:

		Regular Retail Price
1 Special High Grade Genuine Louis Lowendall Violin, Stradivarius Model, made of specially selected curly maple back and sides, choice old resonant spruce top, highest grade solid ebony trimmings. The tone is of the superior quality, found only in the Lowendall violins		$50.00
NOTE—Every instrument bears the label, countersigned by Louis Lowendall with his own autograph. (Beware of imitations.)		
1 Tourte Model Bow, with full German silver trimmings and best quality Brazil wood		5.00
1 Solid Wood Case, Exposition Shape, full flannel lined, provided with lock and spring clasp		3.50
1 Piece of Genuine Gustave Barnadel Rosin, the best manufactured, and imported by us direct from France		.25
1 Instruction Book, complete in every respect and teaches how to play correctly		1.00
1 Set of Acme Professional Strings, imported by us direct from Europe		.85
1 Latest Patent Violin Chin Rest, used by most players		1.50
1 Fingerboard Chart, which is valuable to beginners and advanced players		.25
1 Set of Violin Tuning Pipes, by the aid of which the instrument can be tuned accurately		.50
1 Violin Mute, required when playing soft music		.15
1 Choice Collection of violin music		.50
Total value of outfit		$63.50

SHIPPING WEIGHT, 10 POUNDS.

The above outfit could not be procured from your local dealer, nor any music dealer at less than $50.00 to $75.00. Our special price, complete..........$19.85

FINGERBOARD CHART.

With each Violoncello or Double Bass we give free of charge one of these fingerboard charts. They are of great value to either beginner or professional player, for they tell at a glance the proper place to press the strings to produce the note desired. Beginners can become proficient in a very short time, with the assistance of this chart. It can be firmly gummed to the fingerboard, and in no way interferes with the tone or playing of the instrument.

...VIOLONCELLOS...

OUR LINE OF VIOLONCELLOS includes only the productions of the best manufacturers. We quote the instruments both with peg head and with patent head. In tone, model and finish these violoncellos have no superior at any price. **OUR LIBERAL GUARANTEE.** If any violoncello proves defective in workmanship or material, it may be returned to us at our expense, and we will cheerfully refund your money. Weight, packed for shipment, about 45 pounds.

Our $9.25 Violoncello with Patent Head.

No. 12R400 Our $9.25 High Grade Violoncello. This Violoncello at $9.25 is excellent value, being made of good model and material, and the best care used in its construction and finish. We furnish it complete with perfect fitting canvas bag, violoncello bow, a piece of fine rosin in pasteboard case, and a complete instruction book, and the instrument is ready to play as soon as received by you. Special price..........$9.25

No. 12R406 At $11.20 we offer a violoncello which will compare very favorably with anything ordinarily carried in retail stores and for which retail dealers will ask from $15.00 to $18.00. This instrument is of excellent quality and has handsome inlaid edges which add very greatly to its general appearance. It has patent head as shown in illustration. It is fitted with a complete set of the best strings, and with it we furnish free a perfect fitting canvas bag, a handsome violoncello bow, an extra large piece of fine rosin and a valuable instructor, by the use of which anyone can learn to play the violoncello without the aid of a teacher.
Our special price..........$11.20

No. 12R412 At $12.95 we offer a Violoncello which will seldom, if ever, be sold by retail dealers at less than $25.00, and found in the finest retail stores in large cities. It has beautiful inlaid edges, a decoration which adds wonderfully to the handsome appearance of the instrument; superior in quality and material, fine workmanship and superb tone. It has best peg head, the pegs and fingerboard being made of solid ebony. It is furnished complete with a perfect fitting canvas bag, valuable instruction book, a handsome violoncello bow and a large piece of excellent rosin.
Our special price..........$12.95

No. 12R414 Same description as our No. 12R412, only fitted with best quality brass plate patent head. Our special price..........$14.95

Our Highest Grade Violoncello with Peg or Patent Head.

No. 12R420 This is an instrument which must be seen, examined and tested in order to fully appreciate all its merits. This Violoncello is extra fine quality, beautifully finished. Solid ebony trimmings throughout, including the solid ebony fingerboard and solid ebony tailpiece. The peg head is the very best which is manufactured and the material used in the body is such as is found only in the highest grade instruments. It is made by expert workmen, and the construction is such that it produces a tone such as you would naturally expect only from instruments which retailers sell at from $25.00 to $30.00. We also include a perfect fitting canvas bag, valuable instruction book, a violoncello bow, and a large piece of fine rosin in pasteboard box, so that the instrument is ready to play as soon as received. Our special price..........$15.45

No. 12R422 Same description as our No. 12R420 but fitted with best quality patent head on brass plates. Price..$17.85

DOUBLE BASS VIOLS.

Buying as we do these desirable instruments in quantities from the leading manufacturer, we offer them with the assurance that they will compare favorably with the very finest that are made, in fact, there is no line of double bass viols manufactured which is superior in tone and workmanship to these which we quote and illustrate on this page. These instruments are furnished complete with a splendid double bass bow and complete instructor. Each instrument is packed with great care, and when ready to ship, weighs 125 pounds.

Our $18.95 One-Half Size Double Bass Viol.

No. 12R450 At $18.95 we offer a four string Double Bass Viol, one-half size, with bow, and complete instruction book. This double bass viol is of the very best model, is dark red shaded, very highly polished, and is superior quality in every respect. Best patent head. Our special price..........$18.95

Our $20.50 Four String Bass Viol.

No. 12R454 Our One-Half Size Double Bass Viol with four strings at $20.50 will compare favorably with any double bass viol on the market offered by retail dealers at from $28.00 to $30.00. This instrument has the best iron patent head, is red brown in color, is beautifully polished and of excellent quality. The workmanship employed on this instrument is of the very best. Furnished complete with strings, double bass bow and a complete instructor, by the use of which anyone with any taste for music whatever may learn to play without the aid of a teacher. Our special price....$20.50

Our Three-Quarter Size Double Bass Viol.

No. 12R462 A High Grade Three-Quarter Size Double Bass Viol for $19.50. This double bass has four strings finest iron patent head and is beautifully shaded and colored. In finish it is wonderfully fine, being highly polished throughout. In model and quality it is decidedly superior and possesses a remarkably fine tone, a tone which you will ordinarily find possessed only by the most expensive instruments. Complete, with excellent double bass bow, and a valuable instruction book.
Our special price, each......$19.50

$22.85 Double Bass Viol.

Three-Quarter Size.

No. 12R466 This Double Bass Viol has four strings, high grade iron patent head, solid ebony fingerboard. The inlaid purfling is very handsome and adds greatly to the attractiveness of the instrument, giving it the appearance of the most expensive and highest priced viols on the market. A particularly fine model and possesses a tone which is superior to the instruments ordinarily carried by retail dealers at any price. We furnish free with each instrument, a good double bass bow, and complete instruction book.
Our special price, each......$22.85

Commerce in 1871 counted 2843 employees in the musical instrument trade in 30 towns around Markneukirchen. The annual production at that time was 3200 dozen violins (12–600 Taler/dozen), 40–50 dozen cellos (6–100 Taler/piece) and 700–800 double basses (10–150 Taler/piece). Neighbouring Schönbach recorded an annual production of 146,000 violins, 2,200 cellos and 1,300 double basses for 1907; in addition 200,000 necks, 300,000 violin ribs, 25,000 violin bodies, 1,000 backs and ribs for double basses and cellos. About two thirds of the production went from Schönbach to Markneukirchen to be sold from there.

Fig. left side:
Sears, Roebuck & Co. was already one of the largest mail order companies in the world at the beginning of the 20th century. The printed catalogue consisted of well over a thousand pages.

The 20th century

The most important market for instrument makers in Europe since the end of the 19th century were the U.S.A. Up to 70 percent of all musical instruments imported into the U.S.A. came from the region around Markneukirchen. France and Czechoslovakia followed at a considerable distance with 10 percent each. After the First World War and the resulting economic crises, sales of industrially manufactured stringed instruments fell sharply. Thus the two traditional Mittenwald manufacturers Neuner & Hornsteiner and J. A. Baader ceased production in the 1930s. Simultaneously, companies in the U.S.A., the most important export market, began to manufacture more and more of their own string instruments in the years between the world wars. The demand for double basses was now also met by American manufacturers such as King, Epiphone and above all Kay with their rigid plywood instruments. But unlike Europe, America cannot look back on a centuries-old tradition of violin making. Until 1900 there were only a few inexperienced violin makers in the U.S.A. who made rather simple instruments from local woods. With the arrival of numerous violin makers from Europe towards the end of the 19th century, instrument making in America

With the Saxon Trade Act of 1861, freedom of trade was introduced in the Vogtland: anyone who had reached the age of 24 could now practise a trade as a self-employed entrepreneur. This resulted in a significant upswing for the Vogtland musical instrument industry. The law also regulated child labour for the first time—it limited work hours to a maximum of 10 hours per day and allowed employers "paternal punishment" of school-aged workers. Anyone who did not show up for work or left without permission could be punished with a prison sentence of up to eight days or a fine of three talers (equivalent to around 3 to 4 weeks' wages).

Luthier Egid Sommer at Absroth near Schönbach

became more professional, but it took until the 1970s for two violin making schools to be founded.

Due to the world economic crisis, German exports of musical instruments fell to less than 20 percent of their original value. Whereas in 1928 instruments worth 111.7 million Reichsmarks were exported, the number came down to only 20.3 million Reichsmarks in 1934. The trade value of stringed instruments in the 1930s was so low that it could barely secure the existence of the makers. To "create orderly conditions", the Nazi regime decided in 1939 to set up a forced cartel with fixed prices. Vogtland instrument makers had to join guilds which fixed binding prices for each instrument category. The *Musikinstrumenten-Zeitung*, a newspaper for instrument makers and dealers, wrote: "A manufacturer who exports today and undercuts minimum prices is acting just as criminally as a currency pusher. The musical instrument industry must reclaim its place in the sun. Germany and the Führer [Adolf Hitler] expect every factory manager to do more than his duty."

Workdays for Bohemian and Saxon instrument makers were long, and the wages meagre: the usual working hours were from 6 a.m. to 8 p.m.; in autumn often until after midnight. Women and children also worked in order to feed the family. The tuberculosis mortality rate was very high (50 %). The owners of Markneukirchen export companies, however, came into great wealth: around 1913, out of a population of about 10,000, Markneukirchen had 138 millionaires—apparantly the highest density of millionaires in Germany.

MIRECOURT (Vosges)
Usine THIBOUVILLE-LAMY - Atelier de fabrication des violoncelles

J.T.L. was one of the largest manufacturers in Mirecourt. At peak times, 1000 workers produced up to 150,000 instruments per year.

Soon after the price cartel came into effect, the German invasion of Poland started World War II. Soon there was a general shortage of goods. Many manufacturers reacted with (forbidden) price increases. The German Reich Commissioner for Price Formation therefore ordered a price freeze in 1940: "The ban on price increases must be strictly observed, even if cost increases reduce the supplier's own profit. It is imperative that prices are kept at the level they were at before the war." But little by little all German industries had to subordinate themselves to the war economy. Those who were not called up to the military service at the Wehrmacht themselves had to convert their production to goods more important to the war effort. But at the point, there were hardly any possible destinations for the export of musical instruments anyway.

Richard Herold, bass builder in Brunndöbra near Klingenthal (Vogtland), with a giant plane more than two meters long, as it was used to assemble double bass backs.

Even in Mirecourt, France, instrument making gradually came to a standstill and never returned to its former glory after the war. The world economic crisis had already weakened many companies. After the war many of the workshops and factories bombed by the German Wehrmacht were not rebuilt. The few companies that still existed struggled to keep up with the productivity and innovations of their competitors. In the 1960s, the last traditional companies closed in Mirecourt: in 1967 Couesnon filed for bankruptcy. Jérôme Thibouville Lamy (J.T.L.), where during its peak 1000 workers produced up to 150,000 instruments a year, closed its factory in 1968. And Labarte Magnié had to close in 1969 when Philippe Labarte died and no successor was found. The name Jérôme Thibouville Lamy was purchased by a British company and survived as a trademark until today.

As a result of the Second World War, over 3 million Sudeten Germans were expelled from former Czechoslovakia. About 2000 Sudeten German instrument makers, who had settled around Schönbach and Graslitz in Egerland, had to leave their homeland, as well. A few resettled in Mittenwald, but the majority moved to the new instrument making centres near Bubenreuth (near Nuremberg) and Nauheim (near Frankfurt am Main).

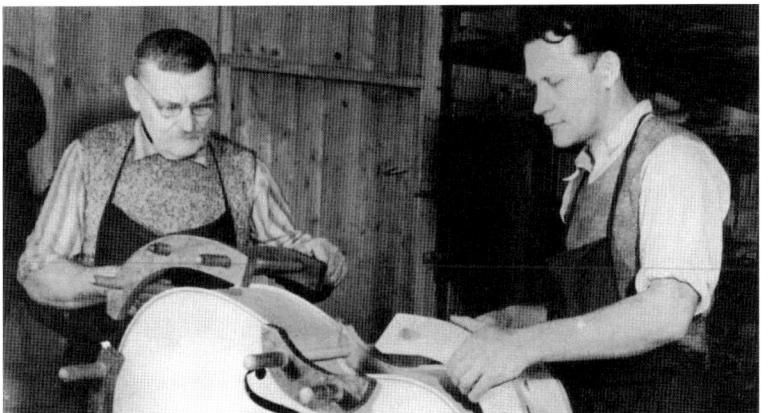

The double bass workshop of Emanuel Wilfer was forced to move from Absroth near Schönbach to Möhrendorf near Bubenreuth after the Second World War. Many other instrument makers from Schönbach settled there, as well. In the 1960s the region around Bubenreuth was the most important instrument making center in Europe.

exhibition booth of Framus, 1953

Fred Wilfer from Schönbach was one of the first to support the re-settlement of expelled violin makers in Bubenreuth, Franconia. After the end of the war Wilfer found work with the US Army. His duties included transport journeys between the 3rd US Army depots in Erlangen and his home in Egerland, which at that time was also under American occupation. It quickly became apparent that the already expropriated Germans would soon be expelled from the Egerland. He therefore started using his trips with the army truck to smuggle tonewood and tools from Schönbach to Erlangen, thus creating initial conditions for resuming production at a new location.

It was important for these very strongly organized instrument makers to stay together even after the expulsion and to find a new home together, as this was the only way to continue, as well as rebuild an efficient production of musical instruments. Fred Wilfer had already founded the company "Fränkische Musikinstrumentenerzeugung Fred Wilfer KG", or "Framus" for short, in Erlangen in 1945. Now he got politically involved in an effort to get the Schönbachers to settle in the district of Erlangen. In the meantime, the Bavarian state government pushed for the expelled workers to settle in Mittenwald, but in the end these plans were rejected due to the resistance of the local population, and in the end the majority of the Schönbachers came to Erlangen. The Framus company served as the first point of contact and employer for most of the newly arriving displaced. Around a dozen experienced double bass builders, including Anton Wilfer, Emanuel Wilfer, Otto Wilfer and Andreas Kohl, worked for Framus at that time. Initially, the principle of working from home, which is typical for the industry, was continued. Finally, at the end of 1949, the foundation was laid for a violin maker's settlement with 500 houses in the village of Bubenreuth, a village of

E. M. Pöllmann in his workshop in Adorf near Markneukirchen.
His nephew and successor Günter Krahmer left Adorf in 1959 and opened a workshop in Mttenwald, Bavaria.

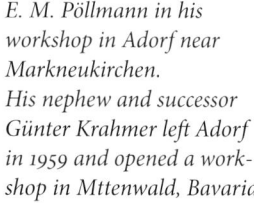

700 inhabitants near Erlangen. Framus and Karl Höfner also had modern factory buildings built in "Neu-Schönbach" ("New Schönbach"). During the years of the post-war economic miracle, demand and production in Bubenreuth grew rapidly. In the 1950s, with the growing popularity of rock'n'roll and beat music, a veritable guitar boom set in, so that large manufacturers such as Höfner and Framus concentrated increasingly on the production of guitars; bowed string instruments took a back seat.

In the 1970s, however, Framus experienced increasing financial difficulties. The company had taken on major debt for a new factory, and contrary to expectations, sales of guitars declined. The reasons were manifold: the guitar boom was over, the competition from the Far East was cheaper, and the strong D-Mark and taxes weakened exports. In 1975 Framus had to file for bankruptcy. With a staff reduced to 30 employees, production in Pretzfeld continued for several more years.

During this time, Höfner initially succeeded somewhat better in asserting itself in a market, where the focus was once again more on string instruments. However, the 1990s brought turbulent times for Höfner; the company was resold several times until it was finally taken over by two long-standing Höfner managers.

In Markneukirchen in the Vogtland region, which was now on the territory of the soviet occupation zone (GDR), instrument production continued after the Second World War as well. The Migma cooperative, founded as early as 1943, became a government-controlled cooperative of craftsmen ("Produktionsgenossenschaft des Handwerks"), which numerous independent instrument makers joined more or less voluntarily. Since the state claimed the foreign trade monopoly, both the import of raw materials and the export of instruments was only possible through the cooperative.

Hopf "Showbass Tabarin", 1950s. The company of guitar maker Dieter Hopf has been based in Taunusstein-Wehen (near Frankfurt) since the post-war period, and also employed the bass maker Ehrfried Wunderlich from Markneukirchen in the 1950s. Max Hoyer, who had been driven out of the Egerland region, also found a new home in the Taunus region.

CHARLIE MINGUS
Down Beat
International Critics Poll
Number 1
JAZZ BASSIST
Plays and Praises
framus
Write Today for FREE Full-Color Catalog
EXCLUSIVE NATIONAL WHOLESALERS OF FRAMUS PRODUCTS
PHILADELPHIA MUSIC co.   LIMERICK, PENNA.

During the years of the German economic miracle, Framus quickly grew to become one of the largest manufacturers of bowed and plucked instruments. Among the prominent endorsers of Framus were jazz guitarists like Jim Hall and Attila Zoller, as well as bassists Charles Mingus and Gary Peacock.

Auf besonderes Verlangen sende ich Bässe in Holzleisten verpackt und berechne hiefür K 3.50; diese Versendung geschieht jedoch nur auf Gefahr des Empfängers und meistens per Eilgut.

Die Bässe feinerer Art werden auf Wunsch in der Form der Violoncelli oder in einer Form gebaut, welche im unteren Teile des Körpers der Violoncelloform, im oberen durch Abplattung der gewöhnlichen Baßform entspricht, oder auch mit Carnisleisten außerhalb der Zargen.

Ich erzeuge die Violons auch noch in Zwischengrößen von $^5/_8$ und $^7/_8$ Größe, der Preis ist dann der mittlere zwischen $^1/_2$—$^3/_4$ resp. $^3/_4$—$^4/_4$.

Cello oder Violoncello.

Violon oder Kontrabaß.

Violon oder Kontrabaß.

Violon oder Kontrabaß.

Preise ohne Bogen, jedoch mit Maschine und mit Besaitung.
Mit kräftigem vollen Ton in solider Bauart.

No.		Größe	$^1/_4$	$^2/_4$	$^3/_4$	$^4/_4$
2	Von Ahorn, glatter Boden, mit eiserner Maschine, bessere . . per Stück K	46.—	50.—	55.—	60.—
3	Eingelegt mit eiserner Maschine, mit Messingplatten . . . . „ „ „	50.—	55.—	60.—	65.—
4	„ „ Messing-Maschine und Rand, Boden eingelegt . „ „ „	55.—	60.—	65.—	75.—
5	„ „ Ebenholzgriffbrett „ „ „	60.—	65.—	70.—	80.—
6	Boden gewölbt, feinste Ebenholzadjustierung, ausgesuchtes Holz „ „			80.—	90.—	100.—
7	Modell nach berühmten Meistern, feiner italienischer Lack, mit feinster französischer Maschine . . . . „ „				120.—	150.—
8	Bestes Orchester-Instrument . . . . „ „				150.—	160.—
9	Instrument für Solisten, nach Barthol. Christophori, Ferd. Gagliano, Venturi Linarolli etc.				180.— bis 250.—

Die Nummern 4, 5, 6 mit französischer Maschine per Stück K 12.— mehr.

Violons, 3saitig sind per Stück K 3.— billiger.

1 Kiste zur Verpackung eines	$^1/_2$	$^3/_4$	$^4/_4$ Violons
	K 6.50	7.50	8.50

In addition to these private and semi-public enterprises, it was above all the state owned company (VEB) Musima that produced instruments on a large scale. Musima was founded in 1952; raw material and machines were supplied by the expropriated companies Eroma (Heinrich Roth II), C.A. Götz from Wernitzgrün and Wenzel Rossmeisl (Roger Guitars). Eroma and C.A. Götz left the GDR after their expropriation and moved to Bubenreuth, as well. Musima was considered a model company of the GDR and was equipped with the most modern machines to achieve large production quantities and high quality. In the 1960s, double basses accounted for the second largest share of production value after guitars (61 %) with about 17 %. In addition to mass production, affiliated Musima master workshops existed, as well. The one founded by Alfred Meyer in 1904, which he had given up in 1970 due to retirement, was revived in the 1980s under the direction of bass builder Günter Focke as a Musima custom workshop. From 1983 onwards, the "Johannes Rubner Sonderwerkstatt" continued the tradition of the double bass workshop founded by Otto and Josef Rubner in 1883. The number of Musima employees grew to 1,200 by 1989, but with the reunification of Germany, demand from Eastern Europe collapsed—the production and number of employees fell rapidly. Ownership changed several times until Musima was finally wound up in 2003.

Although the majority of violin makers from Schönbach (today's Luby u Chebu) were driven out in the post-war years, musical instruments continued to be made in Bohemia. The Strunal company, which is still based there today, was at times one of the largest manufacturers of stringed instruments and guitars in Europe and can look back on an eventful history. After the war, 40 luthiers founded another cooperative under the name Cremona. It was nationalized in 1950 and merged with the wind instrument manufacturer Amati in 1958. Most of the instrument makers continued to work in their workshops for a long time before production gradually merged into one central company. In 1962, however, a fire destroyed the newly built factory building—production was once again distributed among smaller workshops, and industrialization slowed down once again. The number of employees, the production figures and also the quality sank continuously during this period—also because there was a lack of experienced skilled workers. In 1992 Cremona was privatized again and from now on it operated under the name "Strunal", and since 2016 "Strunal Schönbach".

Fig. left side:
catalogue from Hermann
Trapp, Bohemia around 1910

The city name "Cremona" is used inflationary in instrument making. There is also a manufacturer in Bulgaria called Kremona (founded in 1924).

Gustaf Alfred Meyer, Markneukirchen, 1938

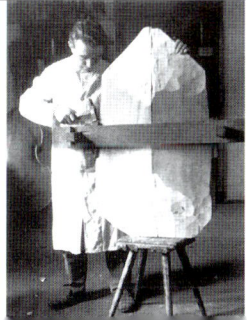

Double bass manufacturing at Höfner in Bubenreuth.
Höfner was one of the companies that had to leave Bohemia after the Second World War and settled in the region around Bubenreuth. Around 1965, about 2,000 people were employed in and around Bubenreuth by about 100 companies in instrument making; the Franconian region was the leader in Europe. At the beginning, the main focus was still on string instruments, but with the rise of rock music, guitars became more and more important. A rapid decline followed in the mid-1970s, triggered by cheap imports from Japan. After the turn of the millennium, only about 130 people were still employed in Bubenreuth's music industry.

Double bass manufacturing at Höfner in Bubenreuth: A fingerboard is glued onto the neck.

Bass maker Rudi Glaßl, Höfner

Cello- and bass maker Ewald Sommer, Höfner

Ribs in outer molds, Höfner

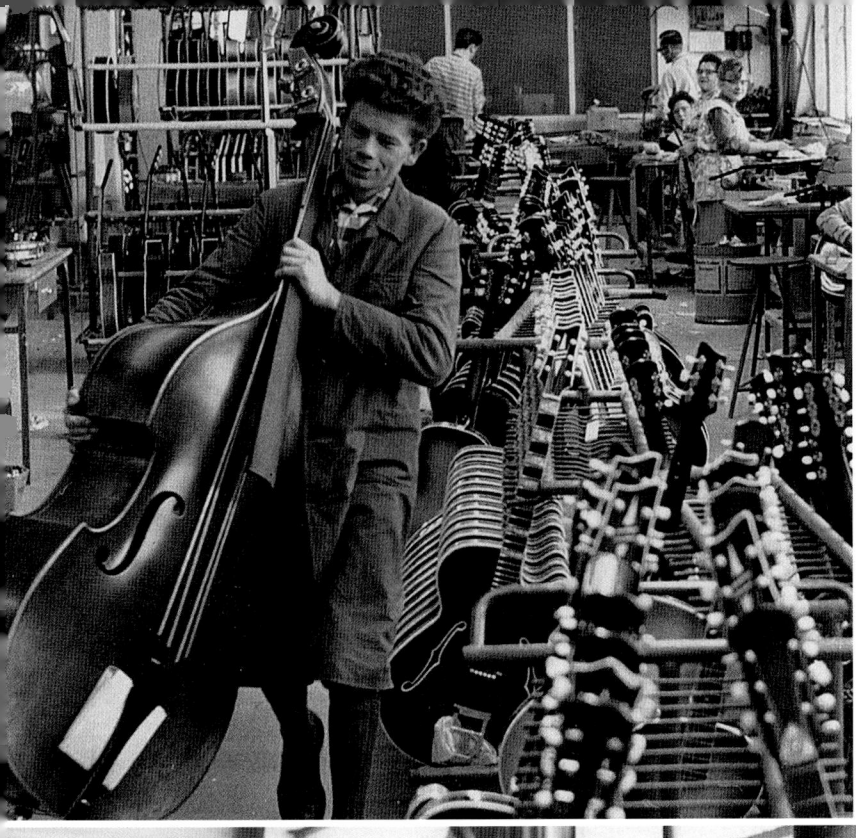

Fig. top: Luthier Paul Schelhorn brings a bass for set up, Framus

Fig. bottom: Anton Wilfer, Double bass department of Framus, 1960s

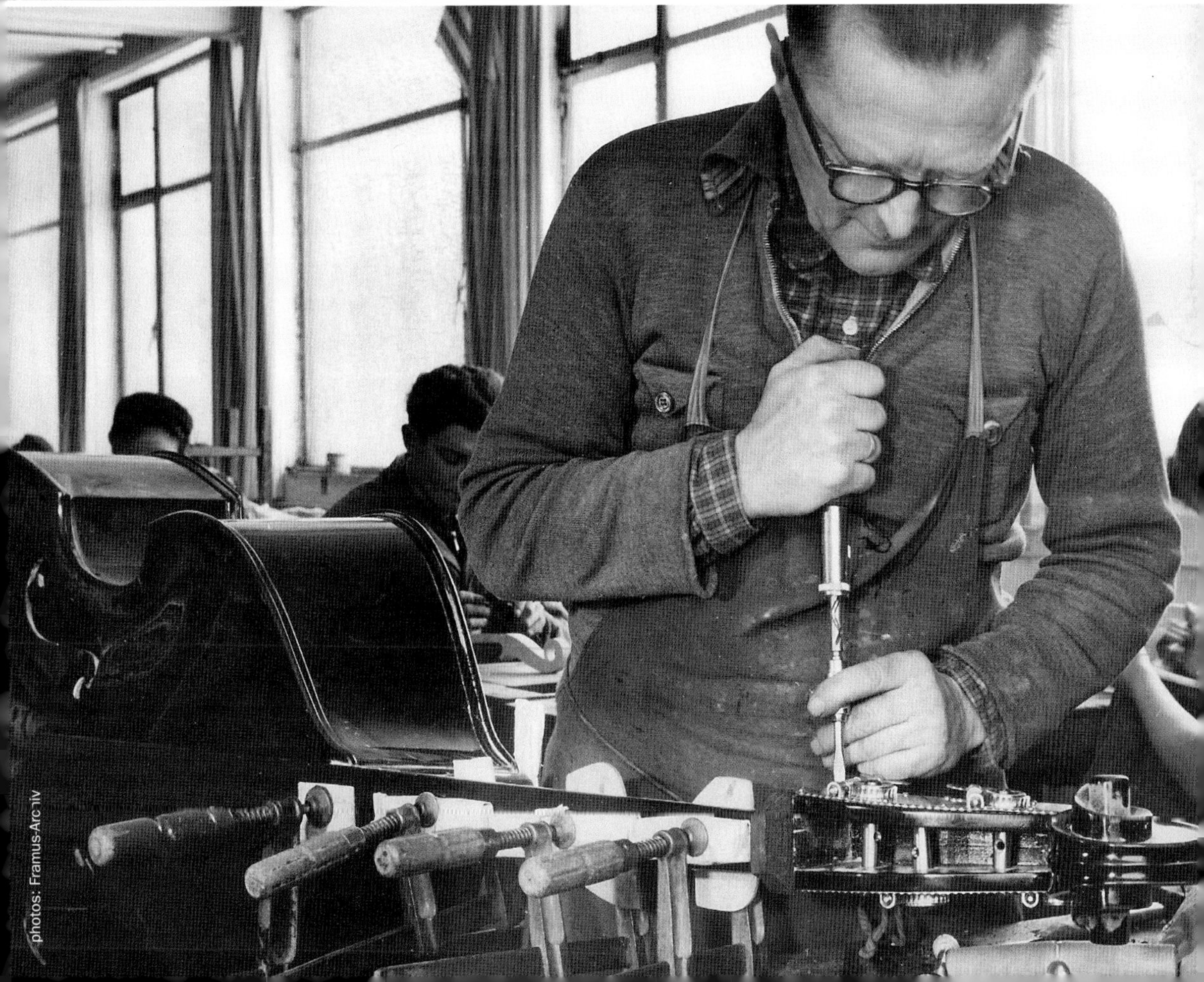

photos: Framus-Archiv

In the 19th century, England and the U.S.A. introduced rules that required imported goods to carry a designation of origin—the famous "Made in Germany". Today the wording of this designations not only allow conclusions to be drawn about the country of origin, but also about age.

Sachsen.. bis 1891
Deutschland, Saxony 1891–1914
Made in Deutschland 1914–1921
Made in Germany .... 1921–1939*, after 1990
* from 1939 to 1945 there were almost no exports from Germany

U.S. Zone / US Zone Made in Germany................. 1945–1950
Made in West Germany .... 1950–1990 (FRG)
Made in Germany, Made in GDR,
Made in German Democratic Republic................... 1950–1990 (GDR)

Bohemia.. 1891-1914
Checoslovacia, Cecho-Slowakia 1918-1921
Made in Bohemia... 1914–1918
Made in Czechoslovakia 1918–1993
Made in the Czech Republic .... since 1993

Fig. left: Otto Wilfer, luthier at Tennelohe near Bubenreuth
Fig. right: Walter Klier, varnisher at Framus

Labeling fraud

Already in the 18th century, imitation labels were commonplace in violin making. At that time, however, nobody considered this practice as plagiarism or even piracy. These mostly printed labels usually refer to the model of the violin—German made violins often bore Stainer labels; French violins from Mirecourt mostly bear the names of Italian masters such as Amati and Stradivari. To this day, these labels still excite inexperienced amateurs, who believe that they are holding a precious Stradivarius in their hands. However, these notes (which often bore little resemblance to the originals) are rarely based on deception. At the time when these instruments came on the market, customers were well aware that they were not authentic old master violins, but that the labels simply served to identify the model.

American dealers have always liked to put fake labels with German or Italian-sounding names on the string instruments imported from Europe. Names, which usually have little to do with the actual manufacturer, but are intended to give the instrument the appearance of coming from a European master workshop. In the U.S.A., there are numerous "German" manufacturer names that are rather unknown in Germany. One of the biggest double bass importers in the U.S.A. for a long time was the company Metropolitan Music of John Juzek from Prague; basses with this label come from Emanuel Wilfer and other Schönbach makers.

Basses by Emanuel Wilfer in the catalogue of the John Juzek company (around 1935)

A Stradivarius note from a violin by the Mittenwald wholesaler Neuner & Hornsteiner. This instrument should not be considered a real Stradivari. The label serves as model designation.

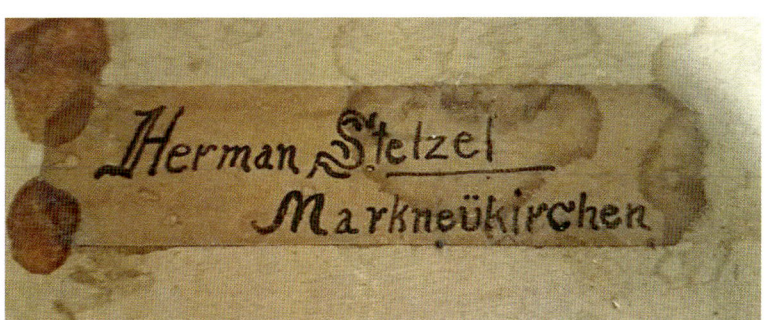

With this label, the intent to deceive is obvious. The forger was a bit over-whelmed with the German spelling of "Hermann Stolzel, Markneukirchen". The blotches, which were applied overlapping on the note and the bottom, are an indication for an intention to deceive, as well.

84

Giovanni Lazzaro

Messina anno 19.....

Jo: Baptista Ceruti Cremonensis
fecit Cremonæ An. 18

Fait par Georges Apparut
A Mirecourt en 19   n°

Gastone Bargelli di Giuseppe
allievo del Padre
fece in Firenze anno 19

Paul Didier
Luthier
Médailles d'Or — Grand prix
N°   rue du Faisan
à Metz, l'an ......

Fait par Paul Blanchard
à Lyon en 18   n°

Marinus Capicchioni
Fecit Arimini A. D. 19

Albertus Aloysius Blanchi
Augustini filius fecit
Nicæa Civitas Anno

ORESTE CANDI
Fece in GENOVA
l'anno 19

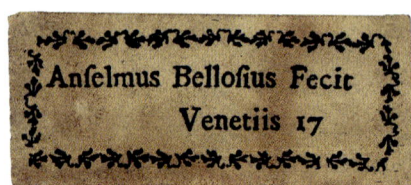

Anselmus Bellosius Fecit
Venetiis 17

GIOVANNI CAVANI
di SPILAMBERTO (Modena)
l'anno

John Juzek
Violinmaker in Prague
N°:   yr: *1930*
Master art copy of:
MADE IN CZECHOSLOVAKIA

FRIEDRICH KOCHENDÖRFER
ATELIER FÜR GEIGENBAU
STUTTGART 19

FAIT DANS L'ATELIER DE
CHARLES BRUGÈRE
PARIS 18

EUGEN GÄRTNER
Atelier für Kunstgeigenbau
KGL. WÜRTTBG.   FÜRSTL. HOHENZOLL.
HOF-GEIGENBAUER   HOFLIEFERANT.
fecit   STUTTGART

photo: William P. Gottlieb

Bassmaking in America

Jazz bassist Chubby Jackson with a Kay bass. The extremely high string action is clearly visible.
Further details the Ampeg pickup (mounted into the endpin assembly).

American-made plywood basses

After the First World War and the resulting economic crises, sales of industrially manufactured stringed instruments from Europe fell sharply. The export-strong Mittenwald manufacturers Neuner & Hornsteiner and J. A. Baader ceased production in the 1930s, and many companies from Markneukirchen and Mirecourt had to close down, as well. Simultanously, the production of musical instruments in the U.S.A. grew, making the market less dependent on imports from Europe.

Like old American guitars, double basses from the U.S.A. are sought-after collector's items today. Although they are comparitively simply crafted and industrially manufactured, good basses from Kay, King or Epiphone in their original condition are traded among collectors at values of fully carved basses of much higher quality.

Founded in the mid-30s by German-born Henry Kuhrmeyer in Chicago, Kay began building up production of basses and cellos in addition to importing string instruments from Germany. They started out with models Concert (gamba model) and Maestro (violin model), and added top models Supreme and Swingmaster in the 1950s. A five-string version of the top model Swingmaster was available under the name Chubby Jackson. Jackson, bassist for Woody Herman and others, was involved in the development of that five-string model and endorsed Kay basses. In cooperation with bassist Ray Brown, Kay designed a cello for jazz bassists, launching it under the name "Ray Brown Jazz Cello".

Unlike a classical cello, it was tuned in fourths, had a wider fingerboard, and double bass mechanics. Besides Ray Brown, several other popular jazz

Plywood basses have the advantage over more expensive carved basses of being more rigid and were therefore very popular in touring big bands.

bassists such as Sam Jones and Percy Heath utilized these piccolo basses as solo instruments. In 1969 the company Kay Musical Instruments was dissolved, and the name and the means of production such as the special tools, templates and moulds were sold. The Engelhardt-Link company has been using that equipment to build their basses more or less identically by following Kay's original patterns.

The King company was founded by H. N. White in 1893 and quickly made a good name for itself in wind instrument construction. In 1935 White started to produce double basses. They offered two models, the violin-shaped King "Mortone" and the gamba-shaped "American Standard". In 1965 White sold its entire string instrument production to competitor Kay, who surprisingly stopped producing the King models. However, American bass luthiers Arnold Schnitzer and Wil de Sola still offer an instrument based on the "American Standard" model, the "Cleveland", but the bass is now manufactured in Germany, prior to beeing varnished and set up in the U.S.

In the 1930s, the companies Gibson and Epiphone competed for leadership in the guitar market. In 1939 Gibson entered the market for stringed instruments and began manufacturing violins, cellos and double basses, as well. Epiphone responded in 1941 with a series that included five different double bass models. Although these were plywood basses, Epiphone was not shy in their advertising: "A superb instrument for the exacting artist who requires the very finest. Of the most choice woods …

King Mortone from 1957 with blonde (clear) varnish

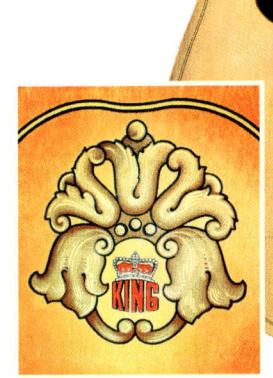

straight-grain spruce arch top, select curly maple full arched back and sides, finest maple neck, natural Brazilian rosewood fingerboard and rock maple tailpiece. Hand polishing brings out the beautiful flame of the wood. Exquisite hand inlaid triple purfling ornaments top and back. Gold plated, full plate engraved machine heads. Adjustable end pin. Famous George Van Eps adjustable bridge, sloping shoulders, narrow fingerboard. In shaded (rich Cremona brown) or natural finish. Three quarter size only."

But soon after, production at Epiphone and Gibson was interrupted due to the war. Many workers were drafted, and instead of musical instruments, Epiphone had to build parts for the aircraft industry. In 1943 Epaminondas "Epi" Stathopoulo died of leukemia, leading to his younger brothers Orphie and Frixo taking over the management of Epiphone. After the war, Gibson initially concentrated on guitars, while Epiphone also resumed the production of double basses. In 1949 Frixo left Epiphone and

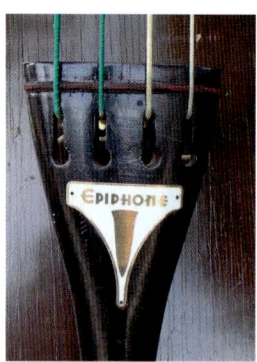

*H. N. White produced two
model series of double basses:
the simpler „American
Standard", and the „King
Mortone".
„Buy American Instruments
—Increase employment":
In this advertisement the
American origin is empha-
sized as the main selling
point besides the robustness
of the instrument—a rather
political argument in times
of economic depression.
These basses were made
completely of local woods in
the U.S.A., only the ebony
for the fingerboard was
imported.
The price for an American
Standard Bass in 1936 was
$ 110, which was about the
average monthly income of
an American.*

A NEW **AMERICAN MADE** WOOD BASS

TO MEET THE POPULAR LOW PRICED FIELD

Every part of this Bass is **American Made**, including the strings. Neck is made in our own factory from native Ohio Maple. All wood used in the body is grown in the states and fabricated in our own factory. Ebony used in finger board and tail piece must be imported from Africa, but it, too, is fabricated in our own factory.

The strings are an American-made product and we manufacture our own gear mechanism.

American Standard

Priced lower than other swell back wood string basses. Excells all previous medium priced string Basses . . . better tone . . . more volume . . . easy playing. . . Built to stand more hard usage.

Thru entirely new methods of construction, the **American Standard** String Bass saves repair costs and practically assures against cracking or becoming unglued thru ordinary usage. Less repair costs and upkeep can be guaranteed.

JOBS FOR AMERICAN WORKERS

"We sacrifice countless jobs of American workers to foreign labor. simply because . . . every dollar's worth of foreign manufactured products imported into the United States last year replaced at least three dollars worth of domestic products and represented a proportionate loss in jobs to American workers."

"Foreign governments are not interested in putting our unemployed back to work. We, ourselves, must do this. And, until we do, taxes will become heavier and heavier and the buying power of the nation less and less."

Made in America Club, Inc.
420 Lexington Avenue, New York, N.Y.

Buy American Made Instruments . . . Increase employment . . . Reduce relief rolls and thereby reduce your taxes . . . American Made instruments are better instruments . . . Buy American Made instruments and receive more for your money.

¾ SIZE

SPECIFICATIONS

Outside—Back and sides maple.
Top—Special tone top wood selected for fine tonal qualities. Through special treatment will not crack.
Neck—Domestic hard maple—thoroughly seasoned and fabricated in our own factory.
Gear mesh and plates—made of special hard brass fabricated in our own factory.
Finger board and tail piece—finest ebony obtainable and fabricated in our own factory.
Finish—Velvet sheen finish, in the finest of lacquers, more durable. Color blended, looking like the most costly violins.

Price, F. O. B. Cleveland	$110.00
Button Mackintosh Fleece Lined Cover	12.00
"Zipper" Mackintosh Fleeced Lined Cover	14.00

BASS BOWS

	Each
Butler Model. Birchwood stick, red finish, ebonized frog.	$ 4.50
Butler Model. Brazil wood, round stick, dark red color, ebony frog with pearl eye and pearl slide. Good model.	8.50
French Model. Good quality Brazil wood round stick, highly polished dark brown color, genuine ebony, full mounted frog.	9.00
French Model. Genuine Pernambuco round stick, finished in rich brown, finely polished. Full mounted ebony frog. A well balanced bow.	15.00

5225-33 Superior Ave. *The* **H. N. WHITE** *Co.* Cleveland, Ohio

began to produce double basses under his own name without much success. In the 1950s the quality and reputation of Epiphone guitars declined; only their double basses were still selling well. In 1957 Gibson finally took over its archrival Epiphone and continued double bass production until 1963 with the acquired moulds and tools.

The large demand in the U.S. market convinced European companies to offer plywood basses, as well. Karl Höfner from Schönbach already had experience producing plywood archtop guitars. By order of their American importer, the Gratz company from New York, they started to design basses and cellos in this new construction method, as well. For this purpose Höfner made positive and negative molds out of concrete. Five layers of veneer were coated with glue, lined up on top of each other and shaped into form in a large spindle press. However, due to the dimensions, pressing laminated double bass backs and tops was much more demanding than preparing guitar parts. The glue has a certain hardening time, which can be shortened by heating the press moulds – but this was hardly possible due to the size of the double bass moulds. Over time, Walter Höfner developed a feeling for how long the glue had to set and planned the process of pressing and adding new veneers in a way that fit efficiently into the daily routine. Höfner was eventually able to produce up to 20 plywood basses per month, almost all of which were exported to the U.S.A.

Today's high asking prices for old Kays are rather the result of American national pride then of constructional quality, since these instruments usually have several typical weak spots. The main issue is the neck: it is very slim and easy to play, which some bassists prefer. However, this may lead to the warping of the neck under the tension of contemporary steel strings. Most American plywood basses use a concealed dovetail joint for the neck, as is common in guitar building. These were machined to high tolerances and are prone to get loose over the years. The dovetail joint also makes it difficult to adjust the neck angle, in order to set up the instrument properly for today's needs. With too flat a neck angle and a regular proportioned bridge, a lower string action and proper string angle cannot be achieved.

Kay basses are very simple in construction, which is especially noticeable at the scroll. The pegbox is sawn, milled with a template and not further carved by hand. To save material, the scroll's ears (plastic or wood) are glued on. Many old Kay basses lack these ears—but they are available as spare parts.

Frixo Stathopoulo left Epiphone in 1949 and made basses under his own name for a short time.

„Mr Rogers Shows How To Make Bass Violins": This episode of the children's television series was broadcast in 1985 and shows how the company Engelhardt-Link (Chicago/U.S.A.) makes basses.

The pre-bent rib segments are assembled and glued together on an inner mould to form the ribs. The moulds and tools came from the bankruptcy assets of the former Kay company.

The pegbox was not carved by hand, but by means of a router.

Kay Maestro,
1939

The finished ribs were inserted into an outer mould …

… and glued to the top and back. Then the neck was inserted by means of a routed dovetail joint, like it is common for guitars.

The finished bass was finally spraypainted with nitrocellulose lacquer – without using a protective mask …

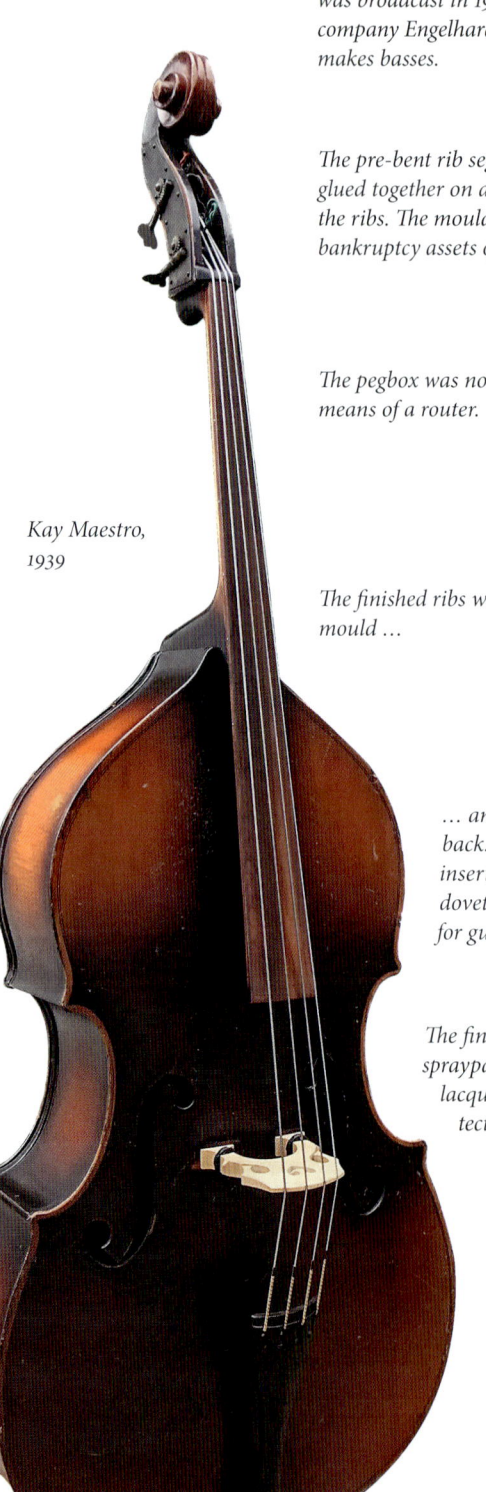

Strings

Strings and their quality play a crucial role in the sound of a double bass—they produce its tone. The corpus of the instrument (as well as the pickups, microphones and amplifiers) only serve to amplify the vibrations generated by the strings. Choosing the right string for an instrument is an important step towards the realization of an optimized and personalized sound.

Today's bass player has the choice between string brands made of different materials and material combinations. In addition to gut (sheep gut or cheaper beef gut), silk and plastics (nylon, perlon, polyester, carbon fibre, PEEK etc.), various steels, ferrous and non-ferrous metals (such as aluminium and copper, gold, silver, tungsten, titanium) and mineral fibres are used in string manufacturing.

String making in the 17th century, copperplate engraving from Christoph Weigel, Regensburg 1698

Using plant fibres and animal tendons as strings originated in prehistoric times. In the early advanced civilizations of the Middle East, horsehair, silk and gut were also used, and the ancient Mediterranean peoples used gut for string manufacturing, as well. When scientist discovered the tomb of the famous musician Harmosis, who lived at the time of queen Hatshepsut (1520 to 1484 B.C.), his lute was found largely intact. The instrument of the artist, who died around 1500 B.C., is exhibited in a museum in Cairo, Egypt, with its gut strings well preserved to this day.

Gut strings are still being referred to with the misleading term "catgut". The origin of this term can be traced back to this anecdote: around 1300, Italian saddle makers in the small town of Salle/Pescara discovered, that the gut of regional wild mountain sheep, which they used for sewing saddles, was particularly suitable as a string for musical instruments. The production of strings quickly became the most important industry of the village. To protect themselves against competition, the string makers concealed the true origin and instead claimed that the gut was derived from cats. Cats were the subject of many superstitious myths at the time, and killing them was considered to be disastrous—this way they hoped to deter potential imitators.

Diderot & Alambert's Encyclopedie, Paris 1750–67

An article in the "Zeitschrift für Instrumentenbau" (magazine for instrument making) in 1881 describes the construction of a low C string for a 5-string double bass: "The C string has a diameter of 10 mm [sic!]. A core of steel wire, which is about 2 mm thick, is covered with silk threads along its length. Simple iron wire is then spun onto the silk layer. This layer of iron wire is again covered lengthwise with silk threads. On top of this, simple iron wire is again wound tightly, which in turn is covered tightly with a layer of silk, and over this layer silver-plated or nickel-plated copper wire is spun as the last covering material.

Around 1650 the production of wound strings began. A sheath of thin wire was wound spirally around the core. Wound strings have a lower stiffness than comparable plain strings. This winding increases the vibrating mass of a string without impairing its elasticity, making thinner string diameters and shorter gauges possible.

It is known that Giovanni Bottesini preferred wound strings with a silk core. Under the conditions of tropical and subtropical climates, in which he frequently spent time, silk was a more resilient string material than gut, that was commonly used until then. In addition, silk core strings met his technical playing requirements. When the first steel strings appeared, silk core strings initially disappeared from the market.

Today, depending on the manufacturer and model, gut, natural silk, nylon, plastic (synthetic) multifilaments, steel cable (strand) or steel or bronze wire are used for the core of a string. A wire core does not necessarily have to be circular. Hexagonal or longitudinally slotted profiles provide better grip for the braiding. The braiding is made in one or more layers with round or flat wire, or a combination of both. When using round wire, the string usually is being polished at the end, to create a smooth surface for a more pleasant feel.

Kontrabaß-Saiten.

	G (I te), Darm		D (II te), Darm		A (III te), Darm	
	No.	Mk.	No.	Mk.	No.	Mk.
Gute Qualität . . . . per Stück	7760	1.50	7770	1.80	7780	2.80
Feine Art . . . . „ „	7761	2.—	7771	2.50	7781	4.—
Ausgewählt, Marke „**Krone**“ . . . . „ „	7762	3.50	7772	4.50	7782	6.—
Quintenrein, für Solospiel, Marke „**Senza Pari**“ . . „ „	7763	6.—	7773	8.—	7783	12.—

	A (III te), besponnen		E (IV te) besponnen	
	No.	Mk.	No.	Mk.
Gute Qualität . . . . per Stück	7785	2.50	7790	3.20
Feine Art, rote Seiden-Enden . . . . „ „	7786	3.50	7791	4.50
Ausgesuchte Solo-Qualität, rote Seiden-Enden . . . . „ „	7787	5.50	7792	7.—

Baß-Saiten

	I.	II.	III.	IV. Qualität			
G Darm . . . Stück RM	4.—	2.10	1.60	1.30	116 A versilberter Kupferdraht, grünend . . . . Stück RM	3.50
D Darm . . . „ „	6.—	3.30	2.70	2.20	118 A garantiert drahtsicher, voller Ton, blauend „ „	6.—
A Darm . . . „ „	8.—	4.10	3.30	2.70	120 E versilberter Kupferdraht, grünend . . . . „ „	4.50
					122 E drahtsicher, voller kräftiger Ton, blauend „ „	8.—

Fig. above: The selection of bass strings until the middle of the 20th century was rather limited, consisting of mainly gut *(German: "Darm")* strings, either plain or with wound *("besponnen")* A and E strings.

Fig. right: E-strings in comparison—a gut string wound with silver round wire (left), a plain gut string (middle) and a steel cable string with flat wire winding (right).

Before being wound, the core is often braided with silk or synthetic threads. This serves both to ensure a tight fit of the braid and to dampen the string. When the string is bowed, this damping eliminates unwanted vibrations and thus ensures a good response. At the same time it also reduces the sustain of the string, which in turn impairs pizzicato playing.

In addition to the damping of a string, its torsional stiffness (or torsional resistance) is another characteristic that is decisive for the suitability of a string for bowing or plucking. When playing with the bow, the strings are "taken along" by the bow hairs and twisted in the longitudinal direction. At a point specific to each string, the torsional resistance is greater than the friction of the bow hairs. The string "tears loose" and turns back until it is twisted again by the bow, and the process is repeated. This jagged oscillation of the bowed string is also known as sawtooth oscillation. For bowing, therefore, torsion-resistant strings are better suited, while more flexible strings are often used for pizzicato.

Sound and playability of a string depend on various physical properties. The most important one is the string tension. For a given pitch, it is derived from the variables length and mass. While the length of the string is determined by the scale of the bass, its mass depends on the force used to tune it to a certain pitch. The string tension results in the pressure it exerts on the bridge and thus on the soundboard. String pressure on the one hand and the properties of the soundboard and bass bar, as well as the position and size of the soundpost on the other hand, are the important variables which, in interplay, determine the vibrational behavior of the soundboard, and thus the sound. The following applies to playability: the lower the tension of a string, the greater the amplitude of its vibration. Soft strings (e.g. gut strings) therefore need a higher string action than strings with high tension.

In the 1950s, steel strings gained acceptance and replaced the gut string.

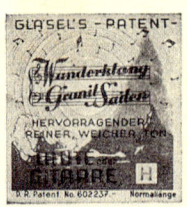

Contrabaß-Saiten Stahl

	G	D	A	E	C 5.	Satz
Romana gebeutelt . . . . Stck.	4.80	6.40	8.—	9.60	—	28.80
Kämpffe-Royal Edelstahl . . . . . . „	6.—	7.50	9.—	10.50	—	33.—
„ Omega Flachdraht . . . . . „	8.—	10.50	14.—	16.—	—	48.50
Weidler-Nürnberger Präzision . . . . „	9.40	10.70	11.50	13.40	18.—	45.—
„ Nürnberger Künstler . . . . . „	12.—	13.—	14.50	16.50	18.—	56.—
Wiener-Thomastik . . . . „	10.80	11.80	13.—	15.—	17.—	50.—
„ Infeld-Seil . . . . „	12.20	13.—	14.20	16.50	18.60	55.—
„ Spiralkern . . . . „	14.10	15.—	16.40	19.—	21.40	63.30
LYCON-Dänisches Fabrikat . . . . . „	12.50	13.10	14.50	16.50	18.50	56.60

Bei Contrabaß-Saiten immer schwingende Länge angeben.

Different string strengths have a direct effect on the sound: a light, thin string may vibrate more strongly and longer due to its lower mass, but it transmits less energy to the bridge and the instrument. This results in a good response and long sustain, but also to a rather quiet tone. Stronger or thicker strings with a higher tension produce a louder and brighter tone, but require more effort when playing.

Too much pressure on the soundboard can have a negative effect on the sound. Some older basses, originally made for the lower pressure of (sometimes only three) gut strings, no longer resonate well when strung with steel strings. If the balance between string tension and instrument is not optimal, two approaches to improving the sound and playability are common. On the one hand, the string tension can be altered by changing the string make. On the other hand, the string pressure resulting from the string tension can be adjusted by applying subtle changes to the bridge and/or saddle. A lowering of the bridge reduces the string pressure on the top, and vice versa. An elevated lower saddle flattens the angle of the tailpiece and thereby lowers the pressure on the soundboard.

To find out whether the sound improves with higher or lower tension, the strings can be tuned up or down half-tones for simulation. Depending on the result, you can then make a calculated choice for a type of string: if the bass sounds better after tuning down, try thinner, lighter strings, and if it sounds better after tuning up, stronger ones. Many manufacturers offer their strings in different strengths, such as light, medium, strong or heavy. These thickness specifications are relative, and "soft" strings from one manufacturer do not necessarily match the "light" or "low tension" strings from another. A little more reliable are specifications in physical units such as kg, lbs or kp.

Ray Brown was one of the first popular bassists to switch from gut to steel strings. The Danish company Lycon offered a Ray Brown version of their strings, which was accompanied by an autographed card.

On this record cover the red colored gut strings of the brand Red-O-Ray, which bassist Bill Crow played, are clearly visible.

The same string has a lower tension on a bass with a shorter scale length than on a bass with a longer one. The difference in scale length between a ¼-bass with 112 cm and a ¾-bass with 106 cm corresponds approximately to the semitone interval E to F. The tension of a ¼-string on a ¾-bass is therefore equal to the tension on a ¼-bass tuned down by a semitone.

However, not all types are offered in several different gauges. Some bassists alternatively use solo strings, which they tune down by a whole step to orchestra tuning in order to lower the string tension.

The string brands available today are separated into three categories according to the nature of their core: gut, steel and synthetic strings. Gut strings are somewhat delicate, and also tend to be more expensive than steel strings. Being a natural product, they tend to react strongly to weather influences, and do not hold the tuning well when subject to fluctuations in temperature and/or humidity. Gut strings have a rather low tension and therefore require a higher string action than most steel strings. They are characterized by a dark and mellow, yet assertive sound, and were standard on all stringed instruments until the First World War. Due to a shortage of material, however, steel strings eventually prevailed. Initially, steel strings started to be used only for violins and cellos, and the sound was considered to be a matter of getting used to. The double bass followed that trend by the early 1960s. Nylon strings first entered the U.S. market in 1946, with nylon threads and ribbons being used both as the core and for winding around gut or steel strings.

Even though gut strings were pushed out of the market with the emergence of steel strings, some bassists still like to use them despite their high price. Today, they are mainly used in bluegrass and rockabilly (slap bass), as well as for baroque music with authentic instruments.

A traditional set of gut strings consists of bare G and D strings spun from gut alone, and A and E strings wound with round wire (silver or copper). Bare gut surfaces are sensitive to hand perspiration and tend to

For the production of gut strings, the intestines are washed and cut into strips. Several of these strips are then twisted into a string and dried.

fray or develop uneven surfaces. For this reason, the strings are oiled, or in some cases available lacquered. Any unevenness that does occur can be smoothed out with fine sandpaper.

In contrast to gut strings, steel strings are insensitive to weather influences or hand perspiration and have a long life expectancy. Due to their thinner diameter they allow a low string action and can also be used with magnetic pickups. Compared to gut strings, they usually have a longer sound duration (sustain) and a brighter, sometimes metallic sound.

Stringmaker Mimmo Peruffo stretches gut strings for drying

New strings for an octobass: In 1996 the Musée de la Musique in Paris commissioned two sets of strings from the Italian string maker Mimmo Peruffo (Aquila corde armoniche) to re-string the Vuillaume octobass. The octobasses have a vibrating string length of 2.15 m, the tension of one string is about 35 kg. The diameters of the original plain gut strings are C (32.70 Hz) 4.0 mm, G (24.50 Hz) 5.3 mm, C (16.35 Hz) 8.0 mm. Even for an experienced string maker such as Mimmo Peruffo, the task of producing strings with these dimensions was a challenge: the length of a raw string was 4.5 meters, and 4.1 kilometers of gut material were needed for one set.

… more about the Octobass on page 32

Rosin

Rosin is made from tree resin, mainly pine resin. To extract the resin, tree trunks are stripped of their bark in places and provided with V-shaped grooves that lead to a collection container. The resin that the tree produces in effort to close the wound flows into this container. During the subsequent processing, the actual rosin is obtained by distillation of the resin. It is used for lubricants, technical fats, cosmetics, pharmaceuticals, adhesive plasters, chewing gum, varnishes, paints, and much more. For use with stringed instruments, other components are added to the raw rosin, such as turpentine, waxes, resins and also metals or metal dusts of gold, silver, copper, tin, lead, meteo iron. These admixtures are responsible for the different properties of colophonium.

To clean the bow hair of rosin residues you can use rectified alcohol and a clean toothbrush. However, the alcohol must not come into contact with the bow stick or the bass, as this would dissolve the varnish. As a less risky solvent, lighter petrol can be an alternative.

Rosin is not unlimited in its use. Over time it dries out and becomes unusable. If you store it in a jar with a screw cap, you can delay the aging process a little. You can also put a cloth soaked in alcohol or water in the glass to freshen up the rosin. But don't let it get too soft, because it would become unusable, as well.

The still liquid rosin is filled into cups.

Depending on the maker, rosin has different hardness and consistency. Bass rosin is generally softer and has a better grip than the brands offered for violin and cello.

Orchester-Anordnung

1. Dirigent, 2. Erste Geigen, 3. Zweite Geigen, 4. Bratschen, 5. Celli, 6. Flöten,
7. Oboen, 8. Fagotte, 9. Klarinetten, 10. Hörner, 11. Kontrafagott, 12. Englisch
Horn, 13. Trompeten, 14. Posaunen, 15. Harfen, 16. Kontrabässe, 17. Schlagzeug,
18. Tuba. — Die Skizze zeigt die im allgemeinen gebräuchliche Sitzanordnung des
Theater-Orchesters, doch sind auch andere Anordnungen möglich.

Important bassists

*Orchestra arrangement: 1. conductor, 2. first violins, 3. second violins, 4. violas, 5. celli, 6. flutes,
7. oboes, 8. bassoons, 9. clarinets, 10. french horns, 11. contra-bassoon, 12. English horn, 13. trumpets,*

Johann Matthias Sperger – *1750 †1812

The double bassist and composer Johann Matthias Sperger was born in Feldsberg (Moravia; today: Valtice, Czech Republic) in 1750. At the age of 17 he moved to Vienna, where he received lessons in music theory and instrumental instruction. In 1777 Sperger was employed as a double bassist in the chapel of the Archbishop and later Cardinal of Hungary, Joseph Count von Batthyany in Bratislava (capital of the Slovak Republic). From his relatively high annual salary of 600 florins (compared to 180–400 fl for other orchestra members), one can conclude that Sperger's reputation was excellent. In addition to seven concertos for the double bass, he wrote six more for various other instruments, 18 symphonies and a fair amount of chamber music. After the dissolution of the Batthyan Chapel in 1783, Sperger was offered a position in the court orchestra of Count Ludwig von Erdödy in Kohfidisch near Eberau (then Western Hungary, now in Burgenland, Austria). In 1786 this chapel was also dissolved and Sperger moved back to Vienna. In his search for employment he travelled extensively and also auditioned for the cello-playing King Friedrich Wilhelm II in Berlin.

During his Viennese years without a permanent orchestra engagement (1786—1789) he wrote numerous works: 13 symphonies and three double bass concertos. In August 1789 Sperger was finally able to take up the hoped-for position in the court orchestra of Duke Friedrich Franz I of Mecklenburg-Schwerin in the Ludwigslust Residence, following a promise by the latter. This orchestra, with its outstanding musicians, offered Sperger an artistic home which fulfilled and satisfied him. In the "Diarium" alone, run by concertmaster Massouneau from 1803, Sperger appeared seven times as soloist in his double bass concertos; numerous of his symphonies and chamber music pieces were being performed, as well. Immediately after his employment, Sperger received permission to purchase a double bass from Vienna suitable for solo playing. Documents show the strict separation between orchestral and solo instrument, for which Sperger used particularly "fine, precious strings". From Ludwigslust, Sperger undertook several concert tours (1792 Lübeck, Music Academy, exclusively with his own works; 1793 Berlin; 1801 performance of two of his double bass concertos with the Gewandhaus Orchestra in Leipzig). On May 13, 1812 Sperger died of nervous fever in Ludwigslust, Mecklenburg-Schwerin. His 40 compositions for solo double bass (18 concertos, chamber music), which even by today's standards require great technical skill, are evidence of his impressive abilities as an instrumentalist. His repertoire covered the entire concert literature for double bass of the Vienna Classic musical epoch and was found to be preserved almost in its entirety in the archives of his estate.

Johann Matthias Sperger: "... for this I have chosen such a strong instrument, which requires a decent way of life in order to maintain strength..."

The International Johann-Matthias-Sperger-Society organises a double bass competition in Ludwigslust (Germany) every two years, which bears his name. In 2018 the city of Ludwigslust erected a monument in honour of its famous son.

Bronze sculpture: Andreas Krämmer; photo: Sylvia Wegener/Stadt Ludwigslust, Illustration: Milan Drujic

Domenico Dragonetti – *1763 †1846

Domenico Dragonetti is considered the first double bass virtuoso of international standing. Being a composer himself, he was friends with many of his famous contemporaries such as Haydn, Beethoven and Rossini. The emergence of sophisticated double bass parts in 19th century music is largely attributed to his influence.

Dragonetti was born on April 7, 1763 in Venice. He came from a simple background and enjoyed only a rudimentary education. He learned to play the violin and the guitar autodidactically and eventually took lessons with double bassists of the chapel of San Marco. In his early years Dragonetti earned his living playing music in the streets, cafés and hotels. First engagements in the theatres of Venice followed, before he finally got a permanent position in the prestigious orchestra of San Marco. There he quickly made a career, leading to offers from abroad, which he initially turned down. In light of Venice's economic decline he eventually accepted an invitation to the King's Theatre in London. Originally just on a five-year contract, Dragonetti remained in the English metropolis until his death as a very successful and prosperous musician and composer. From London, he travelled several times for longer periods to Vienna, the musical centre of his time, and also to his Venetian homeland.

Dragonetti at the age of 80. Notice the bow held in the lower grip.

Sources describe Dragonetti as a dazzling personality, who knew how to market himself skilfully. His fees were far above the level of those usually paid to an orchestra musician. He spent a large part of his income on his collections of dolls, snuffboxes and musical instruments. It is also known that he used to communicate in a difficult to understand gibberish, a mixture of Venetian dialect, English, French and German.

Compared to other musicians such as Mozart, Paganini or Bottesini, Dragonetti rarely went on concert tours. Nevertheless, in 1845, at the advanced age of 82, he travelled to the Beethovenfest in Bonn, where he took part in a performance of the 5th Symphony as the principal of 13 bassists. The strains of the journey, however, affected his health. He had to withdraw from the concert business after his return to London and died there on April 16, 1846.

Dragonetti owned numerous valuable basses. Dragonetti's preferred instrument was a violone by Gasparo da Salò from 1590, converted into a three-string double bass, which he received as a gift from the Orchestra San Marco in gratitude for his loyalty. Today the instrument is on display in the Museum of St. Mark's Cathedral in Venice.

Dragonetti played his Gasparo da Salò with only three strings. This bass was his favourite: if he lost it, he would immediately stop playing forever and break his bow, he said about this instrument.

photo: Sergio Scaramelli

Václav House (Wenzel Hause) – *1764 †1847

In 1764, one year after Dragonetti, Václav House was born in Raudnitz on the Elbe in Bohemia. Comparatively little is known about his life – he first worked as an assistant teacher, and from 1792 on as a violinist in the chapel of Prince Lobkowitz. Later he was hired as a double bassist at the Prague Estates Theatre, where he made a name for himself as a virtuoso. In 1811 he was appointed as a teacher at the newly founded Prague Conservatory, where he trained a number of outstanding double bassists until his retirement in 1845.

It is mainly his pedagogical work and the conception of the first serious method that makes him a key figure for the double bass. House's "School of Double Bass Playing" was published in two parts (1828 and 1829) and was later supplemented by a third part "School of the Virtuoso" (1844).

Giovanni Bottesini – *1821 †1889

Giovanni Bottesini first learned the violin and viola as a child. When he was 13, his parents tried to get him accepted at the Milan Conservatory, but depended on a scholarship for financial reasons. Scholarships were only available for bassoon and double bass, however, so Bottesini prepared for the audition for admission to the double bass class within only a few weeks. When he was considered one of the best students as a result of his rapid progress on the new instrument, he abandoned his original plan of returning to the violin and remained with the double bass. He graduated after only four (instead of the usual six) years, and was awarded a cash prize for his solo playing, as well.

He used a part of this money to purchase his double bass, a Carlo Antonio Testore from 1716. Bottesini reported that he discovered the instrument in a storage room of a Milan puppet theatre and was able to buy it from the trustee of the estate.

With a concert tour through several Italian cities and Vienna, he very successfully began his career as a solo bassist in 1840. Upon his return, he initially took up various orchestral posts in order to improve his ensemble playing. In 1846 he was contracted for an engagement in the Cuban capital Havana. This marked the beginning of a long period of travel for Bottesini; he spent practically the rest of his life on tour.

In Havana he worked at the Teatro Tacón and also started making a name for himself as a conductor and composer. From Cuba, Bottesini made several tours to Mexico and the U.S.A. In 1849 he visited England for a few months, but did not return permanently to Europe until his move to Paris in 1856. In the 1860s Bottesini played and conducted in almost all major cities in Germany, Italy and Scandinavia, as well as in Monaco, Lisbon, Madrid and Barcelona. Additionally, he gave concerts

SIGNOR BOTTESINI.

Giovanni Bottesini with his preferred instrument, the Testore bass dated 1716. Bottesini discovered this bass in the junk room of a puppet theater; he had it converted from a 4-string to a 3-string.

in 1866 in St. Petersburg at the court of the Russian Tsar Alexander II and in 1873 in Istanbul before Sultan Abdülaziz. Through the mediation of his friend Giuseppe Verdi, he finally took up the post of chief conductor at the Khedivian Opera in Cairo. There he conducted the world premiere of Verdi's opera "Aida" on December 24, 1871. When the opera house was closed in 1878, he set out to travel again, this time to South America. In 1888 he returned to Italy to become director of the Regio Conservatorio di Parma, but died the following year.

Franz Simandl – *1840 †1912

Franz (or František) Simandl was born in Bohemia. He studied at the renowned Prague Conservatory with Josef Hrabě. After his graduation he took a position as 1st double bassist of the K. K. Court Opera in Vienna. In addition to double bass, he also played the trombone and worked as a choir director. In 1871 he became professor at the Conservatory of the Society of Friends of Music in Vienna, where he taught for over 40 years. Along with Bottesini, he was considered the leading double bass virtuoso of his time; concert tours took him all over Europe. Richard Wagner appointed him as principal bassist at the orchestra of the Bayreuth Festival.

Franz Simandl

He also enjoyed a stellar reputation as a teacher and was responsible for bringing the trend-setting Prague Double Bass School to Vienna. His method books, "Newest method of double bass playing", "30 Etudes for Double Bass" and "Gradus ad Parnassum" became standard works for double bass teaching and are still being used in music schools all over the world today. His system uses the first, second and fourth fingers of the left hand to grip the strings in the low register, with the third and fourth fingers operating together. In addition, he introduced a position system, which is still virtually standard today. It derives the positional designations from the notes of the G minor scale played on the G string. Thus one plays the note A with the 1st (index) finger in 1st position, B♭ with the index finger in 2nd position, C in 3rd position etc. The positions in between are labeled half positions.

Simandl played a double bass from the workshop of Giovanni Paolo Maggini from the early 17th century.

Serge Alexandrovich Koussevitzky – *1874 †1951

The double bassist, composer and conductor Koussevitzky grew up in Oblast Tewer, 250 km northwest of Moscow, Russia. His parents were both professional musicians and let him learn the violin, cello, piano and the trumpet. At the age of 14 he left his home town to study music in Moscow. There he began with the double bass, as he was dependent on a scholarship, which was only available for that instrument. His teacher Josef Rambousek came from Prague and, like Franz Simandl or Gustav Láska, was a student of the pedagogue Josef Hrabe. After his studies he took up a position at the Bolshoi Theatre. In 1903 he gave his first guest performance in Berlin and moved there in 1905 to study conducting with Arthur Nikisch. Upon his return to Moscow in 1909, he founded the publishing house Éditions Russes de Musique and published works by Rachmaninoff, Alexander Scriabin, Sergei Prokofiev, Igor Stravinsky and Nikolai Medtner. After the Russian Revolution he became conductor of the State Symphony Orchestra in Petrograd (St. Petersburg) before leaving the USSR for good in 1920 to live in Berlin and Paris. In 1924 he accepted the position of musical director of the Boston Symphony, elevating it to one of the leading American orchestras over the course of his 25 year tenure. In 1929 he gave his last public concert as double bass soloist in Boston.

Koussevitzky is considered to be the first sonically documented double bassist. He recorded his own compositions, as well as works by Gustav Làska and Henry Eccles in the early 1920s.

Koussevitzky owned double basses by Maggini, Guarneri and an "Amati", which Koussevitzky's widow Olga passed on to Gary Karr (see also page 232). For his performances, however, he mostly used a double bass from the Glässel & Herbig factory (Markneukirchen) from 1889.

Serge Koussevitzky

In 1929, the German „Kontrabassisten-Bund" (Club of Bassists) was founded and published a regular newspaper

The Double Bass in Jazz

*Eddie Safranski (*1918 † 1974) in concert (1948)*

The double bass in Jazz

Pops Foster is considered the first important bassist in Jazz. From 1907 on he worked as double bassist and tuba player in the bands of Louis Armstrong and King Oliver.
In 1942 he started working for the New York subway.

For the first couple of decades in the history of jazz, a bass instrument was not yet a natural part of the instrumentation of a band or orchestra. Many groups managed to function without one—such as Louis Armstrong's Hot Five or the early bands of Duke Ellington. This changed at the end of the 1920s, when newly introduced electronic recording technology made it possible to record bass instruments for the first time. At first the double bass still shared its place in jazz and dance bands with the tuba, which dominated the marching bands of New Orleans. It was not until the Swing era that the double bass started to assert itself and take over—one of the reasons were faster tempos, which were easier to play on the bass than on the cumbersome tuba. Nevertheless, many bassists doubled on both instruments until the 1930s. The function of the tuba and double bass is the same within the band: as part of the rhythm section, the bass instrument provides a continuous pulse. At the same time it establishes a harmonic reference point or a contrapuntal melody line. Over the course of the stylistic evolution of jazz—from Dixieland to Swing and Bebop to Free Jazz—the role, techniques and range of expressions of the double bass developed continuously.

In the early days of jazz, the Two-Beat rhythm was predominant. To accentuate the rhythm more strongly, the bass was not only bowed (arco) or plucked (pizzicato), but also slapped. When being "slapped", the string snaps back onto the fingerboard with a "clack", giving the bass a concise percussive component. The most famous bassists of this era were Bill Johnson (King Oliver), Steve Brown (New Orleans Rhythm Kings, Jean Goldkette,

The Original Creole Orchestra with bassist Bill Johnson

Committed to the tin: When John Kirby (Fletcher Henderson Orchestra) switched from the tuba to the double bass in the early 1930s, he played a double bass made of aluminium for the first few years.
(excerpt from the Billboard Magazine 1924)

String Bass Replacing Tuba

All over New York it has been noticed that, with most of the prominent bands, the string bass, alias "bull fiddle", alias "dog house", is replacing the tuba.

Leaders agree that the string bass has a far greater carrying power than the tuba, and that it blends much more effectively. Practically all of the exponents of the tuba double in string bass, so the only inconvenience resulting from the switch will be the difference in sizes of the instrument cases, which take our word for it, is plenty.

Paul Whiteman), Wellman Braud (Duke Ellington), John Lindsay (Jelly Roll Morton, Louis Armstrong), and especially George "Pops" Foster (King Oliver, Kid Ory, Louis Armstrong, Sidney Bechet).

One of the first orchestra leaders to hire a full-time bassist in replacement of the tuba was Duke Ellington, who had a life long affinity for the instrument. His first bassist was Wellman Braud, who joined the band in 1927. ; that same year they recorded "Washington Wobble" together, which contains what is believed to be the first recorded jazz bass solo. In 1934, Ellington hired a second bassist, Billy Taylor, and when Braud left the band in 1935, he hired a second bassist again, Hayes Alvis. The musical concept behind this double line-up, however, remains unclear from a historical point of view: Ellington only allowed both bassists to play together on a few recordings, mostly they alternated. There is no record of sophisticated two bass arrangements—perhaps he simply wanted to increase the bass volume at concerts, since pickups and amplifiers did not yet exist. Composer and Ellington researcher Andrew Homzy suspects: *"When Duke had the two players he liked the heavy sound he got live. It's possible, though, that they had problems playing in tune together, and that came out more clearly on record. So when he recorded he had them do more simple things."*

From 1925 on, the new electrononic recording technology made it possible to record the plucked bass. Prior to that, the plucked or slapped double bass, as well as the bass drum would force the recording needle to jump off of the wax matrix. Furthermore, the mechanical recording technology had been virtually insensitive to frequencies below 168 Hz (two octaves above the low E string).

Bowing, plucking or slapping?

How early jazz bassists made themselves heard is not that easily answered. Sound recordings did not yet exist, and photos were mostly staged, and therefor not very relieable. However, one can assume that most bass players were still mainly using their bow until World War I and were initially quite reserved towards the new plucking and slapping techniques. New Orleans veteran Albert Glenny (*1870 †1958) said about slapping: *"That's not playing the bass—pick, pock, pick?!"* Around 1918, however, slapping became so popular, that most bassists quickly adjusted and only picked up the bow for slow pieces or waltzes. It is not clear who was the first who introduced this new technique in New Orleans. Bill Johnson (*1872 †1975) claims authorship for himself: when his bow broke before a gig and no replacement could be found in time, he started plucking and slapping without further ado. For jazz historian William Russel, however, the story of the broken bow belongs to the realm of legends: *"It seems that every bassist I ask claims to have played this style first"*. Ed Garland probably got it right with his assessment: *"I don't know who was the first. It somehow automatically came to us: we were slapping because we saw someone else slapping."*

Al Morgan, bassist with Cab Calloway (1934)

1930–1940: The Swing era

In the 1930s, also known as the Swing era, things changed dramatically: Wellman Braud and Walter Page (Count Basie) heralded the transition from the plucked and slapped Two Beat feel to the walking bass or Four Four feel (⁴⁄₄), where all four quarter notes of a measure are being played. Other important bassist, who helped shape the style of the Swing era were John Kirby (Fletcher Henderson, Chick Webb), Bob Haggart (Bob Crosby), Milt Hinton (Cab Calloway), and Slam Stewart (Slim & Slam). The function of the bass, which until then had been little more than a tuned percussion instrument, began to evolve from pure time-keeping. While the bass accompaniment was initially still characterized by tone repetitions, triads and scales, the walking bass became harmonically more intricate towards the end of the 1930s. A walking bass line is derived from the tonal material of the underlying chord progression and its corresponding scales, with the root usually appearing on the first quarter note of each measure, or beat "one", and the third or the fifth on beat "three". With a diatonic, or ideally chromatic passing note on the fourth beat of a bar, the bass line leads into the next chord. Apart from octave jumps, larger intervals are avoided to allow for a smoothly progressing line. With the emergence of the walking bass style, the Slap Bass more or less disappeared and was considered old-fashioned and antiquated since the 1940s. In Bluegrass, Hillbilly and Rockabilly genres, however, it still shapes the style today.

Bob Haggart led the jazz polls as the most popular bassist in the 1930s. In 1938 he achieved a huge jukebox and top ten success in the radio charts with "Big Noise from Winnetka", the recording of an instrumental double bass/drums duo. He is also the composer of the jazz standard "What's new", and the publisher of the first jazz bass method in 1942.

Milt Hinton's career encompassed almost all eras of jazz history. He is an accomplished slap bassist and played with Louis Armstrong and Cab Calloway, but was also at home at Minton's Playhouse, the birthplace of Bebop. From the 1950s on he worked mainly as a studio musician—

Many Jazz standards of this time are played in the keys F, B♭ and E♭—not least because the tuba's natural overtone series makes these keys particularly easy to play.
Music from "stringy" bands, such as Django Reinhardt's Hot Club de France (violin, guitars, double bass), on the other hand, is preferably played in sharp keys (D, G), which allows the use of open strings.

Wellman Braud (Fig. right) and Duke Ellington with his two bassist Hayes Alvis and Billy Taylor (Fig. left)

his proverbial reliability earned him the nickname "The Judge". Hinton was active as a musician until his old age.

Slam Stewart's trademark were bowed solos, which he sang along with in unison, an octave above the bass line. He became popular together with guitarist, pianist and singer Slim Gaillard as Slim & Slam.

1940–1950: The Bebop revolution

The modern jazz bass style begins with Jimmie Blanton. Blanton was born in 1918 as the son of a pianist and initially played the violin, then switched to the (three-string) double bass in college. During a performance with Fate Marable in 1939 he was discovered by Duke Ellington, who was so impressed, that he hired him on the spot. At the time, the bass chair in Ellington's orchestra was already filled prominently with Billy Taylor. Since Ellington did not want to dismiss Taylor, he temporarily used both bassists, as he had done before. In 1940 Taylor quit the band, leaving the position solely to Blanton, who had been turning into a sensation with his spectacular playing.

Blanton possessed outstanding technical skills and was the first bassist to imitate the flowing melodic lines typical of wind instruments, filled with refined rhythmic ornaments of eighths, sixteenths and triplet notes. By expanding the range of technical, rhythmic and melodic possibilities,

Jimmie Blanton

Billy Taylor: "I'm not going to stand up here next to that young boy playing all that bass and be embarassed."

photo: William P. Gottlieb

Bob Haggart achieved a great jukebox and top ten success in the radio charts in 1938 with "Big Noise from Winnetka", the recording of an instrumental double bass/drums duo. In 1942, Haggart released the first Jazz bass method book.

Jimmie Blanton's biography coincides with that of Charlie Christian, Bebop pioneer and innovator of the Jazz guitar: both hit the Jazz scene in 1939, and died of pneumonia in 1942.

he singlehandedly turned the bass into an accepted solo instrument. He also set new standards in terms of sound: he discovered the stylistic device of sustain, i.e. long resonating plucked notes. Blanton discovered that he could lengthen the sound of a note by plucking the string with as much flesh as possible—i.e. holding the index finger of the right hand parallel to the strings (at the end of the fingerboard) versus just using the fingertips (in the middle of the string).

In the two years Blanton played with Ellington, he participated in about 130 recordings, including duo sessions with Ellington on piano, and additional ones with members of the Ellington band (Johnny Hodges, Rex Steward, Barney Bigard) as leader. Some titles in the Ellington repertoire featured Blanton as a soloist (Ko Ko, Pitter Panther Patter, Jack the Bear). In 1941 Blanton was diagnosed with congenital tuberculosis. He left the Ellington Band and was sent to a sanatorium in California, where he died in 1942 at the age of only 23 years.

Blanton's successor in Duke's band was Junior Raglin, followed by Oscar Pettiford. Pettiford is considered the first bassist of Bebop, which replaced Swing as the main style of jazz in the 1940s. In the 1930s big bands were commercially very successful and toured constantly all over the country. This changed in the 1940s, when the musicians' union called for a strike in dispute over a minimum wage for studio work, as many musicians had

Slam Stewart is known for his bowed bass solos, to which he sang or hummed simultaneously.
Bassist Keter Betts recalls a concert by Slam Stewart: "The entire Boston Symphony bass section was sitting up front trying to figure out how the hell this guy could take a Kay bass and a Kay bow and get that kind of sound! That's when I realized you have to hear the sound in your mind first, and only then can you make it come out of your instrument. (…) I always tell my students that when you make yourself one with the bass, you're not playing the instrument—you're playing yourself."

Jazz Jam Sessions—breeding grounds of Bebop

Jam sessions were very popular in New York clubs from the late 1930s onwards. They offered musicians, who earned their money in commercial entertainment and studio orchestras the opportunity to meet, make contacts and try out new musical ideas. So jam sessions were at the same time an after-work hangout, a job exchange and a musical laboratory for experimentation. The club owners simply hired a house band (usually a rhythm section consisting of bass, drums and piano) to open the session. Other musicians joined after hours—a fixed fee was only paid for the house band, for all other musicians there was (if at all) only a tip, or free food and drink. Many musicians played there primarily for themselves, and not for the audience or the club owner.

Bassist Milt Hinton, who played with Bebop pioneer Dizzy Gillespie in Cab Calloway's band, reports in Gilliespie's autobiography "To Bop or not to Bop": *"Everybody used to come to Minton's to blow at night. I lived right across the street from Minton's, so I was kind of like the house bassist. I was the handiest one, just because I lived there and eventually wound up living in the Cecil Hotel. But so many kids from downtown, kids that couldn't blow, would come in and they would interrupt. Monk would be there, and Diz would be there, and I'd be there, and kids would come in there that couldn't blow, just bought a horn. And we're getting ready to blow 'How High the Moon', and these kids would jump in and they would just, you know, foul up the session. So Diz told me on the roof one night at the Cotton Club, 'Now look, when we go down to the jam session, we're gonna say we're gonna play, 'I Got Rhythm', but we're gonna use these changes. Instead of using the B♭ and D♭, we're gonna use B♭, D♭, G♭, or F and we change'. We would do these things up on the roof and then we'd go down to Minton's, and all these kids would be up there. 'What're y'all gonna play?' We'd say, 'I Got Rhythm' and we'd start out with this new set of changes, and they would be left right at the post. They would be standing there, and they couldn't get in because they didn't know what changes we were using, and eventually they would put their horns away, and we could go on and blow in peace and get our little exercise."*

Fig. left: The 52nd Street Clubs of Manhattan;
Fig. right: Thelonious Monk, Howard McGhee, Roy Eldridge and Teddy Hill in front of Minton's Playhouse in Harlem (1947)

In his book „The Real Jazz", published in 1942, French Jazz author Hugues Panassié wrote:
"String bass is really not a solo instrument; in fact, most bass solos are quite boring, for even if the musician has interesting ideas, they do not come out in an attractive way on a bass fiddle."

been called up for military service during WW II. Since skilled workers were now scarce it seemed like a good opportunity to enforce this demand on record companies. This recording ban was in force from 1942 to 1944 and resulted in loss of income for both labels and bands. In addition, dance and entertainment bands were subject to special levies related to the war effort, making large orchestras unprofitable and forcing leaders to lay off their musicians. The small bands or combos that were playing the new Bebop style, however, were not considered entertainment bands, and the New York clubs that presented them were therefore exempted from the special tax. Of central importance for the emergence of Bebop were the after hours sessions. The most important breeding ground was Minton's Playhouse in Harlem (New York), where jam sessions were held regularly. Musicians such as guitarist Charlie Christian, pianist Thelonious Monk, drummer Kenny Clarke, trumpeter Dizzy Gillespie, and especially alto saxophonist Charlie Parker created a jazz style there that no longer functioned primarily as dance or entertainment music, but rather as art music. Bebop is faster and harmonically more complex than Swing, presenting new challenges to bassists. While the drums previously provided a continuous pulse, the bass now takes over this task, relieving the drums of their purely supportive function and allowing them to interact more freely. In addition to already common alterations and the insertion of intermediate and passing

The two Ellington bassists Oscar Pettiford and Alvis Junior Raglin.
Although Junior Raglin was one of the best Jazz bassists in the early 1940s, he always stood in the shadow of his predecessor Blanton and his successor Pettiford.

photo: William P. Gottlieb

dominant seventh chords the use of so-called extension or coloring notes to the original harmonies represents a further evolution. Even more than before, the walking bass now builds the harmonic and rhythmic skeleton, that allows interplay to happen and pianists to exchange left hand stride patterns for more independent and accentuated comping figures. At the same time, however, the bassist is experiencing more freedom, as well: the walking bass line is not merely limited to the corset of root, third and fifth anymore, but instead develops into an extended improvised melodic line that can stretch horizontally over several bars. In addition, the walking bass is now enriched with rhythmic ornaments (drops).

Oscar Pettiford was born on an Indian reservation in 1922. His mother was a music teacher and his father gave up his original profession as a veterinarian to form an orchestra with his wife and 11 children. In it, Oscar Pettiford first played piano, before he switched to the bass.

In 1941 he joined Charlie Barnet's orchestra (as second bassist besides Chubby Jackson), and in 1943 he moved to New York together with Roy Eldridge, where he quickly advanced to a first call bassist. His first engagement in New York took him straight to 52nd Street, where he appeared with bandleader Dizzy Gillespie in of the first Bebop combos. His style was not limited to Bebop, though: he also recorded with Rhythm'n Blues musicians and worked with Duke Ellington's orchestra from 1945

The first pickups and amplifiers for double bass came on the market in the 1940s.

Tommy Potter with saxophonist Charlie Parker at the Three Deuces. Besides Potter, bassists like Curley Russel, Gene Ramey, Nelson Boyd and Percy Heath played with the Bebop bands in the New York clubs of the 1940s.

photo: William P. Gottlieb

Bandleader Harry James was known for his passion for baseball. The musicians in his big band did not only have to make themselves available for rehearsals, but also for baseball workouts; for games they'd be wearing James' own orchestra jerseys.
During a game against the not-so-trained baseball team of the Woody Herman Band, bassist Oscar Pettiford broke his arm while throwing the ball and had to pause playing bass for a while.

to 1948. Due to a broken arm in 1949, he had to take a leave from playing the bass and practiced the cello instead. Tuned like a bass, he played it pizzicato and helped to introduce it as a jazz instrument. In the 1950s he was certainly one of the busiest New York musicians, although—untypical for a bass player—he was very egocentric and often insulted his fellow musicians (especially when he had too much to drink, which was the case frequently). Pianist Dick Katz reports: *"Pettiford had this amplifier, which he didn't need. It was tuned up so loud that it was louder than the horns. I couldn't hear what I was playing. 'I'm the leader, and I want to be heard', he would say. I would sneak in and turn it down, and he'd turn it up"*

Pettiford moved to Europe in the late 1950s—first to Baden-Baden (Germany), then to Copenhagen (Denmark), where he died in 1960 from the long-term effects of a car accident.

Charles Mingus, like Pettiford, was born in 1922. In the 1940s he worked in Los Angeles with, among others, Illinois Jacquet, Lucky Thompson, Red Norvo, Tal Farlow, Billie Holliday and the Lionel Hampton Big Band. In the early 1950s he moved to New York, where he ran his own record label together with drummer Max Roach (the first one operated by musicians). He was a sought-after sideman and bandleader and as such deliberately ignored the limitations of jazz styles: Swing, Bebop, Third Stream, avant-garde. He is considered one of the most important composers of jazz, but was also

Ray Brown (here with vibra-phonist Milt Jackson) was one of the first Jazz bassists to switch from gut to steel strings.
He was an endorser for the Danish brand Lycon, whose strings were accompanied by an autograph card signed by Ray Brown.

photo: William P. Gottlieb

notorious for his quick-tempered and choleric nature: it was not unusual for him to insult his audience from the stage, and he once knocked out a tooth of his trombonist Jimmy Knepper's mouth in a dispute, earning him a suspended sentence and a temporary ban from performing. In the mid-1960s he was voted best bassist in both the Downbeat Readers Poll and Critics Poll. Mingus was also a politically very involved person, resulting in many composition titles with political reference. For example, the title "Fables of Faubes" refers to Orval E. Faubus, the governor of Arkansas, who in 1957 tried to prevent racial integration in the School of Little Rock with the help of the National Guard. About his composition "Haitian Fight Song" (also published as "II B.S.") Mingus said: *I can't play it without thinking of prejudice, hatred, political persecution and how unfair it all is. There's a sadness and an outcry (of despair) about it in this song, and usually it ends with me feeling 'I've said it'—I hope someone hears me."*

Probably the most popular bassist of the 1950s was Ray Brown. By the mid-1940s he was already part of the inner circle of Bebop pioneers around Charlie Parker and Dizzy Gillespie, playing in Gillespie's Big Band. In 1948

Oscar Pettiford had put together a 13-piece band for an engagement at New York's Club Birdland, which included Whitey Mitchell, a second bassist, and harpist Betty Glamann.
The arrangements were written by Lucky Thompson, Gigi Gryce and Benny Golson. In this band Pettiford played both bass and cello.

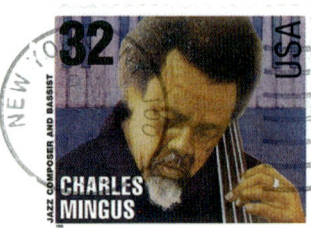

The American postal service honored Charlie Mingus with a stamp

At Stein On Vine, the legendary music shop, double bass workshop and jazz musician meeting point in Hollywood, Ray Brown met Bobby Haggart again after many decades. Haggart was the most popular jazz bassist of the 1930s and author of the first method book for jazz bass.
„You know Bobby, I actually studied your book."—
"Really? May be I should take another look at it myself."
(from: Gary Chen, "They Call Me Stein On Vine")

he married the singer Ella Fitzgerald and acted as her musical director. In his playing, he carried on the quintessence of what bassists such as Jimmie Blanton and Oscar Pettiford had initiated and is still considered a musical role model for many bassists today. From 1951 on he played in the Oscar Peterson Trio for 15 years. In 1963 he published "Ray Brown's Bass Method", which is still available today. For more than a decade he dominated the Readers jazz Polls of Downbeat and Playboy magazine and won several Grammy awards. After leaving Peterson's trio, he moved to the West Coast in 1966 and worked as a studio bassist, composer, writer, teacher, publisher, producer and manager. Until his unexpected passing in 2002, he was constantly touring the world with his own trio and other projects.

Formative bassists

Milt 'The Judge' Hinton already played in various successful Swing bands in the 1930s. In 1936 he took the position of bassist in the Cab Calloway's orchestra, where he featured the bass as a solo instrument both bowed and plucked in a special number with Ebony Silhouette. In addition to Cab Calloway, he worked with Lionel Hampton, Billie Holliday and Teddy Wilson during this time, and regularly played sessions at Minton's Playhouse Bebop hatchery. In 1951 he left the Cab Calloway Orchestra and worked with Count Basie, Duke Ellington and Louis Armstrong. He became a full-time studio bassist with CBS, where he was involved in countless recordings for records, radio, film and television. His career spanned the entire history of jazz. He was one of the few bassists who, in addition to pizzicato and bow, repeatedly used and perfected the slap technique, which had actually gone out of fashion with the Swing era. Milt Hinton died in 2000 at the age of 90.

Israel Crosby played in the orchestras of Gene Krupa, Fletcher Henderson and Benny Goodman. He became known as the bassist of the Ahmad Jamal Trio, which was very successful in the 1950s and whose sound he helped to shape. In 1962 he left the trio and joined George Shearing's Band, but died that same year.

Percy Heath came to New York in 1947 with his brother, saxophonist Jimmy Heath, to play with Howard McGhee. He quickly became part of the Bebop scene around Charlie Parker, Thelonious Monk and Miles Davis. From 1950 om, he played with Dizzy Gillespie. With members of this band, he eventually founded the Modern Jazz Quartet, which became a style-defining and extremley successful ensemble of Cool Jazz for decades.

George Duvivier switched from violin to double bass at the age of 14. After finishing school, he began studying music at New York University, but soon after went on tour with bands lead by Coleman Hawkins, Lucky Millinder and Jimmie Lunceford, while also writing big band arrangements. From the 1950s on he worked mainly as a studio bassist and played

Red Mitchell about the bass scene of the 1950ies

In December 1957 the record *Presenting Red Mitchell* was released. The bassist had moved from New York to Los Angeles three years earlier and was now one of the busiest bass players in the local studios. In the LP's liner notes, Red Mitchell talks about his influences and the bass scene of the late 1950s. And not surprisingly, these liner notes read like a who's who of jazz bass. What makes this source especially interesting is the fact, that some of the names mentioned in it are rarely mentioned by jazz historians. The importance of some of the musicians was evaluated differently back then than it is today.

Not surprisingly, Mitchell names the bassists first, who were most formative for his generation, and whose great influence is undisputed today: Walter Page, Jimmie Blanton, Oscar Pettiford. But some names that are lesser known today like Chubby Jackson and Eddie Safranski had a great influence on Mitchell and other musicians in the 1940s.

Red Mitchell became a professional on the New York jazz scene when Bebop was at its peak. The bassists around Charlie Parker and Dizzy Gillespie were his next role models: Ray Brown, Charles Mingus, but also today's less common names like Keter Betts, Curly Russell, Al McKibbon, Tommy Potter, Nelson Boyd, Red Kelly. A meeting with Milt Hinton made a lasting impression: *"Milt is very exceptional in that he can do everything and do it well. He can bow, he can read, he can walk, he can play solos. He's really my idea of the kind of bass player I'd like to be, an all-around player."* But also the *complete professional* George Duvivier, who even then was often overlooked by the critics, impressed him: *"George just scared me to death. He was getting that real big sound and executing all kinds of fantastic things"*. Many of the names Mitchell subsequently mentions are hardly found in jazz history books today. Teddy Kottick, Bob Carter, Joe Carmen, Dante Martucci, Kenny O'Brian, Clyde Lombardi, Chet Amsterdam and others are bassists who have fallen into oblivion today, but who made an impression back then. Mitchell says about Arnold Fishkin: *"… his solidity of time, and I think too, he's the only guy I've ever heard really make very successful use of a three-finger plucking technique"*. Another of his favourite bassists is only known to insiders today: Leroy Vinnegar *("one of the best rhythm feelings of any bass player I have ever heard; one of my top few favorite bass players")*.

Red Mitchell recognized the talent of two bassists who are still highly respected today and were in the early stages of their careers at the time of the interview. About Paul Chambers, he says: *"… underrated as a rhythm player, also the best of the new guys solo-wise."* And Mitchell was also spot on with his assessment of Scott LaFaro (who had only been playing bass for two years in 1957) *"I believe he's going to be recognized as one of the best in a very short time"*.

The Jazz critic and author Nat Henthoff writes in the introduction to the liner notes that by the age of thirty, Red Mitchell had listened to all the important and less important modern bassists, resulting in a personal style that outlines the history of modern jazz bass.

in bands of TV shows like NBC Today Show, Tonight Show, Dick Cavett Show and Ed Sullivan Show. He accompanied such diverse jazz musicians as Louis Armstrong and Eric Dolphy, and singers such as Billy Eckstine, Lena Horne, Frank Sinatra and Barry Manilow.

1950–1960: Modern Jazz

From the end of the 1940s onwards, Modern Jazz branched out further into numerous different developing directions. From the injection of Bebop with elements of Latin American music Afro Cuban Jazz was born, with Dizzy Gillespie being its main pioneer. Another trumpeter, Miles Davis, shaped yet another new style called Cool Jazz with his *Birth of the Cool* recordings. In contrast to Bebop, with its brilliant soloists improvising over breakneck tempos and intricate chord progressions, Cool Jazz redirects the focus to a group sound that is a result of good ensemble playing and thought-out arrangements. Solos are still an important element, though, corresponding to improvisation techniques established during the Bebop period. These somewhat more pleasing sound aesthetics were

With Leo Fender's "Precision Bass", the first commercially successful electric bass was launched in 1951. Prominent musicians switching from double bass to electric bass were Buddy Montgomery, Steve Swallow and Bob Cranshaw.

also adopted by the West Coast style, which emerged in the metropolises of the West Coast in the 1950s. Stylistic elements of Cool Jazz and West Coast Jazz flowed into Bossa Nova in the early 1960s, combinig Brazilian rhythm with jazz harmonies. However, Hardbop became the new mainstream jazz style from the mid 1950s onwards. It is more influenced by traditional Blues and Gospel music than Bebop, resulting in yet another essential stylistic trademark, its strongly driving rhythmic nature. Within the Hardbop style, Miles Davis and John Coltrane developed their modal improvisation technique. In modal jazz, the musician's improvisations are not based on the tonal material of a song-related chord progression, but on one or more ususally simple modal scales. Bebop, with its complex melodies and rapidly changing chord sequences, was countered by modal jazz with quieter, often almost minimalistic tone and chord sequences. Miles Davis' LP *Kind of Blue* (1959) was a style-defining influence and the best selling album in jazz history. Paul Chambers can be heard playing the theme on the opener, the iconic composition *So What*.

Art Blakeys Jazz Messengers, Max Roach/Clifford Brown Quintet, Cannonball Adderly Quintet, Horace Silver Quintet, as well as bands lead by saxophonists Sonny Rollins and Dexter Gordon are regarded as the defining ensembles of the Hardbop style.

Formative bassists

Bill Haley & His Comets with bassist Al Rex (lying on the floor): In the mid 1950s, Rock'n'Roll, a mixture of black Rhythm and Blues and white country music, became increasingly successful, especially among young people

Paul Chambers played with Kenny Burrell, the trombonists J.J. Johnson and Kai Winding, before he became a member of the Miles Davis Quintet for eight years in 1955. His distinctive bounce and melodic sense in his walking bass lines, as well as his typically bowed solos made him one of the most recorded jazz bassists of the early 1960s.

Wilbur Ware arrived in New York from Chicago in 1956. He played with Art Blakey, Sonny Rollins and Thelonious Monk, whom he complemented congenially with his playing. For bassist Charlie Haden, Ware is *"the most underrated, most fantastic musician of all time"*.

Red Mitchell was initially a pianist and picked up the double bass during his time at the armed services in Germany, after he had traded a double bass on the black market for some packs of cigarettes. In 1949 he started working with Woody Herman, and later with Red Norvo, Gerry Mulligan and Hamton Hawes. In 1955 he moved from New York to the West Coast to work in the studios. In the 1960s he began tuning his bass in fifths instead of fourths.

Sam Jones came to New York from Florida in the mid-1950s, playing with Kenny Dorham, Bill Evans, Thelonious Monk, and from 1959 on in the Cannonball Adderly Quintet. He won the Down Beat Critics Poll in 1960, and the Playboy All Star Jazz Poll from 1961 to 1964. In 1966 he succeeded Ray Brown as bassist in Oscar Peterson's Trio.

In addition to New York, California's club and studio scene increasingly offered job opportunities for jazz musicians. Besides Leroy Vinnegar, who is known for his incredibly swinging beat, people such as Monty Budwig, Curtis Counce, Monk Montgomery and Joe Mondragon were formative for West Coast Jazz bassists.

1960–1970: Free Jazz and Avant-garde

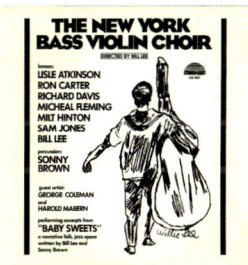

Bill Lee (father of film director Spike Lee) founded the "New York Bass Violin Choir" in 1968, to which besides Lee also Lisle Atkinson, Michael Fleming, Milt Hinton, Richard Davis, Ron Carter and Sam Jones belonged.

In 1960 Ornette Coleman's record *Free Jazz: A Collective Improvisation* was released. It was recorded with a double quartet, featuring Scott LaFaro and Charlie Haden as the two bassists of the session. The album had such an impact on the scene, that the new, avant-garde jazz style was named after it. In Free Jazz, the musicians deliberately broke away from traditional jazz harmonies, while initially still holding on to a rather conventional rhythmic concept. The bassist still had the task of setting the pace, laying the foundation with his walking bass. With Free Jazz pioneer and pianist Cecil Taylor, however, bass and drums become equal improvising dialogue partners. The musical spectrum of Free Jazz thus ranges from well-conceived playing structures with limited free passages to completely freely improvised communication structures, whose musical course is determined spontaneously, in the moment decision making. Basic harmonic structures and tonal centres on the one hand, and the conscious avoidance of any tonal reference on the other, co-exist in various Free Jazz forms.

This bass by Abraham Prescott (New Hampshire/U.S.A., ca. 1825) was played by Scott LaFaro on the Village-Vanguard recordings.
The sides and back are made of lightly flamed maple, the top is made of three piece slab cut fir.
Red Mitchell discovered the bass and passed it on to Scott LaFaro, who had it completely restored and set up with flat string action and "Golden Spiral" gut strings. The bass was damaged in the car accident; neck and parts of the top and rib were burned.

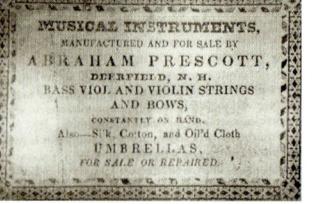

Abraham Prescott is one of the few bass builders who were already active in the U.S.A. in the 19th century. Besides basses he also made umbrellas.

Formative bassists

Scott LaFaro is considered the most influential bassist after Jimmie Blanton. After his schooldays he first studied the saxophone, before discovering the double bass. Shortly afterwards he quit college to go on tour with Buddy Morrow's big band. In 1959 he moved to Los Angeles and played with Chet Baker, Victor Feldman, Stan Kanton, Benny Goodman and Ornette Coleman. At times he shared appartment with bassist Charlie Haden; and together they worked on Ornette Coleman's LP *Free Jazz*. In 1959 he joined Bill Evans' trio. LaFaro was a virtuoso technician, which allowed him to play extended solos in the higher register of the instrument. Instead of the classic walking bass of his predecessors, he developed a much freer and independent style of playing, that often resulted in a counter melody to Evans' piano part. Together with Paul Motian, he developed a new way of trio playing, where bass and drums do not merely accompany the pianist, but act as equal partners. LaFaro died in 1962 in a car accident near his birthplace Geneva (near New York)—two days after he had played with Stan Getz at the Newport Festival, and less than two weeks after the legendary Village Vanguard recordings with Bill Evans. The recordings were released as *Sunday at the Village Vanguard* and *Waltz for Debby*. Scott LaFaro played a double bass by American bass builder Abraham Prescott on these recordings. The bass was severely damaged in the accident, and Sam Kolstein, the New York bass builder, who had previously set up this instrument for LaFaro, purchased the remains of the bass with the promise of making it playable again. However, this task was completed by his son Barrie Kolstein, who presented the restored bass to the public in 1988 at a congress of the International Society of Bassists (ISB) on the 25th anniversary of Scott LaFaro's death. Today it is owned by the ISB, which occasionally makes it available to selected members for recordings and concerts.

Saxophonist John Coltrane was one of the most influential jazz musicians of the 1960s. From 1955 to 1960 he was a member of the Miles Davis Quintet. In 1960 he founded his own quartet and recorded the album *Giant Steps* with Paul Chambers on bass. As he shifted more and more away from the Hardbop idiom he experimented with a variety of players such as Steve Davis, Reggie Workman and Art Davis, before settling on Jimmy Garrison, who became the bassist of *the* classic quartet. This group also featured pianist McCoy Tyner and drummer Elvin Jones and went on to record the LP *A Love Supreme*. On some records, Coltrane used two bass players, as well.

Ron Carter came to New York in the late 1950s and quickly made a name for himself. In 1963 he succeeded Paul Chambers in the Miles Davis Quintet, and stayed for five years. During this time he developed into a sought-after studio bassist, who since then has been involved in well over 2000 recordings. Until his retirement, he also taught at the City College of New York, the Eastman School and Juillard School.

Richard Davis is a very versatile bassist, who is at home in both traditional and avant-garde Jazz as well as in classical orchestras. He has performed with such diverse personalities as Benny Goodman, Eric Dolphy, Igor Stravinsky and Frank Sinatra. From 1967 to 1974 he led the jazz polls and became the head of the University of Wisconsin Jazz department in 1977.

After Scott La Faro's death, Bill Evans first played with bassist Chuck Israels (1961–1966) and Gary Peacock (album *Trio '64*), before establishing a long-lasting relationship with Puerto Rican born Eddie Gomez. Gomez stayed with Evans for 10 years, before moving on to working with pianist Chick Corea, as well as the band *Steps Ahead* around vibraphonist Mike Manieri and Michael Brecker.

The Dane Niels Henning Ørsted Pedersen (or NHØP, as he called himself) was the first of a number of European bassists, who were able to make a name for themselves in the motherland of jazz. By the age of 14 he was already playing with the best Danish musicians, and at the age of 16 he was offered to stay, accompanying many guest soloists such as Ben Webster, Dexter Gordon and many others as a member of the house band of the Copenhagen jazz club Montmartre. From the early 1970s until his passing in 2005 he was a regular member of Oscar Peterson's trio.

With Mirouslav Vitouš and George Mraz, two outstanding bassists from the Czech capital Prague came to the U.S.A. at the end of the 1960s. Mraz stands in the tradition of Ray Brown, toured with the Thad Jones-Mel Lewis Orchestra, and played with Dizzy Gillespie, Oscar Peterson, Stan Getz and Tommy Flanagan. Vitouš became known as one of the founding members of the ground-breaking Jazz Rock/Fusion band *Weather Report*.

Most recorded bass player of the world:
The Guinness Book of Records lists Ron Carter as the jazz bassist with the most recordings. By the cut-off date in 2015, participation in 2221 recordings had been verified.

1970: The electrification of Jazz

While the decade of the 1960s was characterized by commercially not very successful trends such as Free Jazz and avant-garde, the emergence of Jazz Rock and Fusion Jazz in the 1970s reintroduced a larger audience to improvised music. Until then, jazz had been largely dominated by acoustic instruments—this changed with the rise of Fusion Jazz, since its sound was an electric one compromised of keyboards, electric guitars and basses.

The electrification of musical instruments took place in several phases. In the 1930s, first musical instruments that required electricity to produce sound appeared: the pedal steel guitar, the vibraphone, the Hammond organ and, above all, the electrically amplified jazz guitar. In the 1950s,

124

the solid-body electric guitar had its breakthroug has the main voice in Rock'n'Roll music, which had developed as a blend of black Rhythm'n'Blues and white Country music. With Rock, music became louder, since guitar amplifiers were designed to become more and more powerful. The arrival of this newest style of Fusion Jazz was again marked by an LP by trumpeter Miles Davis: *Bitches Brew* from 1969, which featured British bassist Dave Holland and Ron Carter. Herbie Hancock's LP *Head Hunters* (1973) sold millions of copies. The band Weather Report was also very successful, initially featuring Prague-born Miroslav Vituoš, and later electric bassists Alphonso Johnson and Jaco Pastorius. Jaco Pastorius is perhaps the most influential electric bassist of all time, and was also one of the first to play a fretless electric bass. Another popular and very influential fusion band was *Return to Forever*, founded by keyboardist Chick Corea. The band's bassist Stanley Clarke introduced the electric bass slap technique to the fusion vocabulary, while also being an excellent, classically trained double bassist. Unlike when slapping a double bass, with the electric bass the lower strings are struck with the thumb by turning the wrist, and rhythmically combined with the pulling of a higher string.

„The bass guitar was the instrument that let you know the 50s were over and music was going to some new places." Marcus Miller

Technological Backlash

Although the achievements of electronics opened up new possibilities for bassists in terms of sound and playing technique, many soon found the amplified double bass sound of the 1970s unappealing. Pianist Ethan Iverson judges: *"The simple fact is that at least 80% of the swinging acoustic jazz records made between 1970 and the advent of Wynton Marsalis [mid-1980s] have a godawful bass sound. In performance it was all amplified pick-up, and when recording the bass the engineers usually put that pick-up directly to tape. To compound the problem, often the strings of the bass were far closer to the fingerboard than in the 60s and 50s, making for a walking line that was heard but not felt. This 70s bass set-up did enable the player to 'liberate the bass' and perform melodies and take long solos more like a guitarist. But the ultimate aesthetic value of this liberation—at least in the context of straight-ahead jazz—was questionable."*

Trumpeter Wynton Marsalis represents a neo-traditionalist style of jazz that emerged in the 1980s, and also redefined the role of the bass. Marsalis and other Young Lions wanted to return to the pure sound of the unamplified double bass. For bassist and author Peter Dowdall, however, the issue was not technology itself: *"Rather, it was technology's excessive use in a style whose successful rendering was not well served by its indiscriminate employment. The pulse of the unamplified string bass was transformed into something entirely different by the electronic pickup and amplifier resulting in a louder and brighter but less propulsive rhythm section underpinning."*

About the backlash of the 1980s, he states: *"The Young Lions advocated a return to a more vigorous, forceful approach to the string bass, one that produced an aggressively swinging undercurrent unmediated by technology. This vision of the heroic, unamplified bassist powering the ensemble with sheer determination and muscle was as idealistic as it was unrealistic."* (See also page 150.)

Bassists and the Cello in Jazz

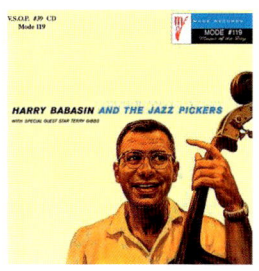

In contrast to its relatives violin and double bass, the cello is still an exotic instrument in jazz music. Initially, the cello was thought of as the "little bass", since the first musicians to use the cello were jazz bassists. One of them was Harry Babasin, who made his first recordings playing the cello pizzicato with pianist Dodo Marmarosa in 1947. While he initially remained in the role of bassist even as a cellist, he added a bass player to later recordings, allowing him to use the cello as melody and solo instrument only. After breaking his arm while playing baseball with band mates in 1949, Oscar Pettiford was temporarily unable to handle the bass and settled for the physically less demanding cello. Prior to the accident, he had already used the cello occasionally in solos with the orchestras of Duke Ellington and Woody Herman. This led him to showcasing the cello consistently in small groups as a melody and solo instrument. In 1952 a joint session of the two "Pizzicato Jazz Cello" pioneers Babasin and Pettiford took place. Bassists Charles Mingus, Harry Babasin and Whitey Mitchell (Red's brother) are featured on some of the numerous albums, that Pettiford recorded with the cello. After his move to Europe, guitarist Attila Zoller would frequently take over the bass part. Starting in 1954, Pettiford experimented with the new multitrack recording technique, laying down both the bass and cello parts. In the following years, Keter Betts, Sam Jones, Percy Heath, Eldee Young and Ray Brown also recorded as cello soloists, tuning their instruments not in fifths as usual, but in fourths as is customary for the bass—only an octave higher.

Together with Ray Brown, Kay designed a cello for jazz bassists, which was eventually marketed as the "Ray Brown Jazz Cello". Ray Brown's dislike of the narrow fingerboard and the unpractical tuning pegs led to the Kay company's design of a cello with a stronger neck, a wider fingerboard, and tuning machines. To match the "Ray Brown Jazz Cello" Kay also offered cello strings in forth tuning.

This is how Percy Heath came to the cello through his friend and colleague: *"I asked Ray Brown, 'Hey Ding, you got one of them things?' He said, 'Yeah, I got one in the garage.' Because all the bass players jumped on it [the jazz cello], and then gave it up. Anyhow, Brown called me from the airport a few months later because I had to find something else to do from*

Ray Brown released an LP in 1960, which he had recorded on the cello accompanied by a big band. The cover photo shows him with a plywood cello by the manufacturer Kay, which came on the market as model K200 and was also advertised as "Ray Brown Jazz Cello". Ray Brown later gave the instrument to Percy Heath.

The double bass shown here is considered an Amati from the 17th century, which is now played in the Toronto Symphony Orchstra. The mixed stringing with steel strings from the Danish manufacturer Lycon (E- and A-string) and bare gut strings (D- and G-string) is clearly visible.

the Heath Brothers. He called me from the airport and said, 'Hey P, I sent that thing on for you.' I said, 'Hey Ding, thanks man.' 'He said, „You're going to have to use three.' I said, 'What do you mean?' He said, 'You'll dig it,' and hung up and split. So here comes this cello in this crate. I'm trying to play it. I sit down and try to play it like the bass. What he meant was: I had to use three fingers, because the thing is so small, if you try to put four fingers in there you're out of tune. It just didn't work mechanically. So that's why I play the thing with three fingers."

Ron Carter also recorded in the 1960s as a cellist, with George Duvivier on bass. Ron Carter had enjoyed classical cello lessons before switching to bass , which enabled him to play his cello (tuned in fifths) with the bow as well on recordings with Eric Dolphy, Mal Waldron and George Benson. Later he used a "piccolo bass" built to his specifications: *"In 1974–1975 I put together a band with two basses: me, another bass, piano and drums. I decided that the audience coming to our gigs should immediately recognize that I was the band leader, but as a bass player it is difficult to be recognized as such. So I had to move forward and needed an instrument that was small enough to cover the range upwards and at the same time big enough to function as part of the rhythm section when the bass player plays a solo. That's where I met Frank Lyman, who became a very good friend of mine and built me a ½ bass. We tuned him in A-D-G-C. It was a bit too bright in sound for me, but it worked for a while. Then I found a real half-bass that I've been playing ever since. I call it 'Piccolo' to distinguish it from the other bass."*

Other more recent cello recordings were released by Dave Holland (with guitarist Derek Bailey, as well as with bassist Barre Philips, both 1971; solo album in 1982) Todd Coolman and Buell Neidlinger. In the mid-1950s the classically trained cellist Fred Katz introduced the bowed cello into jazz. As a member of the quintet of Westcoast drummer Chico Hamilton, he was the first "cellist-only", for whom the cello was more than just a higher tuned bass. In 1958 Nat Gershman succeeded him in that band. Starting in Chico Hamilton's quintet, cellists were able to play their instruments in a way, that broke stylistically from the double bass and allowed it to become an independent jazz instrument in its own right.

Bassists in the Jazz polls

Since the 1930s, the American Jazz magazines Downbeat and Metronome have published Jazz polls—rankings in which the most important instrumentalists in their respective fields are listed. Initially, these polls were pure readers' polls—, allowing them to choose their favorite musicians according to individual taste and personal preferences. The purpose of such polls was of course controversially discussed early on—after all, Jazz is not a sporting competition where there are clear winners and losers. The popular magazine Esquire (which reported on Jazz early on) took a different approach and had the critic Robert Goffin compile a list of three All-American bands (on bass: Al Morgan, John Kirby, Billy Taylor). In 1944, the Esquire Jazz Award was introduced and executed by a panel of critics. Jazz critic Leonhard Feather wrote about the introduction of the Esquire Jazz Award:

"Gradually a plan crystallized. We did not want our poll to wind up like those conducted in Down Beat and Metronome, in which, typically, Charlie barnet or Tex Beneke be the leaders on 'hot tenor', followed by Coleman Hawkisn and Ben Webster; Ziggy Elman would win for 'hot trumpet' and Alvino Rey for guitar; Helen O'Connell or Dinah Shore would be elected No. 1 female Jazz singer while Billie Holiday wen unhonored. 'The only way out,' I said, 'is to put togehter a panel of experts, rather than rely on the readers.'"

The winners of the Gold and Silver Awards appeared in January 1944 the Esquire All American All Stars; they included Billie Holiday, Roy Eldridge, Jack Teagarden, Barney Bigard, Coleman Hawkins, Art Tatum, Al Casey, Sidney Catlett and bassist Oscar Pettiford. In 1946, however, the award was already discontinued.

Starting in 1953 a critic poll was initiated to compliment the Downbeat Magazine reader poll, and in 1962 the categories "Artist deserving wider recognition" and later "Rising Stars" were added. The immensely popular Playboy Magazine, which was owned by its editor, the enthusiastic Jazz fan Hugh Heffner, also published a Readers Jazz Poll in 1957, with 430,000 participating readers. The winner in the bass category was Ray Brown,

In Germany, the men's magazine "Die Gondel" published an annual jazz poll in the 1950s.
In the double bass section, the winner from 1950–1953 was bassist Hans Last, who was also appointed bassist in the German Allstar Band of the 1st German Jazz Festival in Frankfurt in 1953. Under the stage name of James Last, he became internationally known in the 1960s as an orchestra leader, arranger and creator of the "Happy Sound".

just ahead of Oscar Pettiford. The Playboy Jazz Poll was accompanied by a prizewinners' concert and record releases, supervised by Leonhard Feather. Over the years, however, the profile became increasingly diluted, and even clearly non-Jazz musicians such as Peter, Paul & Mary, The Beatles and Sting made it into the Playboy Jazz Poll. It was discontinued in the 1990s, but the Playboy Jazz Festival has survived to the present day.

When studying the results of these polls, it is noticeable, that some of the most important innovators and driving forces of the Jazz bass are not mentioned: Jimmie Blanton and Scott LaFaro are nowhere to be found, although this may be due to the fact that both died at a young age. Oscar Pettiford as the formative bassist of Bebop at least made it into the critics polls.

Bob Haggart, who dominated the polls in the early years, is not so well-known today. He made a major contribution by writing the first Jazz bass method and the much-played standard "What's New", and had a major commercial hit with the recording "Big Noise from Winetka".

Artie Bernstein, who made it to the top in 1943 and 1944, played in the renowned bands of Charlie Barnet and Benny Goodman, but is largely unknown today. Eddie Safranski, born in the same year as Jimmie Blanton, is not the first bassist name that comes to mind for the post-war era. However, he was a very busy studio bassist in the 1950s and certainly benefited from the high popularity of his bandleader Stan Kanton when he got elected.

A recurring pattern in the polls is that one name often dominates a whole era over a long period of time: first Bob Haggart, then Eddie Safranski, Ray Brown, Richard Davis, Ron Carter, and finally Charlie Haden. In the years when there was a change at the top, this was usually anticipated in the critics' polls a year earlier: 1963 with Charles Mingus, 1967 with Richard Davis, 1980 Charlie Haden, 1999 Dave Holland—(almost) always the critics caught on a year earlier than the readers. One exception is Ron Carter, who was in the lead in the Reader Polls from 1973 onwards, but was not acknowledged by the critics until two years later.

Compared to other instrumentalists, bassists in general perform poorly in the polls. Lee Jeske wrote for Downbeat in 1983: *"Of all the instruments commonly used in a jazz band, none is taken more for granted than the acoustic bass. For example, of the 56 members of the DownBeat Hall of Fame only one—Charles Mingus—is a bassist; and it's safe to say that Mingus was elected more for his composing and band-leading than his bass playing. Names like Blanton, Pettiford, LaFaro and Chambers are missing from that list."*

photo: William P. Gottlieb

Jazz Bass Timeline

Vivien Garry (*1920 †2008) with her band at the Dixon's/New York (1947).
She was the only female bass player who performed in the clubs on 52nd Street at the time.

A bass instrument is not yet firmly established in dance and jazz bands. Many groups get by without one until the 1920s – such as Louis Armstrong's Hot Five, or the early bands of Duke Ellington.

In Jazz, the double bass is played with the bow (arco), plucked (pizzicato) or in "slap style"

Walter Page, bassist with Count Basie, heralds the change from the slapped two-beat feel to the plucked walking bass.

Big Band swing is in its prime: numerous dance orchestras travel across the country; swing is very popular in among all age groups

Fate Marable's New Orleans Band on board a river steamer with Pops Foster on bass (1917)

String Bass Replacing Tuba

All over New York it has been noticed that, with most of the prominent bands, the string bass, alias "bull fiddle", alias "dog house", is replacing the tuba.

Leaders agree that the string bass has a far greater carrying power than the tuba, and that it blends much more effectively. Practically all of the exponents of the tuba double in string bass, so the only inconvenience resulting from the switch will be the difference in sizes of the instrument cases, which take our word for it, is plenty.

Billboard Magazine, 1926

Plywood basses from the American companies Kay, King and Epiphone meet the increasing demand for robust, affordable instruments in the USA

The tuba (or sousaphone), the predominant bass instrument in early jazz, is gradually being replaced by the double bass. The orchestras of Duke Ellinton and Paul Whiteman complete the change by 1927. However, many bassists still double on both instruments until the 1930s.

1938 – "Big Noise from Winnetka", a duo recording of double bassist Bob Haggart and drummer Ray Bauduc storm the charts.

1917 – the Original Dixieland Jazz Band releases „Livery Stable Blues", the first ever jazz recording (but without bass)

The Audiovox company launches the first electric bass in 1935, but it remains unsuccessful.

1925 – Electric recording technology for the first time allows recordings of the plucked bass. Prior to that, the plucked or slapped double bass and the bass drum would make the recording needle jump off of the wax matrix.

Jimmie Blanton (*1918 †1942) *"The father of modern jazz bass playing"*. As bassist of Duke Ellington Orchestra, he revolutionizes the jazz double bass

Scott LaFaro (*1936 †1962) As bassist of the Bill Evans Trio he redefines the role of the bass

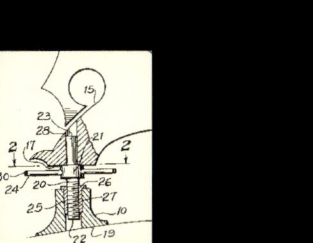

The German double bassist Eberhard Weber makes an Electric Upright Bass his main instrument

1946 – Jazz guitarist George van Eps applies for a patent for the height-adjustable double bass bridge

The Zorko (later named Ampeg Baby Bass) is one of the first commercially made EUBs

First pickups and amplifiers for double bass become available

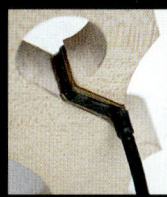

Steel strings are becoming increasingly popular, and are gradually replacing gut strings

Piezoceramic pickups establish the electrical amplification of the acoustic double bass

1942 – Bob Haggart publishes the first jazz double bass method

With Leo Fender's Precision Bass, the first commercially successful electric bass hits the market in 1951. (Popular bassists switching from acoustic to electric bass: Buddy Montgomery, Steve Swallow, Bob Cranshaw)

Fusion jazz appeals to a wider audience; electric instruments are increasingly used: keyboards, electric guitar and electric bass

Bebop replaces Swing as the main jazz style; only a few big bands are left

With the rise of the Brazilian Bossa Nova, Latin American rhythms begin to influence jazz

1950   **1960**   **1970**   **1980**

Leroy Vinegar (*1928 †1999)

Red Mitchell (*1927 †1992)

Ray Brown (*1926 †2002)

Sam Jones (*1924 †1981)

Wilbur Ware (*1923 †1979)

Percy Heath (*1923 †2005)

Charlie Mingus (*1922 †1979)

Oscar Pettiford (*1922 †1960)

George Duvuvier (*1920 †1985)

Israel Crosby (*1919 †1962) – Fletcher Henderson,

Chubby Jackson (*1919 †2003) – Charlie Barnet,

Jimmie Blanton (*1918 †1942) – Duke Ellington

Eddie Safranski (*1918 †1974) – Stan Kanton

Bob Haggart (*1914 †1998) – Bob Crosby

Slam Stewart (*1914 †1987) – Slim & Slam

Milt „The Judge" Hinton (*1910 †2000) – Cab Calloway, *Studio-Bassist*

John Kirby (*1908 †1952) – Bob Crosby, *Bandleader*

Walter Page (*1900 †1957) – Count Basie

Wellman Braud (*1891 †1967) – Duke Ellington

George Murphy „Pops" Foster (*1892 †1969) – Louis Armstrong

Steve Brown (*1890 †1965) – Jean Goldkette, Paul Whiteman

Bill Johnson (*1874 †1972) – King Oliver

| 1900 | 1910 | 1920 | 1930 | 194 |

Miroslav Vitouš (*1947) – Weather Report, Chick Corea

Niels Henning Ørsted-Pedersen (*1946 †2005) – Oscar Peterson, Dexter Gordon

Dave Holland (*1946) – Miles Davis, *Bandleader*

Rufus Reid (*1944) – Dexter Gordon, Thad Jones, Nancy Wilson

George Mraz (*1944) – Oscar Peterson, Mel Lewis/Thad Jones Orchestra, Stan Getz

Eddie Gomez (*1944) – Bill Evans, Miles Davis, Michael Brecker

Charlie Haden (*1937 †2014) – Ornette Coleman, *Bandleader*

Ron Carter (*1937) – Miles Davis, Herbie Hancock, *Studio-Bassist*

Scott LaFaro (*1936 †1961) – Bill Evans, Stan Getz, Ornette Coleman

Gary Peacock (*1935) – Bill Evans, Paul Bley, Jimmy Giuffre, Albert Ayler

Paul Chambers (*1935 †1969) – Miles Davis, John Coltrane

Jimmy Garrison (*1934 †1976) – John Coltrane

Richard Davis (*1930) – Sun Ra, Mel Lewis/Thad Jones Orchestra, Eric Dolphy, Elvin Jones

– Shelly Manne, Stan Getz, Chet Baker, Barney Kessel

– Woody Herman, Gerry Mulligan, Hamton Hawes, *Studio-Bassist*

– Charlie Parker, Oscar Peterson, Ella Fitzgerald

– Dizzy Gillespie, Cannonball Adderley, Bill Evans, Oscar Peterson

– Thelonious Monk, Sonny Rollins

– Dizzy Gillespie, Miles Davis, Modern Jazz Quartet

– Red Norvo, Duke Ellington, *Bandleader*

– Charlie Barnet, Dizzy Gillespie, *Bandleader*

– Coleman Hawkins, Jimmy Lunceford, *Studio-Bassist*

Ahmad Jamal

Woody Herman, *Bandleader*

Free Jazz, Avantgarde, Fusion
Bebop, Hardbop, Cool
Swing
Early Jazz

1950   1960   1970   1980

*Tommy Potter
(*1918 †1988) with
Charlie Parker at
the Three Deuces/
New York, 1946*

photo: William P. Gottlieb

Electrical amplification of the Double Bass

Electrical Amplification of the Double Bass

Before suitable electrical amplifiers were available, bassists had to compete with the volume of entire big bands and orchestras—an often hopeless battle. Today, pickup and amplification systems are taken for granted as accessories for double bass players. Adjusting to a band's volume level is no longer a major issue, since most bassists have their instruments equipped with a pickup. Nevertheless, the electrical amplification of such a complex acoustic instrument as the double bass is anything but trivial. And depending on the situation and acoustic requirements, different pickup methods and reproduction systems are available. Many systems actually do not reproduce the acoustic sound of an instrument very well, but authenticity is not the only criteria by which bassists measure the quality of amplification. The assertiveness of the amplified sound within the band and the volume are other aspects that play a role in the choice of pickup and amplification system.

Microphones

Clamping a microphone into the bridge arch is the simplest way of miking. The picture shows the "Bass Ball"—a foam ball which contains a small condenser microphone. Due to the ball shape, the microphone can easily be aligned for an optimal sound.

The signal generators available for the electrical amplification of a musical instrument, i.e. pickups or microphones, can be divided into three categories of sound conversion. First are microphones: they pick up the airborne sound radiated by the instrument and convert it into an electrical signal. Today, mainly dynamic and condenser microphones are used. Most dynamic microphones are so-called moving coil microphones where a coil is attached to a membrane. When the diaphragm is inspired to vibrate by the incident sound, the coil gets immersed in a ring-shaped slot of a permanent magnet, which induces an alternating voltage (proportional to the vibration). Simplified, this is the reverse principle of a loudspeaker. Dynamic microphones are very robust and are mainly used as stage and vocal microphones for live applications.

Condenser microphones have a diaphragm made of metallized plastic or gold leaf, which forms a condenser together with a counter electrode. The vibrations of the diaphragm caused by airborne sound change the distance between these electrodes and thus the electrical voltage, which is then amplified. Condenser microphones are very well suited for the amplification of acoustic instruments and are preferably used in studios. They have a wider frequency range and a more linear frequency response than dynamic microphones. In contrast to dynamic microphones, very small and lightweight capsules can be made, making them ideal to be mounted on the instrument. However, they always require a power supply from either pre-amp, built-in batteries, or phantom power.

Contact microphones are mounted directly on the instrument. There they do not pick up the airborne sound but the structure-borne sound of the instrument. The microphone capsules are housed in a case that is attached to the top or bridge, where it prevents additional airborne sound from reaching the capsule from outside.

Piezos

Piezoelectric transducers also belong to the category of structure-borne sound transducers (the word "piezo" is Greek and means "pressure"). Certain crystals (seignette salt) and ceramics (barium titanate, lead zirconate titanate) have the property of generating an electric charge on their surface when they are deformed mechanically or subjected to pressure. This phenomenon is used for sound conversion.

Clip-on microphone by the Danish manufacturer dpa

Piezoceramic flexural resonators consist of a ceramic layer applied to metal plates or bending strips (e.g. brass). The popular Fishman BP100 double bass pickup is one such flexural resonator. In piezoceramic thickness transducers, such as the Underwood pickup, a mass on the ceramic layer provides additional force and sensitivity. In addition to piezoceramic sensors, there are also piezoelectric sensors made of polymers such as polyvinylidene fluoride film (PVDF). This plastic, when pre-polarized, has piezoelectric properties and, provided with a metal layer, is suitable as a transducer for contact pickups. Since piezoelectric pickups do not convert airborne but structure-borne sound waves into electrical voltage, they are less sensitive to feedback than microphones. Unlike magnetic pickups, they do not require steel strings—another major advantage. Piezo elements are cheap and can also be found in alarm systems, electronic lighters and quasi "vice versa" as loudspeakers and buzzers in toys and acoustic greeting cards.

Besides the most common piezoelectric pickups, there are other sensor technologies, such as electret pickups (APTflex, BBand Statement), as well as electrostatic (Schertler StatB) and electrodynamic pickups (Schertler DynB). In their handling, however, they are not fundamentally different from other contact pickups.

With all contact pickup models, the positioning is decisive for the resulting amplified sound, in addition to the quality of workmanship and components. Depending on the design, signal components from the strings or the body of the instrument predominate. Through the bridge the strings impact the body of the instrument, and together they allow sound to be born. Due to this central role in sound production, most pickups are mounted on or near the bridge. The vibrations in the bridge can essentially be assigned to three directional forces: the vertical movement between strings and

Piezoceramics are polarized in a strong direct electric field at high temperature. This polarization decreases only very slightly over the years, making piezo pickups very durable. However, thermal or mechanical overload can lead to an audible deterioration of the transmissional behavior. Piezos work as force-to-voltage converters: They generate electrical voltage proportional to the force acting on them. The force does not impact the pickup directly, however, but is filtered mechanically by the pickup's housing and the bridge.

soundboard, the pendulum movement from right to left at right angles to it, and also the movement in the direction of the string tension. While in the upper part, in the immediate vicinity of the vibrating strings, a large number of different oscillations overlap. The vertical oscillations in the direction of the bridge feet increasingly dominate which has a practical significance for the placement of pickups. Depending on the position of the pickup, the different planes have a different share in the amplified sound. Pickups placed in, or on, the upper part of the bridge (i.e. near the string) tend to transmit a high proportion of finger and fingerboard noise. The sound here tends to be richer and more defined, whereas when positioned in the lower part of the bridge or under its feet, it tends to be rounder, but also less transparent.

Magnetic pickups

Finally, magnetic pickups represent a third category. They pick up neither airborne nor structure-borne sound, but the vibrations of the (steel) strings. They essentially consist of one or more permanent magnet(s), that have a coil of winding thin copper wire at the core. As a steel string (or a string made of another ferromagnetic material) comes near this coil, the course of the magnetic field lines alters, resulting in an induced voltage. This creates an induced voltage in the coil. The vibrations of the strings are therefore converted directly into alternating electric voltage.

The electrodynamic StringAmp pickup works in a similar fashion at first glance, but is fundamentally different. "The string is the pickup", as the Danish developer Michael Edinger describes it. For this purpose, carefully calibrated permanent magnets are attached to the lower end of the finger-board, and the strings (which must be conductive for electric current but not magnetic) are individually connected to a special preamplifier. The move-ment of the strings in the magnetic field of the permanent magnets induces voltage in the strings themselves, which is amplified by the preamplifier.

In 1936 Gibson introduced the ES-150, their first jazz guitar with magnetic pickup. Simultaneously, Gibson also produced a handful of prototypes of an "Electric Upright Bass Guitar". These instruments had an acoustic body (but no sound holes), a magnetic "Charlie Christian" pickup, and an adjustable endpin. In order to make the sound more "double-bass-like", the instrument came with an adjustable felt damper on the bridge and a fretless fingerboard. However, this EUB never went into serial production. Gibson made double basses, as well as guitars, but an electric bass was not pro-duced until the EB-1 model was released in 1953.

Schaller magnetic pickup, introduced in the 1950s and still made today

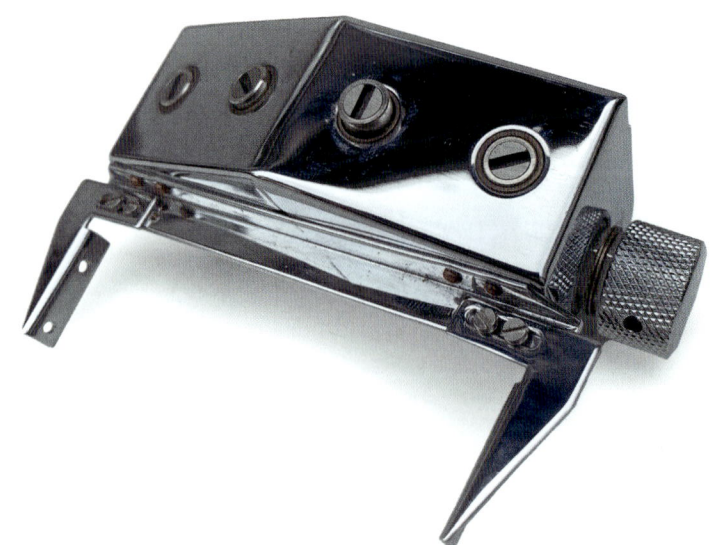

The Fender Precision Bass is considered to be the first successful mass produced electric bass. Fender released it in 1951, after the Fender Tele-caster electric guitar had already been extremely successful on the market. However, the electric bass as we know it today was first introduced in 1936 in form of the Audiovox Model #736 Electronic Bass Fiddle. Before that, Audiovox had experimented with EUBs. The Seattle newspaper Post-Intelligencer wrote in 1935: "Paul Tutmarc invented an electric bass that you can clamp under your arm. It doesn't even need a bow. You pluck the string and a full, deep sound comes out of the amplifier—as if five or six double bass players were masterly bowing. The sustain is as long as you want, even without the bow."

Audiovox produced about 100 copies of the four-string fretted electric bass model #736 until the company went out of business around 1950, three of which are still in existence. The electric bass #736 was $65, the amplifier #936 another $75—a lot of money back then. The #736 with case pictured below was auctioned first hand in 2018 and attained the price of $23,850.

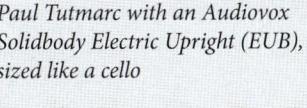

Paul Tutmarc with an Audiovox Solidbody Electric Upright (EUB), sized like a cello

Audiovox Model #736 Electronic Bass Fiddle, 1936

Fender Precision Bass, 1951

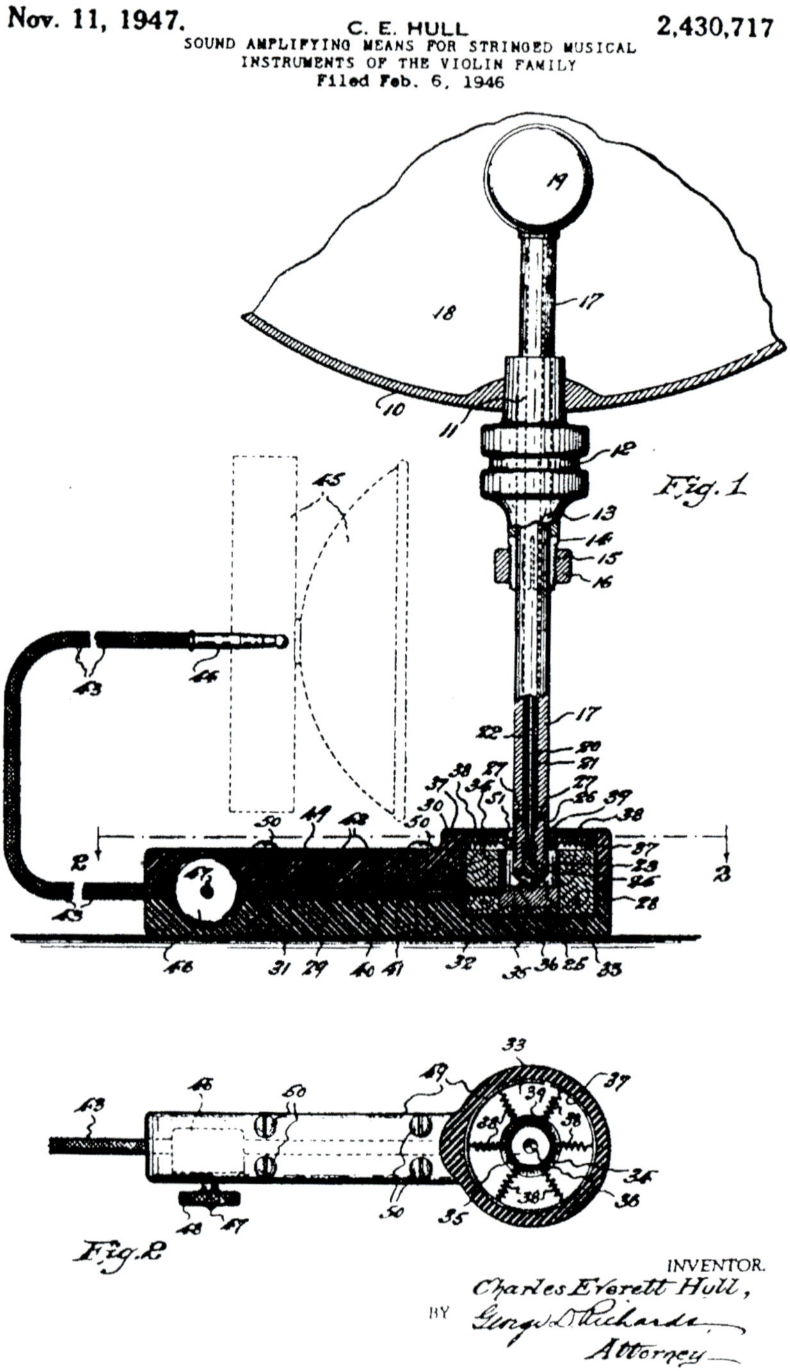

Nov. 11, 1947.

C. E. HULL

2,430,717

SOUND AMPLIFYING MEANS FOR STRINGED MUSICAL
INSTRUMENTS OF THE VIOLIN FAMILY
Filed Feb. 6, 1946

In 1947, a patent application was filed for the "Ampeg": a microphone that was inserted into the interior of the body with the spike ("peg"). The matching amplifier ("amp") was also available.

Actually, the Ampeg pickup had already entered the market a bit earlier. Jazz bassist Chubby Jackson reported on this groundbreaking moment: "On March 26, 1946 at exactly 4:45 p.m., on the stage of Carnegie Hall, I saw my electrically amplified bass for the first time. The rehearsal for 'Ebony Concerto' began at 5 p.m. So I had 15 minutes to finger and inspect it—like a little child inspects a new toy. During the rehearsal, I immediately got excited about the new effects that the amplifier made possible. Everett Hull, a friend and great bass player, had the idea for this amplified bass. It's the greatest thing I've come across in my musical career, and I predict that it will be widely used in a few years."

Fig. 1

Fig. 2

INVENTOR.
Charles Everett Hull,
BY George D. Richards,
Attorney

The development of pickups

In the 1920s and 1930s, many companies began to manufacture electric and electrically amplified instruments. In addition to successful newly developed instruments such as the vibraphone, the electric organ, Hawaiian Lap Steel guitars and especially the electrically amplified acoustic guitar, there were early attempts to produce an electric bass instrument. Around 1924 Lloyd Loar (Gibson company) introduced an electric upright bass (EUB) with an electrostatic pickup, which, however, did not go into serial production. In 1936, Rickenbacker introduced an electric double bass with a magnetic pickup. Since gut strings were still common for double basses at that time, they had to be wrapped with metal in the area of the pickup. Guitar manufacturers like Regal and Vega also produced electric double basses at the end of the 1930s. They had magnetic pickups with movable coils. The Audiovox company produced EUBs with magnetic pickups, as well, and launched an electric bass guitar in 1936—the forefather of today's electric bass.

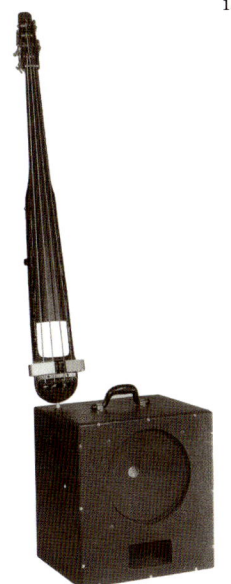

Electric Upright Bass from Rickenbacker, 1930ies

While pickups for acoustic guitars were available for retrofitting earlier, the first pickup for amplifying an acoustic double bass did not appear on the market until 1946: Everett Hull's "Ampeg". Everett Hull, himself a bass player, was introduced to pickup and amplification technology by guitarist Les Paul. His pickup used a crystal microphone attached to the inner end of the endpin rod—hence the name "amplified peg". In addition to this pickup, Hull's company soon offered the matching amplifier—the first dedicated bass amplifier ever. As one of the first prominent bass players, Hull was able to win over Eddie Safranski (Stan Kenton Orchestra, NBC Studio Orchestra) to endorse his products. Safranski increased recognition of Ampeg among New York bassists and received a commission for every pickup and amplifier sold. In addition, Hull was able to get some other well-known bassists as endorsers, e.g. Chubby Jackson (Woody Herman Big Band), Joe Comfort (Nat King Cole) and Oscar Pettiford. In the late 1950s a stereo version was released with an additional microphone near the bridge. Ampeg pickups were available until 1970.

DeArmond contact microphone for double bass

Other manufacturers used microphones as pickup sensors, too. Manufacturers DeArmond, Kent and Spotlight introduced contact microphones in the 1950s. In their designs, the pickup's casing was pressed against the top of the bass by a clamp, which was attached to the tailpiece. Premier, on the other hand, offered a microphone that was put into the body through one of the *f* holes.

The growing popularity of steel strings lead to the introduction of magnetic pickups in the 1950s. The company L&K offered a rather bulky pickup with volume control, which was attached to the end of the fretboard (like all magnetic pickups). The pickup of the German manufacturer Schaller is the

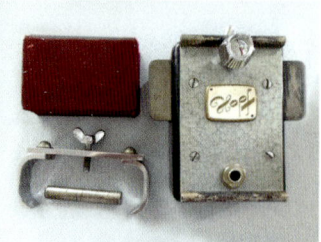

A pickup from the German manufacturer Hopf. The clamp fixated the magnet (red) under the fingerboard, while the casing was mounted onto the strings above the tailpiece.

L&K magnetic pickup

The Ampeg Baby Bass (formerly Zorko) was one of the first series-produced EUBs, and is popular among Latin and Salsa musicians for its percussive sound even today. The pickup consisted of an aluminum bridge that transmitted the string vibrations to two steel membranes, each of which had magnetic coils underneath.

only pickup of this era still on the market today. Magnetic pickups amplify the vibrations of the strings, not of the bridge or body. They are therefore only suitable for steel strings, and many models generate a rather "electric" double bass sound and are therefore not well suited to amplify a bowed bass. On the other hand, they are more resistant to feedback problems.

In 1962, Everett Hull released the Ampeg Baby Bass, which he had previously acquired the rights for from the Zorko company. This electric double bass had a body made of glass fiber (later Uvex plastic), and a new type of magnetic pickup built in. This pickup consisted of an aluminum bridge transmitting the string vibrations to two metal membranes, under which magnetic coils were mounted. In contrast to other magnetic pickups, gut and nylon strings could also be used, because the string vibrations were indirectly picked up by the coils. Nevertheless, this early Electric Upright Bass was not very successful, however, because of this model with its rather dull and percussive sound established itself in the 1960s among Latin and Salsa bassists and is still popular to this day.

Truely satisfying results could rarely be achieved with these early pickup "dinosaurs", since first generation amplifiers were extremely primitive by today's standards. Ampeg's first bass amp, which was launched in 1946, had as little as 18 watts.

Dec. 13, 1966   F. C. CARMAN ETAL   3,291,887

PIEZOELECTRIC MUSICAL PICKUP ARRANGEMENT

Filed Jan. 30, 1964   2 Sheets-Sheet 1

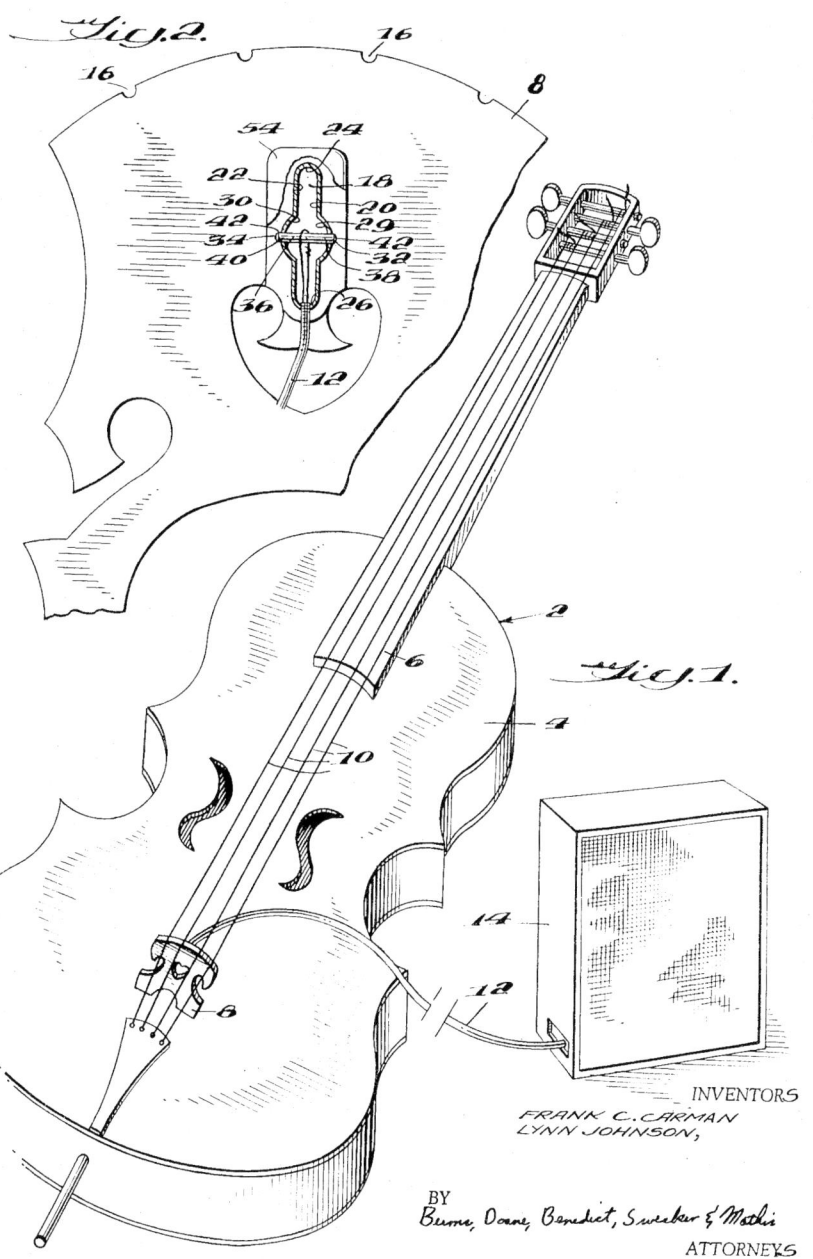

In the 1960s, the first piezoceramic pickups became available.

INVENTORS
FRANK C. CARMAN
LYNN JOHNSON,

BY
Burns, Doane, Benedict, Swecker & Mathis

ATTORNEYS

The Contraphone is a microphone, which is inserted into the double bass body through the ƒ hole.

The first experiments with piezo pickups were made in the early 1960s. Around this time, William Fowler developed and marketed a piezoceramic pickup for the double bass. Towards the end of that decade, companies such as Barcus-Berry and FRAP introduced piezo pickups and preamps for retrofitting acoustic guitars. By the early 1970s, piezo pickups that could be attached to the bridge or top of bowed string instruments with adhesive putty were available, as well. Soon afterwards, Polytone released a pickup specifically for the double bass, which was clamped between the feet of the bridge.

In 1977, the Underwood pickup was launched, which is still very popular and common to this day. Don Underwood was a saxophonist, who began developing piezo pickups, while working as a technician for a manufacturer of electric organs in the 1960s. Initially, he only produced small quantities for local bassists, but thanks to its easy handling and robust sound the pickup soon experienced a much wider distribution. The piezo elements of the Underwood pickup are inserted into the slots under the two bridge wings—a design that was adopted and varied by many other manufacturers (e.g. Shadow, K+K, FWF, Upton). With this design it is of importance, that the elements are neither too tight nor too loose. If the bridge slot is too wide, the PU should be fitted with thin strips of paper or wood (veneer or old saxophone reeds); if it is too narrow, the bridge must be reworked. It is also important that the elements rest flatly against the wings.

In 1980, jazz bassist Larry Fishman launched the Fishman BP-100, which has become similarly popular. It consists of two piezo plates, which

One of the first piezo Pickups for guitar and double bass were launched by the company Strobotronix under the acronym Frap (Flat Response Acoustic Pickup).

are pressed onto the bridge's surface with clamps. Soon, this design was copied as well. However, similar models from other manufacturers usually use double-sided adhesive tape for fastening. With most bridges, mounting is a matter of a few simple steps. If the upper side of the bridge is too curved, it has to be adjusted accordingly. Alternatively, the plates could be attached to the mostly flat down-facing side of the bridge. In the 1990s, Fishman released a two-channel preamplifier, the Bass Blender, as a supplement. In addition to an input for the BP100 (or any other piezo pickup), a miniature microphone can be connected to the second input to make the sound more natural. The idea of a hybrid system that mixes signals from different types of pickups (piezo + microphone, piezo + magnetic, etc.) has since been adopted by other manufacturers.

While the range of double bass pickups was quite manageable for decades, the number of products offered began to grow since the 1980s. Many pickups are imitations and further developments of the Underwood and Fishman models—but some completely new ideas have also been implemented. In 1983, Jørgen Wilson from Danmark released a pickup consisting of four small, cylindrical piezo elements. These are inserted into small holes drilled into the bridge below the strings. (Alternatively, it is also possible to mount a single Wilson element in the bridge foot).

The Swiss bassist Stephan Schertler looked for alternatives to piezoelectric transducers and patented an electrostatic pickup in 1987. Its technology is similar to that of a condenser microphone. Later he developed another model: a dynamic pickup, which is comparable in design to a magnetic

The Polytone piezo pickup is clamped between the bridge's feet

The Underwood Pickup is mounted in the bridge's wings. Inside the sensor, a piezoceramic disc is embedded in a rubber-like insulating layer. It is important for the sound-quality that the sensor fits perfectly in the bridge: not too loose, but not too tight, either.
The construction and assembly of the Underwood has been copied by numerous manufacturers.

Ray Brown with Polytone-amp and pickup (at the bridge)

phonograph cartridge. It is attached to the instrument's top, which acts as a membrane. Inside the pickup housing is a coil which is moved back and forth in a magnetic field by the instrument's vibration, thereby generating electrical voltage.

In 1987, a pickup from the Japanese manufacturer Yamahiko entered the market. In the Yamahiko CPS-DB, the piezos are embedded in the screw of a height-adjustable bridge. This pick-up has remained largely unknown outside Japan, but its design was copied by Fishman and released as the Full Circle Pickup in 2003. Basses that already have a height-adjustable bridge can easily be equipped with this good sounding pickup, as long as the thread of the height adjustment is the same as that of the Full Circle.

The collaboration between bass luthier David Gage and designer Ned Steinberger (who also designed the first "headless" electric basses) resulted in "The Realist" pickups in the late 1990s. The piezo elements embedded in thin copper sheet metal are clamped between a bridge foot and the top. Also in the 1990s, a piezoceramic pickup in the form of a conical brass pin was designed by German luthier Willy Balsereit. It's mounted to a hole, also conical, drilled to the bridge. By turning the pickup in its mounting hole, the sound can be adjusted to that of the instrument.

In addition to the pickups which can easily be installed by the player, some manufacturers offer complete systems in which the piezo elements are permanently integrated. Apart from replacing the complete bridge (Barcus Berry, AKG DB1; both no longer in production), their installation into an existing bridge is also possible (Barbera Multi Transducer Bridge, Rick Turner UB-1). Since bridges must always be individually adjusted for each bass, these usually more expensive systems might not be easily transferable to other instruments.

The Lando pickup clamp for mounting pickup sockets to the tailpiece: The rubber washers dampen the transmission of structure-borne noise and prevent rattling.

Phase cancellation for pickups

In the case of pickups with several transducers, phase cancellation (interference) may occur in some instances. In this phenomenon, the waves or vibrations picked up by the individual sensors superimpose themselves so unfavourably that an unbalanced sound is created. Theoretically, this can even lead to a complete cancellation if two waves are superimposed on each other exactly half a wavelength apart. Some bassists who use an Underwood pickup (or derivative) therefore mount only one sensor and leave the other one hanging freely in the air to achieve a more balanced sound.

Do-it-yourself pickups

Since piezoceramic components are inexpensive, simple pickups can also be self-produced. Depending on the effort, the quality of components and skill of the hobbyist, it is certainly possible to achieve the sound characteristics of commercial pickups.

Very easy to find are piezoceramic bending elements, which we encounter as buzzers or loudspeakers in acoustic greeting cards, toys, alarm clocks, etc. They usually consist of a circular brass plate with a diameter of 20 mm or more and a ceramic layer applied to one side. It is best to use shielded cable for pickups. The ends are first soaked in a little liquid solder and then carefully (without excessive heat) soldered to the piezo. Solder a jack plug to the other end—et voilà! The fragile solder joints can be reinforced with epoxy glue. To protect the sensor against interferences, you can use conductive adhesive tape or thin copper sheet.

For more advanced handicraft projects you can use higher quality piezo material, which is available as a wafer, coaxial cable and PVDF (piezo film). However, these more specific piezo components are less often available in specialized electronics shops, in contrast to the simple piezo buzzers.

Magnetic electric bass pickups can also be used on the double bass, provided steel strings are used. A problem, however, is the curvature of the fingerboard. Here, two-piece double-coil pickups are a good choice, as used in the Fender Precision bass, for example. Usually, magnetic pickups are mounted on a wooden or metal (sheet metal) holder, which can be attached to the end of the fretboard with screws or Velcro.

Piezo sensors are available as wafers of different sizes, as well as a flexible cable.

Amplifier and speakers

Instrumental amplifiers usually consist of four components: the preamp, the EQ, the power amp, and the speakers. Compact amplifiers, where all components are placed in one housing, are called combo or case amplifiers. Amplifier systems that consist of one or more loudspeaker cabinets and a separate amplifier top section (amp head) are called "stacks". The most elaborate variant is an amplifier "rack". The components such as preamplifier, tone control, power amplifier and, if necessary, effect units are installed as individual elements in a housing, usually a standardized so-called 19" rack, and wired together.

For most double bass players, however, compact combo amplifiers are the most convenient solution. A stack or rack can be useful for bassists who use individual components in order to amplify different instruments simultaneously (electric bass, double bass, electric upright) and/or to adjust to the setting (jazz club, arena, gala).

The first electric amplifier for double bass was available, even before the electric bass had been invented. In 1946 the Ampeg company launched the "Bassamp" as a supplement to their double bass pickup. It consisted of a mahogany veneered cabinet with a 12" loudspeaker and an 18 Watt tube amplifier. At the end of the 1960s, the Polytone company came out with the "Mini-Brute" amplifiers, and they quickly became popular with both jazz guitarists and double bass players. Endorsers included Ray Brown, as well as guitarists such as Joe Pass, George Benson and Jim Hall. They were

"The answer to the bass man's prayer"

offered as compact combo amps with 12" or 15" speakers. The early models only had bass and treble tone control in addition to the volume control, with the control of the mid range added later.

The first, and for a long time only, special amplifier for the new piezo pickups was released by Walter Woods in the early 1970s. Over decades of continuous development, Walter Woods still manufactures his by now legendary amp heads by special order and in small seriel runs. His models have two (or more) channels, one of which is optimized for piezo pickups, and above all are very small and compact—an important argument for double bass players.

In the 1980s the Gallien-Krueger company released a very compact combo amp. The amplifier electronics and a 12" loudspeaker are housed in a handy metal case. Despite its popularity among double bass players, the GK MB112 remains in the category of "ordinary" electric bass amplifiers, because the preamp and input impedance are not optimal for most double bass pickups.

While options were limited up until the 1990s, a large number of suitable amps are available today, some of them developed explicitly for the double bass. One such example is Acoustic Image's "Contra", which was released towards the end of the 1990s. A compact, cylindrical housing contains a tweeter, as well as a downward pointing speaker. This speaker is located about 7 cm above the floor and radiates the sound downwards, distributing it more evenly throughout the room.

As an alternative to electric bass and special double bass amplifiers, combinations of PA monitors (or active monitor speakers) and external pre-amps are also available. Conventional electric bass amplifiers are optimized for electric bass frequencies and do not reproduce the sound spectrum of a double bass without discolouration. Depending on the pickup, this can either improve or lower the sound quality.

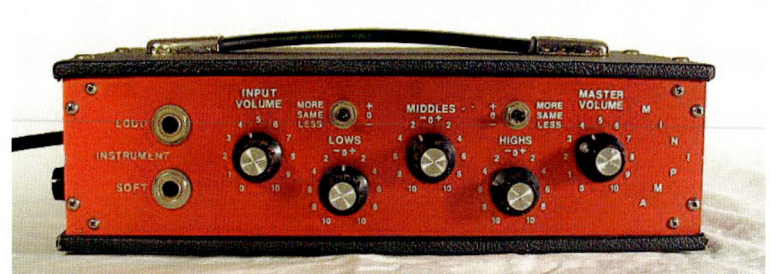

Walter Woods was the first to introduce small transistor amplifiers designed for double bass pickups

Ray Brown about electrical amplification: *"When I started, there were no amplifiers, and hardly any microphones. I mean, you just stood in the back of the band, and you never got to play over the microphone. The microphone was for the vocalist usually, or announcements—and once in a while a saxophone or a trumpet would go down there and play. So you had to be heard; you had to play with a lot of strength and dexterity. But I think that orchestras were aware of that, and you always heard the bass player. You stood in front of an orchestra and you could hear everybody; they blew so that you could, for some reason. I remember standing in front of Lunceford, Basie, Ellington and all those bands, and I could hear the bass as good as everybody else. The only thing that happens, I think, since they got amplification, is that the guys just blow louder. There is a definite difference between bass players now and bass players in my early days. Growing up in the thirties and forties, you were more involved in sound, basically. You couldn't afford to get too involved in technique, because you didn't have any amplification. There was one microphone in front of the whole orchestra, and the bass player was always in the back. Unless you were with Ellington—then you were up front. But it was very difficult to project; the faster you played, the harder it was to hear what you were playing. It was a physical problem in those days. That's one of the reasons the instrument wasn't played as well—certainly not as fast. A guy who's twenty–five years old, at fifteen he started out with amplifiers, so he didn't have to bother specifically with getting a sound—he never had a problem of being heard."*
(Interview by Les Tomkins, 1980)

The New York bassist **Ben Wolfe** still prefers to play gut strings and unamplified: *"I prefer the sound of every one of my favourite bass players—Paul Chambers, Ray Brown, Oscar Pettiford—without an amp. I want to experience the problems that my heroes experienced—the breaking strings, intonation trouble, a drummer playing too loud."*
(Interview by Stephen A. Smith, Allaboutjazz.com)

In the early 1990s, **Christian McBride** also strived for the ideal of playing without an amplifier and with a high string action, which at the time *"seemed to be the new religious experience for young bass players coming to New York"*. McBride recalls a meeting with his maestro and mentor Ray Brown: *"Ray said: 'Why are you young cats playing so hard? You don't need your strings set up that high'. Before I responded, something said, 'Shut up, and listen to Ray Brown. Don't say one word'. Benny and I saw him at the Blue Note a few nights later, and it hit me like a ton of bricks. Ray seemed to be playing the bass like it was a toy. He seemed to be having fun. He wasn't yanking the strings that hard, and he had the biggest, fattest, woodiest sound I'd ever heard, and I could tell that most of it was coming from the bass, not from the amp."*
(Ted Panken, jazz.com)

Ron Carter about bassists who only use a mic without a pickup:

"I think they are making a mistake. They want to sound like we did in the 1950s, but I don't know any bassist who played back then who would want to go back to that setup. They had no chance to be heard— and 50 years later, bass players who prefer that setup still can't be heard. Once the drummer picks up some sticks, the bass player's sound is inaudible. How can that be acceptable to him? Or to the bandleader's manager, or to anyone who's concerned with the group's sound? What's wrong with that picture?"

(Bass Player, Sept, 2003)

The first amplifier for double bass was launched in 1946.

Impedance

Impedance (or output/source impedance) is the electrical impedance of a microphone or pickup. The relatively high output impedance of many piezo pickups (usually between 3 and 10 MΩ) proves to be problematic, if the input impedance (or resistance) of the amplifier is too low. The result is a thin and jarring sound that usually cannot be improved significantly via equalization of the amp or mixing console. Active DI boxes or preamplifiers provide a remedy by matching the high output impedance of the pickup to the lower input impedance of the amplifier. For most piezo pickups, a preamplifier provides a significant improvement in sound. However, amplifiers specially designed for acoustic instruments or the double bass, have an input impedance of > 2 MΩ, which makes an external preamp superfluous.

On some amplifiers with tone control optimized for electric bass, the sound can be improved by bypassing the internal preamp and connecting the pickup with a more suitable external preamp via the effect loop-in path (effect in, slave in, return).

Tone controls and filters

Modern preamplifiers usually have tone controls (equalizer, EQ) for the three frequency ranges—bass, midrange and treble. Some models have so-called parametric tone controls, which allow you to individually determine the frequency range to be adjusted and, in the case of fully parametric circuits, also to specify the width (Q) of the frequency range. With the double bass, certain midrange frequencies of piezo pickups are commonly too dominant—with a parametric tone control, you can lower those particular frequencies and achieve a more balanced sound.

Notch filters have a similar effect, but not as wide as parametric EQs. The notch filter lowers a certain, very narrow frequency range considerably, without changing the sound image significantly. Notch filters are often used to amplify microphones in order to precisely reduce feedback.

High pass or low cut filters reduce lower frequencies below a certain bass frequency. In double bass amplification, a high pass filter might be applied to get a grip on booming lows, making the sound clearer and more resistant to feedback.

A phase switch or phase inversion switch is especially effective in small rooms, where interference (phase cancellation) with sound reflections occurs. In the absence of such a switch, the same effect can (theoretically) be achieved by placing the loudspeaker somewhere else in the room—provided, that the size of the stage permits it.

The Acoustic Image Clarus amp head was designed for double bass. Both channels have a high impedance input, seperate 4-band EQ, low cut filter and phase reverse switch.

Feedback

During the electrical amplification of acoustic instruments such as the double bass, the unpleasant phenomenon of feedback can occur quickly, especially at high volumes. When an instrument or the microphone that is meant to amplify it receives sound waves reproduced by a loudspeaker, it could begin to vibrate and thereby create a closed circuit. This phenomenon usually manifests itself in an increasingly intense and loud booming or whistling sound coming from the PA system.

As a rule, microphones are more sensitive to feedback than (contact) pickups. Available models differ in their stage suitability: studio microphones are much more sensitive than ones designed with a built-in feedback insensitivity for optimized live sound reinforcement.

In general, the main cause is either too little distance between microphone and loudspeaker, or too much distance between microphone and instrument. The distance between microphone and loudspeaker should be as large as possible. In addition, the more indirect the sound, the lower the risk of feedback. This can be achieved, for example, by using several small loudspeakers instead of one large one. The easiest way, of course, is to have little or no sound coming back into the microphones from the speakers at all. A proven strategy is to only use the microphone signal for sound reinforcement in the audience and to use a less sensitive contact pickup for monitoring on stage.

Feedback can also occur when using contact pickups. The sound waves reproduced by the loudspeaker rarely stimulate the pickup, but can cause the instrument itself to vibrate. In this particular case, the distribution of the sound pressure plays a decisive role. The most favourable position for the instrument is in the sound pressure minimum. If the feedback frequency (depending on the instrument) is between 120 and 150 Hz, the distance between the minimum to the maximum sound pressure level is about three meters. Due to space limitations, it is not always possible to choose the optimal position for the instrument, which is why some pick-up systems and amplifiers have phase reversal switches that shift the sound pressure distribution by half a wavelength. In extreme cases it can help to dampen parts of the bass: a towel wrapped around the tailpiece, foam or tape around the strings below the bridge, a tennis ball clamped between the tailpiece and the ceiling or even foam in the f holes can help to tame a bass.

Magnetic pickups are the least critical, as they pick up the sound directly from the strings. However, you should make sure that they are mounted as vibration-free as possible, otherwise feedback can occur even here, if the pickup itself is made to vibrate at high volumes.

Digital signal processing

Today, digitalization has found its way into amplifier technology, as well. "Modeling preamps" offered mainly for electric guitars mimic the sound of legendary (tube) amplifiers via software and processors. They are now also available for acoustic string instruments, but the approach here is different: not a particular amplifier sound is digitally reproduced, but the sound of a particular violin, guitar, or double bass itself. With devices such as Vsound or ToneDexter, the sound of the instrument must first be recorded and stored in the device as a digital template ("WaveMap" or "IR"). After this "training", the signal from any piezo pickup can then be processed and "re-modeled" by the preamp in real time. The amplified sound of the pickup artificially reproduces the natural sound of the instrument by means of computer technology. The ToneDexter uses a studio microphone to record WaveMap templates directly into the device. The Vsound preamp has only volume controls on the device and instead edits and adapts the templates of recorded instruments with additional PC/Mac software. The manufacturer provides templates of historical instruments recorded within an anechoic space, to allow for the reproduction of the sound of a Stradivarius, Guarneri, or Tononi violin by means of a solid body electric violin.

Audiosprockets
ToneDexter

Bassist Miles Mosley is known for his extensive use of guitar effect pedals with the upright bass.
"I started using pedals simply as a means to adapt my sound so that it could cut over a band. I didn't want the drummer, and piano player to be quiet when I solo'd. I felt like it was more fun playing with the band the same way a horn player does. Effects solve a volume issue for me, and additionally create a whole new tapestry of expression."

① ② ③ ④ ⑤ ⑥ ⑦ ⑧ ⑨ ⑩

Setup und sound optimization

Setup and sound optimization

The fingerboard

The fingerboard of a bass is usually made of ebony. In the past, rosewood was used as a less durable alternative, but no longer offers any cost advantages anymore. Instead, black stained hardwoods are used for inexpensive instruments today. Ebony from Madagascar is considered the best choice, but due to strict regulations it can no longer be exported. Exports from West Africa are also becoming increasingly regulated, which is why prices for good quality ebony have been steadily rising. Additionally, raw cuts of the very best quality that are suitable in size have become increasingly rare. The differences in quality of ebony can be significant. Bright spots in the wood are less of a nuisance than knots and irregular growth, which not only require more work when dressing the fingerboard, but can also cause string noise in the long term.

Fingerboards have a curvature in the transverse direction, which increases from the nut (where it is only slightly pronounced) to the lower end of the fretboard. This curvature makes it easier to change from one string to the next and can be less pronounced on basses that are only played pizzicato than on ones that are bowed. In addition, fingerboards have a curve, or relief, which runs lengthwise and takes into account the amplitude of the vibrating string. Without a sufficient dip, the strings would rattle or clatter on the fingerboard. You can feel this dip by pressing down on the strings at both ends of the fingerboard, while regarding the gap between string and fretboard. For conventional steel strings it should not be more than a maximum of two to three millimetres at the lowest point; a greater distance will make the instrument much more physically demanding to play.

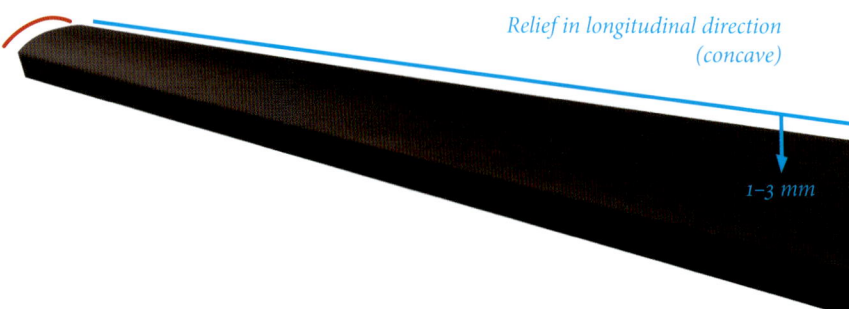

Relief in longitudinal direction (concave)

1–3 mm

Some fingerboards have an edge and a flat area below the E-string. This so-called "Romberg bevel" is intended to give the E-string more room to vibrate, and is actually unnecessary on a properly prepared fingerboard. As a result, it has become increasingly uncommon.

Due to high ebony prices, manufacturers have been looking for alternative woods and materials. Carbon actually has properties that are sought-after in fingerboards—a hard and homogeneous surface, stability and durability. The industrial production of a carbon fingerboard is actually not that difficult, but an individual adjustment and fine-tuning is problematic, since conventional methods and processing tools such as hide glue, plane and scraper are not applicable with this material. Several companies have developed new materials which offer the advantages of conventional setup routines. They are generated from local wood fibres that are dyed through, compressed under pressure, and bound with synthetic resins. These new materials have a similar feel, hardness, and appearance to ebony and are currently used to manufacture piano keys, guitar bridges, and even fingerboards. The use of such new materials is still in its infancy, but will certainly gain momentum in the coming years.

There is comparatively little instruction on how to dress a fingerboard in the relevant violin making literature. This is certainly due to the fact that this is more specific to the double bass. The smaller stringed instruments do not place such high demands on the fingerboard's relief, since the distance between the strings and the fingerboard is much greater in relation to string diameter and scale length than on the double bass. The demands on the bass maker have increased further with the advent of steel strings and bassists' desire for a growling, sustainable pizzicato tone. The lower the string action, the more carefully the fingerboard has to be dressed; even the slightest unevenness leads to annoying buzzing and rattling.

Ebony fingerboards may wear out over time. Grooves have formed in the most frequently played part of this fretboard

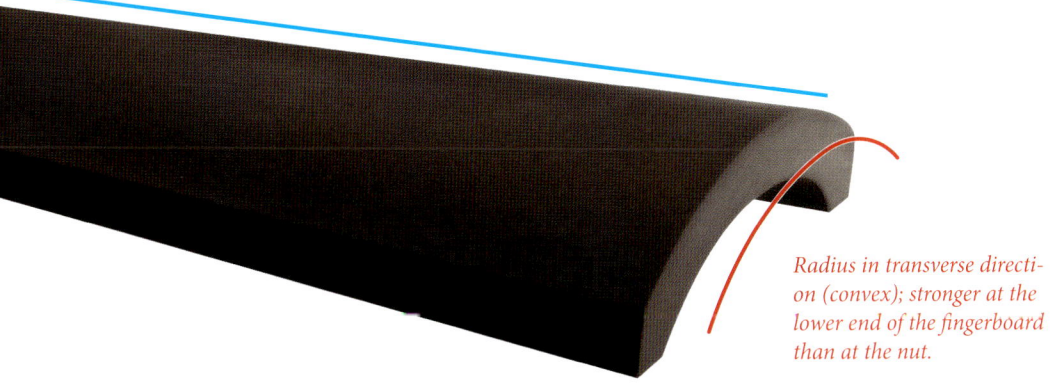

Radius in transverse direction (convex); stronger at the lower end of the fingerboard than at the nut.

Bass luthiers use planes (preferably with narrow mouth openings), scrapers, and sandpaper as tools for fingerboard dressing. To measure and check the final alignment of the fingerboard, a shorter straightedge or ruler in addition to a measure with the length of the fingerboard are required. The long ruler is used to check the shape and dip of the relief. After the fingerboard has been planed and smoothed, the short straightedge can be used to detect any minimal elevations that could cause the strings to rattle. These uneven areas are removed with a scraper or plane, then sanded over again. Only superbly sharpened plane blades will guarantee a smooth surface.

With a short straightedge and backlight, the planed and sanded fretboard is examined for any remaining unwanted elevations.

Small "bumps" that can cause the string to buzz or rattle are leveled with a finely adjusted plane. The scraper is used to smooth the surface.

Double bass luthiers Jim Ham, David Gage und Arnold Schnitzer about how to dress a fingerboard:

Jim Ham: A bowed string vibrates differently than a plucked string, so it is impossible to have an ideal fingerboard relief (hollowness) for both arco and pizz. (…) In the Helmholtz motion, the kink describes a curved path with its greatest displacement at half of the vibrating length. The elevation of the string at the nut provides some extra clearance for the open string so the point of greatest hollowness of the fingerboard for a bowed string should be half the distance between the first stopped note (A-flat on G string) and the bridge. When the string is plucked, the string forms a second kink upon release which travels in a direction opposite to that of the first kink; these two kinks describe a curve with a maximum displacement nearer to the ends so the ideal fingerboard shape for pizz would have the lowest point about one-third of the string length from the nut. I generally make the depth of the lowest point between half the string diameter to one full string diameter, this allows for the greater amount of hollowness needed for the lower pitched strings.

David Gage: I believe that, in principal, one curve will work with all styles of music. Starting with this premise, I will, if necessary, slightly alter the basic curve to fit the player's approach and needs and to the various string types. (…) A properly planed fingerboard with a curve or relief that is not too deep allows for greater vibrato ability and longer note sustain. We plane the fingerboard so that the deepest part of the curve is different for each string. The deepest part for each string forms a diagonal across the fingerboard. The deepest part of the curve and the depth at that point are: E string deepest at A-flat (major third up from open E), depth approximately 1.5 mm; A string deepest point D (perfect fourth up from open A), depth approximately 1.25 mm; D string deepest point A-flat (tritone up from open D), depth approximately 1 mm; G string deepest point D (a fifth above open G), depth 1 mm. (…) While I'm planing this curve or relief, I'm also planing a left to right continuous arc or radius in the fingerboard, about r-72 mm at the bridge end to a lesser r-90 mm radius at the nut.

Arnold Schnitzer: I take into account several things before regraduating and dressing a fingerboard: How hard does the player pluck or bow? Is the neck stiff and stout, or mushy and bendable? What type of strings will be used? (…) A client of mine works in an orchestra that plays very aggressively. He complained that when playing hard sforzandos he would get a nasty fingerboard rattle. He thought he needed more camber (scoop) planed into the board, but when I checked it, I found that the camber was more than adequate. The problem was that the amount of bow pressure he used was causing the string to slam down against the bottom end of the fingerboard. This was verified by greasing the string up with a white China marker and having him play the offending notes. The marker left white patches at the end of the fingerboard, which had a fair upward curve.

The bridge

The bridge is of great importance for the sound quality and playability of a double bass. It connects the instrument's tone generator (the string) with its resonator (the body), and acts as a filter, too. Its height determines the distance between strings and fingerboard, and thereby an instrument's playability. The optimum string action not only depends on the bassist's individual preferences and needs, but also on the characteristics of the strings. Before the appearance of pickups and amplifiers, gut strings and fairly high action were common, allowing for powerful playing necessary for that era. Today, steel strings and electronic amplification allow much lower string setups. Most players cope well with string heights between 4 to 6 mm for the G-string and 8 to 10 mm for the E-string (measured at the end of the fingerboard).

Bridges are made of maple, or more rarely, of platane wood. Blank bridges exist in various shapes and models, differing mainly in the proportions and shapes of the ears, hearts and feet. The differences in the silhouettes are not only for optical reasons, but do have a noticeable effect on the instrument's sound. Even though appearing to be mere ornamentation, the ears and the heart of the bridge impact the sound by absorbing or amplifying certain frequencies. Its size and weight play a major role, as well. With mutes that are placed on the upper part of the bridge, specific sound components, as well as the volume can be reduced. The damping

French and Belgian bridge models in maple. The bridge blanks are designed with additional wood on feet and upper edge, allowing for adaptation to the individual instrument.

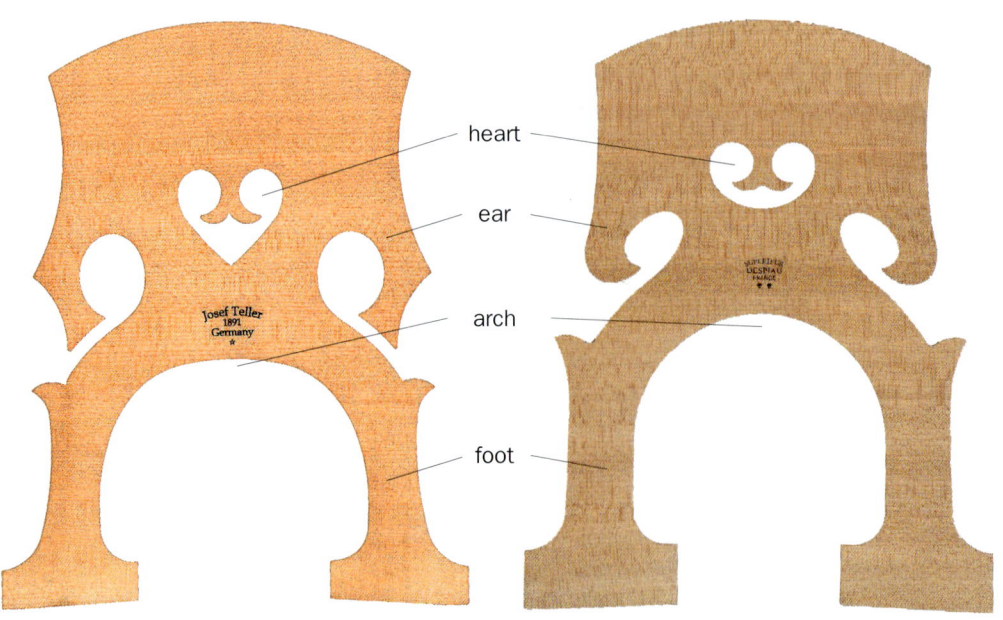

heart

ear

arch

foot

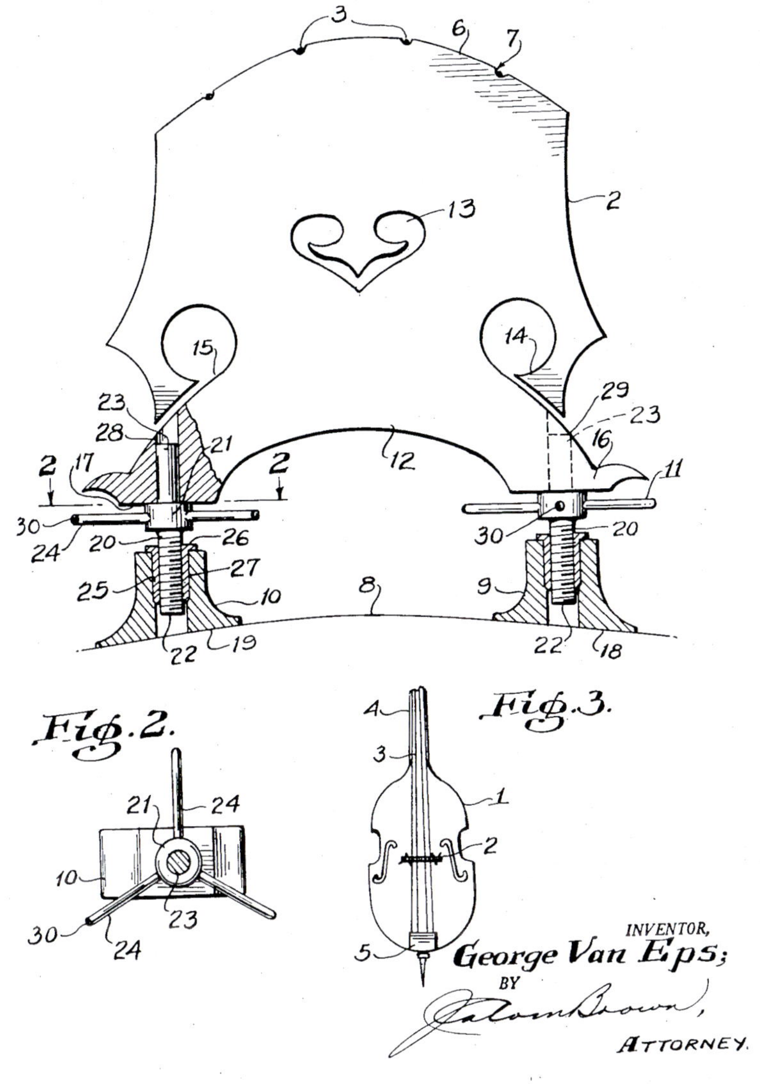

3 6 7

13 2

15 14

23 29 23
28 16
2 17 21 2 12 11
30 30 20
24 20 26
25 27
10 8 9
22 19 22 18

Fig.2.

21 24
10
30 23
24

4 **Fig.3.**
3
1
2
5

INVENTOR,
George Van Eps;
BY
[signature]
ATTORNEY.

Height adjusters for double bass bridges, as used today, were patented in the 1940s by the popular jazz guitarist and teacher George Van Eps. Van Eps came from a family of watchmakers and invented several other parts for musical instruments. In addition, he constructed mechanical components for the U.S. Army, which were used in the development and "successful" application of the first atomic bombs.

Due to its strength, platane wood is also being used for bridges.

effect increases with the weight of the mute. This principle applies to the bridge itself, as well: if it is massive with a wide upper part, it will dampen the sound more than if it is light and slim.

The vibrations in the bridge can essentially be attributed to separate forces working from three different directions. The vertical movement between strings and soundboard, the horizontal pendulum movement from right to left, and also the movement in the direction of the string tension. While a large number of different oscillations overlap in the upper part of the bridge near the vibrating strings, the vertical forces increasingly dominate towards the bridge. This has a practical significance, especially for the placement of pickups.

With Franz Moser's height adjusters, the bridge feet are connected to the upper part of the bridge by means of a ball joint, resulting in an optimized contact with the top due to the design's flexibility.

Height-adjustable bridges make it possible to quickly adapt the string action to changing weather conditions or a different type of string. For this purpose, threads and screws made of metal (aluminium, brass, steel), plastic (Delrin) or wood (boxwood, maple, ebony, Lignum Vitae) are integrated into the bridge legs. They first appeared in the 1940s in the U.S.A., where they are still being used by most bassists today. Due to a less challenging climate, they never became as common and accepted in Europe. The screws' additional weight, and interference with the vibrational structure is known to have a slight, but mostly tolerable affect on the sound of the bass. A positive effect can be that the feet are more flexible with an adjustable bridge and can keep better contact with the top. And last but not least, the increased playability should affect the sound very positively.

An interesting further development are the height adjusters by the Austrian Franz Moser. Their key feature are ball joints, which allow the bridge feet to easily adapt to the curvature of the top. In this way, optimum contact of the bridge feet with the top is ensured even in the event of seasonal or climatic deformations.

The bridge is placed right in the center between the *f* holes; in most cases the notches in the *f* holes can serve as a guide to the correct height. When viewed from the side, the bridge has a flat underside and a slightly curved upper side. In the foot area, its thickness is 22 to 24 mm, at the upper edge it is about 3 to 5 mm. Due to the tension of the strings, the bridge has a tendency to tilt towards the fingerboard. Therefore it is important to make sure that the angle between the lower side of the bridge and the top is no more than 90°. This angle should be checked and adjusted on a regular basis, but especially after putting on new strings. Otherwise, the bridge may warp or even tip over and damage the top. In order to correct the bridge's position, one should lay the bass flat on the floor and pull the upper part of the bridge evenly from below with both hands in the direction of the tailpiece.

various bridge models

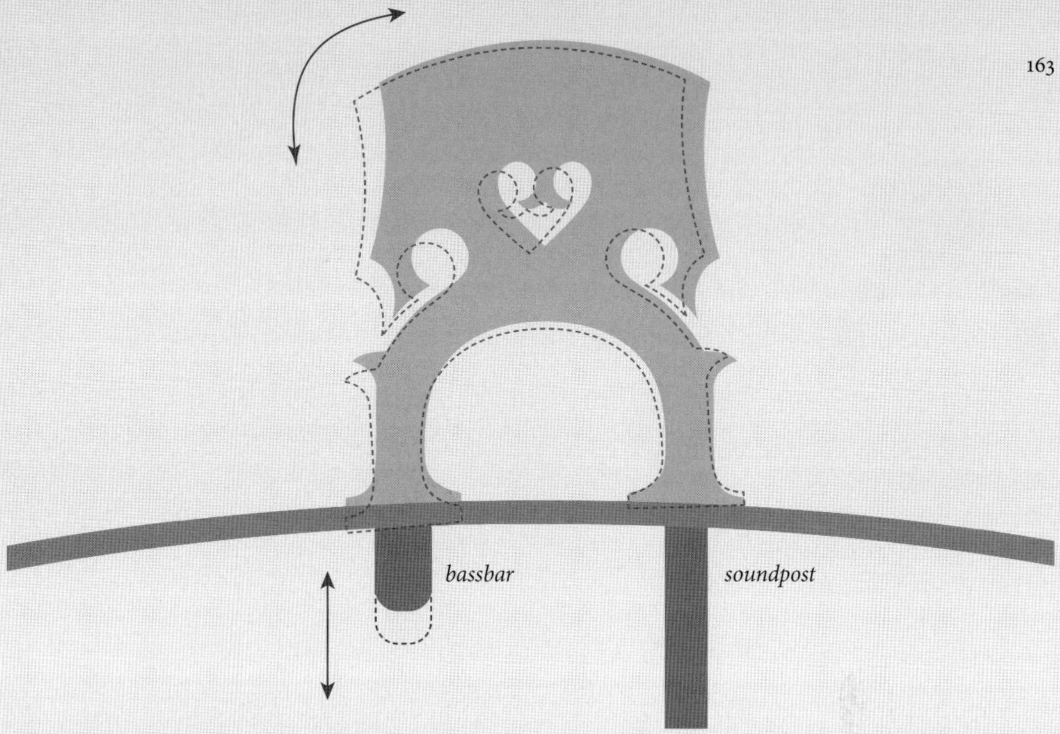

bassbar   *soundpost*

The bridge as a pendulum

Despite their strictly mirror-symmetrical shape, string instruments are asymmetrically built, unlike the guitar or other plucked instruments. To withstand the string pressure, the soft spruce top is arched and supported by the soundpost, sitting on the harder maple back in the area of the treble side bridge foot. The bass bar runs under the bass side foot of the bridge and distributes the vibrations lengthwise over the top. Those string vibrations not only cause the bridge to move up and down, but also in pendulum motion. While the top's area around the soundpost remains relatively still and acts as a nodal point, the area on the bass side plunges heavily and performs a pumping motion.

Bridge of Dragonetti's three-string double bass (with stamp "Kennedy").

The notches through which the strings run across the top of the bridge should be adapted to the strings' diameter for ideal contact. Therefore, changing from thick gut strings to thinner steel strings might pose a problem. But since steel strings can usually be played with a lower string action, there should still be enough extra wood left on the bridge to file the notches again. Should the notches be too tight, they can be widened with a suitable needle file to avoid string damage.

The bridge's height and arch depends on the preferred distance between the strings and the fingerboard. However, it is almost impossible to find a string action that does justice to all styles and playing techniques. For arco playing, the bridge radius must be pronounced enough to allow the bow to reach all strings without touching the adjacent ones even when playing fortissimo. In Jazz pizzicato, on the other hand, plucking is easier when the strings are closer to the fingerboard—the bridge radius may therefore be flatter. In slap bass techniques, however, the string position must not be too flat so that the fingertips can still get under the string. Therefore, the optimal bridge setup depends on the preferred playing technique and structural conditions such as the fretboard radius.

Regardless, the G-string requires a smaller distance from the fingerboard than the E-string, which has a stronger swing. For example, a medium all-round string position is 6 mm for G, 7 mm for D, 8 mm for A and 9 mm for E (measured at the end of the fingerboard). A low string position is one millimetre lower. For gut strings or light synthetic fibre strings, which vibrate more than steel strings, you may need 8 to 9 mm for the G-string.

With the help of a pencil, the shape of the top's curvature is transferred to the blank's feet.

With a saw, the feet are cut, and fitted with a very sharp knife, chisel and fine scraper.

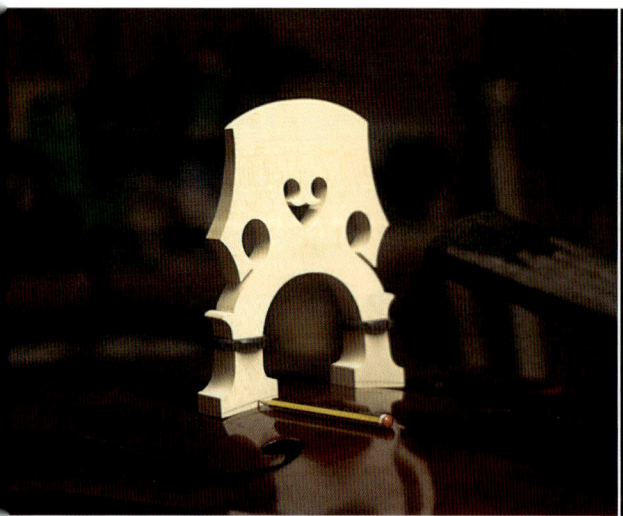

Ray Brown (interviewed by Les Tomkins and Arthur Johnson, 1963):

"I favor a type of string according to what suits the particular instrument. On this bass [Silvestre, France ca. 1850], I have rope–cored steel strings. The Italian bass gives in best results with a gut G and D and a metal A and E. Lots of orchestral players use all metal strings: they're good for bowing. For pizzicato playing, the metal G and D strings tend to cut into the fingers. I prefer the gut; they have a more flexible 'feel'. You have to decide that according to the type of playing you want to do, and how responsive your bass is. The higher the strings, the bigger the tone. But for speed solo playing, you need to press the strings down easier, so they need to be closer to the fingerboard. If I put the third finger of my left hand flat on the fingerboard at the bottom end, and it slides comfortably under the strings, that's the height that suits me.

I wrap the first section of my index finger round the string and snap it back. Usually just the index finger, but occasionally with the second. I come from the older school, where one finger for picking was the thing. The twofinger style has come in with the younger men.

You find out what the instrument will take without killing the tone. The tone has to sing. With the left hand you apply an equal pressure to match the pull of the right hand. In each position, the fingers should be over their respective notes, ready to press when required. I keep my left hand as relaxed as possible, and don't hold the fingers rigidly in position as though a teacher were standing over me."

To check how well the feet fit the top, you can use chalk, carbon paper or (as shown) lipstick.

Then the bridge height and the top edge are adjusted. Finally, the feet are brought to the correct thickness.

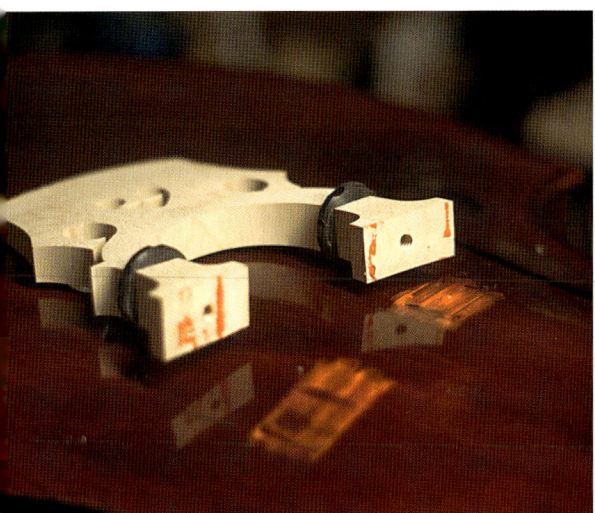

While generally between 22 and 28 mm, most bassists prefer a distance of 25 to 26 mm between strings. The closer the strings are to each other, the stronger the bridge radius must be in order to be able to reach all strings cleanly with the bow. This distance is usually measured between string centers, but there are also bassists who prefer an even distance between the outer sides of the strings. A compass or caliper gauge is recommended for marking and checking—it is more accurate than using a ruler.

In order to fit a new bridge, the top's curvature is transferred to the feet with a pencil, while the blank is placed in its intended position. Then the feet are sawed at the pencil mark with a scroll saw, and carefully trimmed with an extremely sharp chisel or carving knife until they fit perfectly. In order to identify and mark the areas where wood still needs to be removed, apply some chalk to the bass's top. The areas where the chalk shows on the bridge's feet must be reworked. Instead of chalk you can also use graphite, carbon paper or lipstick.

Schematic diagram of a typical bridge radius for pizzicato in relation to the fingerboard radius; the blue contour shows the optimized arch for playing with the bow.

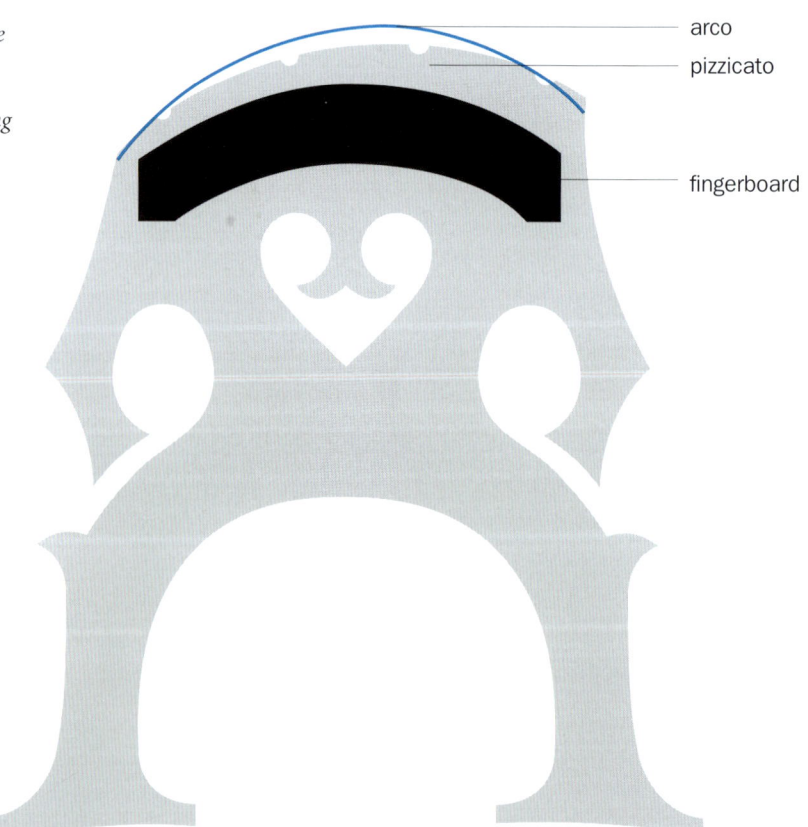

arco

pizzicato

fingerboard

As an alternative to carving, you can also use sandpaper to adjust the bridge's feet, as long as the curvature is mainly transverse. The sandpaper is fixed to the top of the bass while the bridge is being moved back and forth in the longitudinal direction (i. e. following the center joint) until the curvature has been transferred. The bridge must always be held vertically so that the edges do not round off. However, this method does not produce good results with older tops that already show deformations or have a pronounced curvature in the longitudinal direction.

Once the soles have been worked out, the feet are brought up to thickness from the upper side—with a carver, files or a spindle sander. Then the upper part of the bridge is planed to the required thickness. The underside remains flat, while on the upper side (facing the fingerboard) a slight curvature is worked out lengthwise and crosswise (i. e. the bridge is thinner towards the edges than in the middle). As a final step, most luthiers give the bridge an individual look by chamfering some of the edges, usually at the heart and ears. Finally, the wood can be treated with boiled linseed oil to make it look a little darker and older.

In the past it was not uncommon to attach the bridge to the tailpiece with a string to keep it from tipping over when tuning.
Bass: Hans Christoph Zäncker, 17th century (see also page 210)

Height adjusters are available in various designs and materials. Screws made of light materials such as aluminium and Delrin have a lower damping effect than heavier ones (e.g. brass). For one-piece screws without threaded insert, the thread is cut directly into the wood. One-pice bridge adjusters are lighter, but sometimes more difficult to operate.

With these wooden two-piece adjusters, the thread part is mounted to the bridge's feet.
The disadvantage of this design is that the thread rod can press through the foot of the bridge and may damage the top.

Bridge models made of aluminum or steel have remained a curiosity and have never established themselves. The bridge by the American manufacturer Deuce (pictured right) is milled from aluminium and has an exchangeable upper part made of plywood and feet made of cedar wood. With two screws, piezo pickups can be clamped in place.

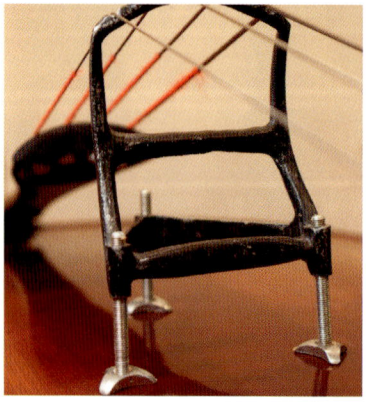

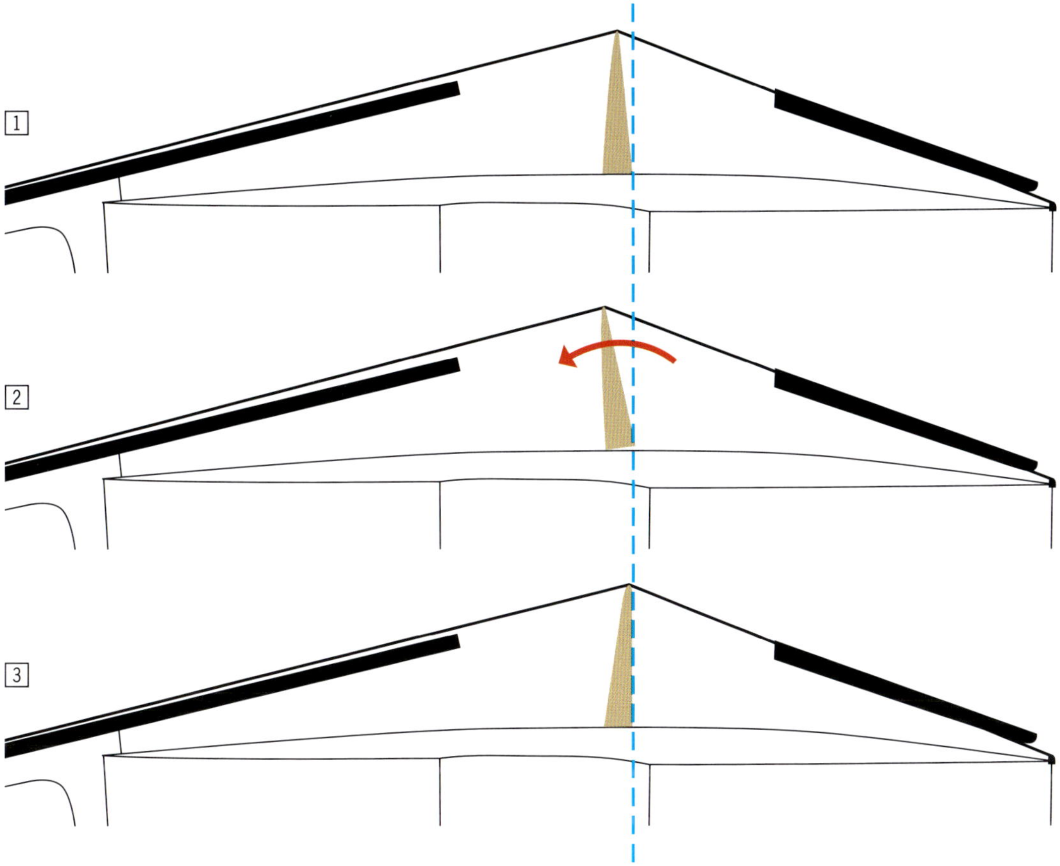

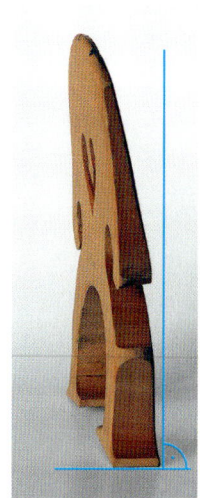

① Bridges that have been fitted to the top in the shape of an isosceles acute-angled triangle tend to move towards the fretboard.

② As this slight tilting progresses, the bridge's feet no longer have full contact with the top, effecting the sound negatively. In addition, the bridge can warp over the years (photo). This process does not only increase the string action, but can lead to the bridge falling over more easily if struck accidentally.

③ A bridge designed as a right-angled triangle is more in line with the force vector resulting from the string tension and therefore more stable.

The nut

If the saddle notches are too high, they can be deepened with a round needle file (or "rat tail"), which covers all string diameters due to its conical shape. For easy playability, the saddle notches should be filed down until a business card fits under the strings. For the E-string, the distance can be a little higher than for the other strings. The width of the notches should be a bit wider than the diameter of the strings so that they do not jam. The notches should not be deeper than half or a third of the string diameter.

When filing the saddle notches, make sure that the edge towards the fingerboard is not round. This edge should be the highest point of contact with the string, with the notch dropping down towards the pegbox. If the highest point is not on the edge, the string's vibration in the notch can cause annoying noises. However, the cause for the buzzing could also be the fingerboard, if it has been dressed with a slight slope towards this end. This can happen easily when the planing and sanding of this area has not been carefully executed.

If the notches were filed down too far, a strip of wood veneer can be glued under the saddle to raise it again a little bit. In preparation, the saddle must be loosened with a few light blows of a hammer. One does not impact the saddle directly, but use a small wooden block as a buffer (allowance). If that doesn't work, you can alternatively use a knife to loosen the glue joint between nut and neck or fingerboard. The knife is placed at the glue line and with light hammer blows to the back of the knife, it works as a wedge. To attach the nut, a small drop of glue or superglue is sufficient, since it is mainly held in place by the string pressure.

The distance between the strings should be 10 to 11 mm, measured from string center to string center. The distance between the outer strings and the edge of the fretboard should also be in this range—symmetrically

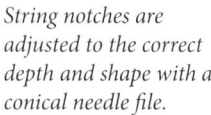

String notches are adjusted to the correct depth and shape with a conical needle file.

for both sides, of course. When starting a new notch on a smooth surface, a narrow triangular file is recommended rather than a round file. With this file the notch can be placed more accurately, while round needle files tend to slip if you have not filed a small "guide" prior. The round file provides the necessary shape and fine grinding at the end of the nut. To make sure that the strings slide well, the notches should be lubricated with some graphite, preferably with a soft pencil.

The soundpost

The soundpost (or ital. "anima" = soul), is a spruce wood stick which is clamped between the top and the back. By adjusting its length, thickness and position, the timbre and response of the bass can be controlled and influenced. In violin making, there are many opinions about its function and effect. Its supporting function is to counteract the pressure which the strings exert on the top via the bridge to prevent it from sinking in—just like the bass bar under the bridge foot on the bass side. In addition, the soundpost transmits vibrations directly from the top to the back. Some recognize that the most important aspect is its role as the central nodal point in the vibration field of the bass. Whatever theory you subscribe to, the fact is that the soundpost is a powerful tool for adjusting the sound of the bass.

Fig. left: This soundpost is improperly fitted.
The narrow sides have to match completely to the arching of the top and back.
Right: If the soundpost does not fit properly or is positioned too tightly, it can leave marks on the inside of the soundboard.

Soundpost setter for inserting and positioning the soundpost

The soundpost should be fitted in such a way that it does not fall over immediately without the pressure of the strings, yet not much firmer. Since the soundpost can easily fall over when putting on new strings, they should be replaced one by one instead of all at once.

Violinmakers often warn musicians not to experiment with the soundpost themselves, since it can cause damages when incorrectly positioned. A soundpost that is too long, too tight or tilted will quickly leave dents in the soft spruce wood of the top and might lead to a cracked top. Such a crack along the grain in the area of the soundpost must be repaired with a soundpost patch, which is one of the more complex and therefore more expensive repairs resulting in a reduced value of a bass.

Nevertheless, with some practice and suitable tools, repositioning an already adjusted soundpost can certainly be executed without having any bass-building experiences. Being self-sufficient in this respect is very useful—not only for re-setting a fallen soundpost, but also for optimizing your sound.

If the soundpost does collapse, it first must be removed from the bass via the *f* hole. The easiest way to do this is with a claw-type gripper, purchased inexpensively from a hardware store.

The most important tool for setting up the soundpost is the S-shaped soundpost setter. Some soundpost setters are delivered flat, and need to be bent to become usable. In most cases, the tip must be sharpened and finished. The tip should not be too thick. Many bass luthiers prefer a wider tip shape that tapers off towards the bottom, as this makes it easier to pull the soundpost outwards without it coming loose immediately. In any case,

The distance between the soundpost and the bridge foot can be checked with a gauge. You can easily make one from a piece of cardboard or plastic. The one shown here was cut out of a plastic folder.

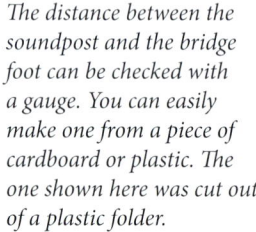

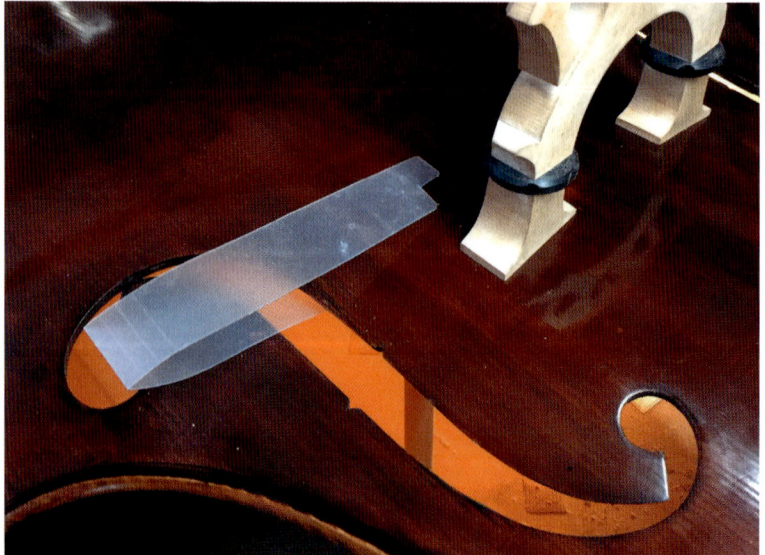

a heavy head is advantageous, since it allows the adjustment of a positioned soundpost as with a hammer. The handle of the soundpost setter should be bandaged to protect the sensitive edges of the ƒ hole. You can use leather, adhesive tape (bicycle handlebar tape), or a cut piece from a shrinking hose. You will also need a gauge to measure the position, which you can make yourself from cardboard or plastic, such as from plastic stationary folders (as pictured on the previous page). Some luthiers also use a thin twine as an additional aid to keep the post connected to the setter while pulling it outwards.

In order to assess the soundpost's vertical position, the corpus should be resting horizontally on the floor with the strings loosened. To hold the bridge in place, it is sufficient to tighten the A-string a little (but not to bring it into tune).

The sound post is then attached to the sound post setter via a slit-shaped groove, usually located in the post's upper third. If the existing groove is not in the ideal position, another one may be created. The soundpost should sit firmly (but not too firmly) on the soundpost setter's tip. It should not fall off during maneuvering, but must still be removable once the post is in its position.

The soundpost should be placed vertically between the back and the top. On many basses the middle bout ribs or the neck block can serve as a visual orientation when looking through the endpin hole.

Moving the soundpost is not as easy as it may seem at first glance. The rib, back , and top are obstacles, which are easily bumped into, causing the post to fall off the setter, and the need to restart the process. Because of the curvature, the bass body is deeper towards the middle than the outside, where the f holes are located. So the trick is to pull the soundpost from the middle towards the ribs to put it in place.

The first step is to line up the soundpost parallel to the f hole and insert it into the bass body with the lower part (the side that will later be on the back) towards the upper block, and the upper end towards the lower block (endpin). Then turn the soundpost in a counter-clockwise motion with the lower part towards the middle of the body, and the shorter upper end towards the rib. Next, the lower end pivots towards its final position on the bottom of the bass, while the upper end moves towards the middle of the body where it has some room for maneuvering. Once the sound post is near its final location, the bottom end is placed first, by pressing it down a little bit. Next the sound post is raised vertically until the upper end connects and locks into the top below the treble side of the bridge. A cord, which is loosely wrapped around the soundpost can be a useful additional tool for this final, delicate move. Once it is in a vertical position, release

The "Anima Nova" carbon soundpost is height adjustable—even when installed. The narrow sides are movable and thus perfectly adapt to the inner sides of the body. This allows the soundpost to be positioned anywhere without having to make several different long wooden soundposts.

the downward pressure so that the soundpost is being pressed up against the top. To release the soundpost setter, hold the post in place by pressing against it from the outside with the flat palm of your hand on the top. The setter should now pull out without moving the sound post from position.

With a mirror and a lot of light the contact surfaces are further inspected, since the soundpost rarely fits perfectly on the first try. With the head part of the soundpost setter, tap, push and pull the upper and lower ends of the post until no gaps exist between the soundpost and the soundboard or back. The soundpost must be perfectly vertical, which can be checked through the ƒ hole or the endpin hole in the lower block. Looking through the ƒ hole, one must direct light at the soundpost from the middle bout as well as from above or from the direction of the neck in order to be able to judge the position correctly. A small LED lamps can be inserted into the bass through the ƒ holes for this purpose.

It is quite common for the soundpost to fall during the readjustment process, especially for those who are inexperienced. A hemostat (surgical clamp) might be a good alternative tool, since it provides a tight grip of the soundpost properly. The unattractive marks that such a clamp leaves are considered somewhat amateurish, but are not problematic. The positioning of the sound post is complete once neither end can be moved, and fits snugly between their contact surfaces.

In traditional violin making it is frowned upon to round the edges of the soundpost. In fact, a sharp edge makes it easier to judge how well it fits. In his book "The Setup & Repair of the Double Bass", Chuck Traeger, on the other hand, advocates rounding the edges considerably, since the resulting smaller contact surface has a positive effect on the sound—a controversial view. It is undisputed, however, that the edge must not have any loose splinters, since they can later result in annoying noises.

Not recommended for replication On this old bass the soundpost probably fell over so frequently that the owner lost his patience and fixated it to the back with a small nail.

The soundpost wood should be fine and have 13 to 15 annual rings. Particularly high-quality blanks are not turned from sawn boards, but from ones that have been split along the grain and therefore have a very homogeneous grain pattern.

Where does the soundpost go?

Most luthiers have their own individual "starting position" for the soundpost. This is where they place it first and where they make adjustments from. Needless to say, opinions differ a lot. Most literature recommends that the soundpost be positioned at its diameter width (about 15 mm) below the bridge (towards the lower block). In the transverse direction, the soundpost is usually set up in the middle of the bridge's foot. You can also use the bass bar as an orientation, since its distance should mirror the distance from the soundpost to the *f* hole. This position is generally considered to be the "neutral" starting position.

As a rule of thumb, the closer the soundpost is to the foot of the bridge, the harder and more focused the sound becomes—a greater distance makes the sound softer and darker. If the soundpost is moved outwards (towards the edge), the E-string becomes more dominant, and if it is moved inwards towards the middle of the soundboard, the G-string comes out more. But here, too, no rule is without exception. In addition, it should always be noted that a new soundpost position usually requires a new adjustment of its length and contact surfaces. A soundpost that is too long sounds hard and compressed, whereas one that is too short sounds undefined and boomy and can be the cause of a poor response.

Cutting a new soundpost

If the soundpost does not fit properly or is too long, it must be reworked. This task is somewhat more demanding due to the curvature of the body. You will need a very sharp carving knife or chisel, with which you carefully remove some wood, and control and rework until the soundpost fits. This requires a lot of patience, because a fraction of a millimeter difference in length might already be too much for a soundpost.

Soundpost blanks made of spruce wood are available in different diameters, with 15—19 mm being the most common. The wood should be fine and have 13 to 15 annual rings. Particularly high-quality blanks are not turned from sawn boards, but from ones that have been split along the grain and therefore have a very homogeneous grain pattern.

The greatest challenge is to fit the surfaces exactly to the inner sides of the top and back, since the soundpost must be adjusted to the body's curvature. From the outside, however, these surfaces are impossible to be measured or evaluated. Therefore, good results can only be achieved by repeated trial and error, reworking and testing.

An existing soundpost that can be used as a sample makes the task a little easier. To copy a soundpost, I use a gauge consisting of two hardwood blocks that are screwed onto a board in a way that still allows them to turn freely. They simulate the angles of the back and top. The soundpost is aligned along a guide line with the annual rings parallel to the board. With a pencil mark, I mark the side of the soundpost that will later point upwards (towards the soundboard). Then both blocks are aligned and fixed to the sloping sides of the soundpost with screws and wing nuts (or clamps). Now you can take the old soundpost out, saw and rework the new one until it fits between the blocks with a few additional millimeters distance to the guide line. That distance to the guide line depends on how much longer the new soundpost should be. Or alternatively: the distance to the guide-line tells you how far the new soundpost is from the old position. The soundpost prepared in this way must then be finely adjusted to the curvature of the top and back in the next step.

The closer the soundpost is to the foot of the bridge, the punchier and more focused the sound becomes, while a greater distance makes the sound softer and more open. Moving the sound-post outwards (towards the edge) gives the E-string more dominance, and moving it inwards towards the middle of the bass gives the G-string more emphasis.

bassbar

soundpost

The Tailpiece

The influence of the tailpiece on the sound of the bass is often understated. Usually tailpieces are made of ebony or other hardwood, while those with fine tuners are usually made of aluminium. Originally, they were attached to the endpin socket (or a separate wooden knob in the lower block) with a gut string. Later it became common to use brass wire which had the disadvantages of being extremely stiff and breaking easily. Better suited is steel cable, which can be fastened with crimp sleeves or screwable connectors, allowing the tailpiece to swing more freely. Even more advantageous are tailpiece ropes made of low-stretch synthetic fibres. They are even more tear-resistant and flexible than steel cables, but can be easily knotted.

The area between the bridge and the tailpiece is called the residual strings or string afterlength section. Resonances of the residual strings can result in wolf tones and booming sounds, especially when electrically amplified. To dampen this resonances, special "wolf-killer" weights can be screwed onto the afterlengths. If you wish to have a somewhat drier sound overall, you can wrap a velcro tape or cloth around his passive section of the strings.

Instead of merely damping these resonances, they can also be used to improve the sound and response of the bass. One possibilty is to adjust the string length between bridge and tailpiece to about ⅙ of the vibrating string length between the nut and bridge. For a bass with a 105 cm string length that distance would come out to 17.5 cm. With these measurements, at least one of the strings could be tuned exactly to the interval of a fifth plus two octaves (29 semitones) above the tone of the open string. This results in the optimum length of the rope with which the tailpiece is attached. (If the tailpiece is the right size for the bass, there should now be a gap of about one or two centimetres between the lower saddle and the lower edge of the tailpiece).

Harp-shaped tailpiece

Wolf tone eleminators which clamp to the afterlength (strings below the bridge)

A newer, "tunable" tailpiece model allows for the length of the string's afterlengths to be adjusted individually. Similar to an electric bass bridge, these tunable tailpieces have adjustable sliders, which allows the afterlengths to be specifically changed. These tailpieces are different from the fine-tuning models commonly used for violin and cello, since they merely provide an additional tuning mechanism without changing the resonant string length.

Conventional tailpieces lead the strings in a parallel continuation past the bridge. Since the strings' attachment points lie outside of the force's path, the tailpiece is pressed sideways especially by the tension of the outer strings. This force dampens the strings' vibrations and may effect the sound negatively. This can be avoided by using tailpieces that do not guide the strings parallel, but rather centrally to the saddle, with the fixing holes of the strings lying on the force paths of the latter. Since this requires the holes to be closer together, they must be arranged at an angle to provide sufficient space for the seals at the ends of the strings. Such tailpieces were common practice for viols in the past, but had been forgotten until German luthier Hans Rödig described them in his book "Geigenbau in neuer Sicht" ("Violinmaking in a new light", published in 1962).

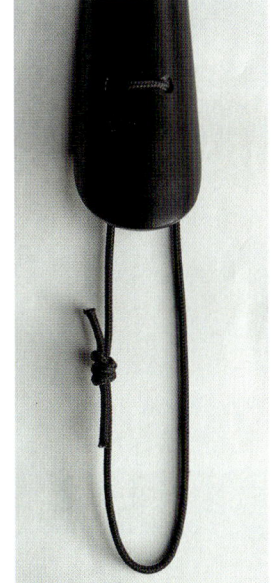

Tailpiece with synthetic tailpiece rope.

tunable tailpieces

The Saddle

In addition to their tension, the angle at which the strings run across the bridge also influences the extent to which they impact the top and how "soft" or "hard" they feel when played. The flatter the angle, the less pressure they exert on the soundboard. This does not only influence the way the instrument feels, but also directly effects the sound. To regulate this angle and thus the string pressure on the soundboard, a raised saddle can be extremely useful especially for older basses that were originally made for the lower pressure of gut strings. Another remedy is to change the neck angle, but this would obviously require a much bigger effort.

A saddle that can be adjusted in height has been developed by the Austrian bass luthier Franz Moser. This sophisticated design consists of two parts: a frame and the actual saddle, which is inserted according to the desired height. The dimensions of the frame have been calculated in a way that allows the length of the tailpiece rope to always remain the same.

Franz Moser's height adjustable saddle

Many basses have the lower saddle fitted directly into the top. Since the saddle and the sound board expand in different directions, cracks in the sound board are typical and very common. They usually start from the lower edge and move their way up parallel to the tailpiece.
To prevent this, the saddle should definitely be some- what narrower than the recess, so that it has some air on either side.

The Endpin

Until the 20th century, basses had simple wooden endpins that were inserted directly into the lower block or a wooden socket mounted there. They were not adjustable, but simply sawn to the right length. Today, adjustable endpins made of steel tube or rods are standard. Wooden endpins are rarely found, despite their advantageous sound properties.

A good fit of the endpin socket in the lower block is also important for the sound. The socket is conically shaped and is only plugged into the lower block, not glued. Usually, the tailpiece rope or wire is led around the endpin, but some basses have a separate end button for this purpose.

When playing while standing up, a bent endpin, as made popular by bassist François Rabbath in the 1980s, can provide a more balanced position. In this design's simplest version, a steel rod angled at about 45° is used for this purpose. In the common, slightly backward tilted position of the bass with a straight endpin, a large part of the weight usually rests on the thumb of the left hand. The bent endpin shifts the centre of gravity forwards. The thumb is relieved, and the instrument tilts much more towards the player. Due to this more cello-typical playing posture, the sound radiates differently to the conventional, more vertical position. Above all, the bass feels much lighter than with a straight endpin and ideally seems to stand on its own.

Height-adjustable endpins (image above) were not established until after World War II. Previously, wooden endpins were commonly used (left image)

Laborie Enpin (top)
and RobPin (bottom)

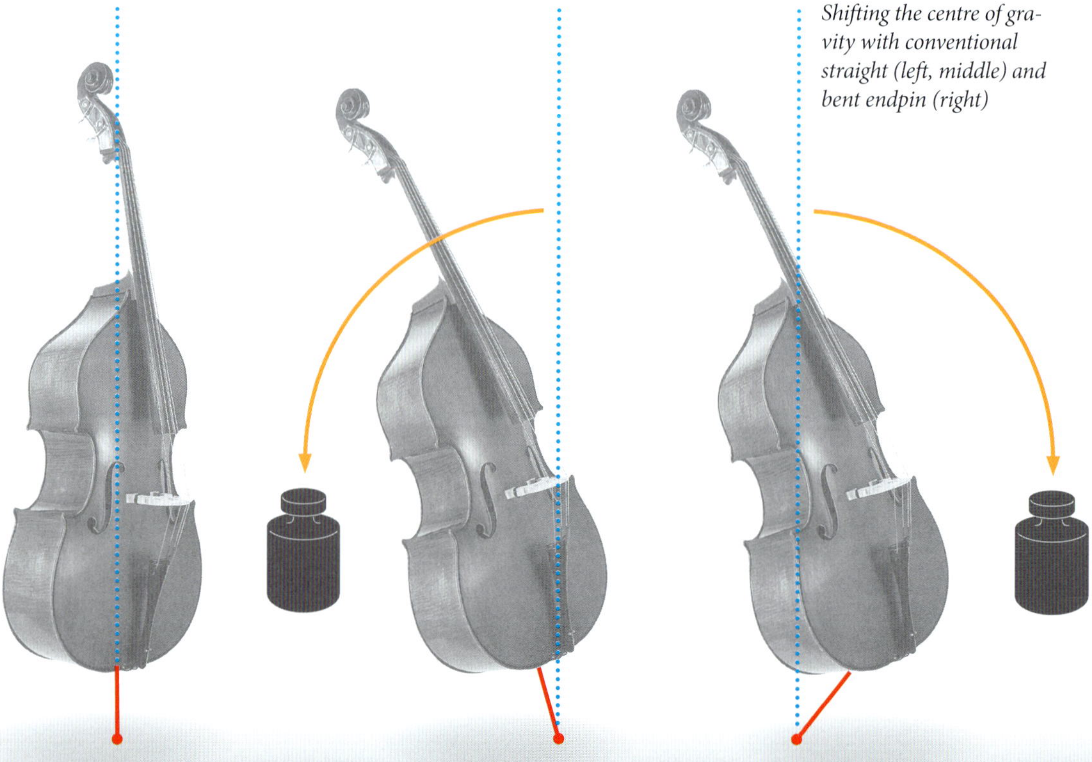

The endpin model by the French bass maker Christian Laborie, which was created in collaboration with bassists François Rabbath, Nicholas Walker and Patrick Neher, is a further development of this simple bent endpin. The wooden socket and carbon endpin form a solid unit here. For mounting, a new hole is drilled in the lower block, at a distance of 2 to 3 cm from the back and not, as traditionally, at a right angle to the rib, but at an angle of 40° to 44°. The endpin, which is not height-adjustable, is inserted directly into the lower block and removed again for transport.

The RobPin endpin is inserted into the existing socket instead of the conventional endpin and screwed into place. For individual height adjustment, rod sections of different lengths are available, which are screwed into the milled aluminium frame. The angle of the endpin can be adjusted to 25°, 35°, or 45°. Unlike for the Laborie endpin, no additional hole needs to be drilled into the lower block, since the weight of the bass resting on the two struts keep the RobPin from turning away unintentionally. Due to its numerous adjustment possibilities, the RobPin allows for an individual adaption to the bassist's posture and playing position.

Shifting the centre of gravity with conventional straight (left, middle) and bent endpin (right)

Climate

Wood has the property to absorb and store water from the air. If the water content in wood increases, it swells, sinks and contracts again. This process also takes place in basses and has a direct effect on their playability. The moisture penetrates through the *f* holes into the interior of the body, where it enters the wood via the unvarnished surfaces. The maple back absorbs more moisture than the resinous spruce top and it becomes longer and (with arched backs) flatter, while the top deforms less. As a result, the fingerboard drops and the string action increases to varying degrees depending on instrument and humidity. In an attempt to adjust to the differing conditions in summer (high humidity, high string action) and winter (low humidity, low string action), some bassists use multiple bridges of different heights (summer and winter bridge) or an andjustable bridge.

But while the varying string action can be compensated for, the influence of the weather can also cause cracks or the opening of glue joints. Therefore, the instrument should be spared abrupt climate changes.

Ideally, the ambient air should have a humidity of about 50 percent and should be checked with a hygrometer on a regular basis. An excessively moist environment is easily adjusted through frequent ventilation, while a too dry one is more difficult to counter. In the winter months the humidity is lower anyway due to the cold, and heaters additionally dry out the air. Specific humidifiers are available to protect the instrument from drying out. Sponge-filled tubes of about 30 cm lengths are soaked with water and hung inside the body through the *f* hole. Additionally, it is advisable to improve the room climate by placing water containers, hanging up damp cloths or using electric air humidifiers.

While extreme dryness poses a threat during the winter months, direct heat and abrupt climate changes can cause damages in the summer. The instruments are especially vulnerable when being transported in black, heat-absorbing soft bags and moisture-extracting car air conditioning systems. Therefore, it is better to drive with a slightly opened window while avoiding direct sunlight on the bass.

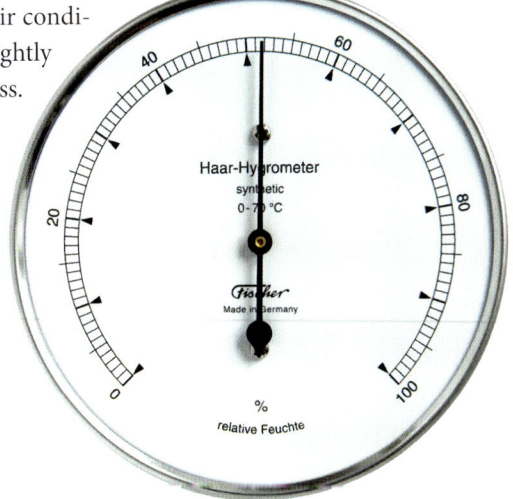

Sharp tools

Many adjustments and small repairs can be taken care of by bassists themselves. Apart from craftsmanship and patience, qualities that bassists usually have anyway, two things are needed above all—practice and good tools. The following applies to all cutting tools: they cannot be sharp enough. Therefore, the purchase of sharpening stones is just as important as the tools themselves. The sharpening of tools is almost a craftsmanship in itself. While some rely on machines, others prefer to sharpen by hand. Diamond sharpening stones have proven to be a good option, as they do not wear out as much and can be used for either dry or wet sharpening. An inexpensive, but not as durable alternative are lapping films (fine sanding

The tools used in violin making have essentially remained unchanged for centuries.

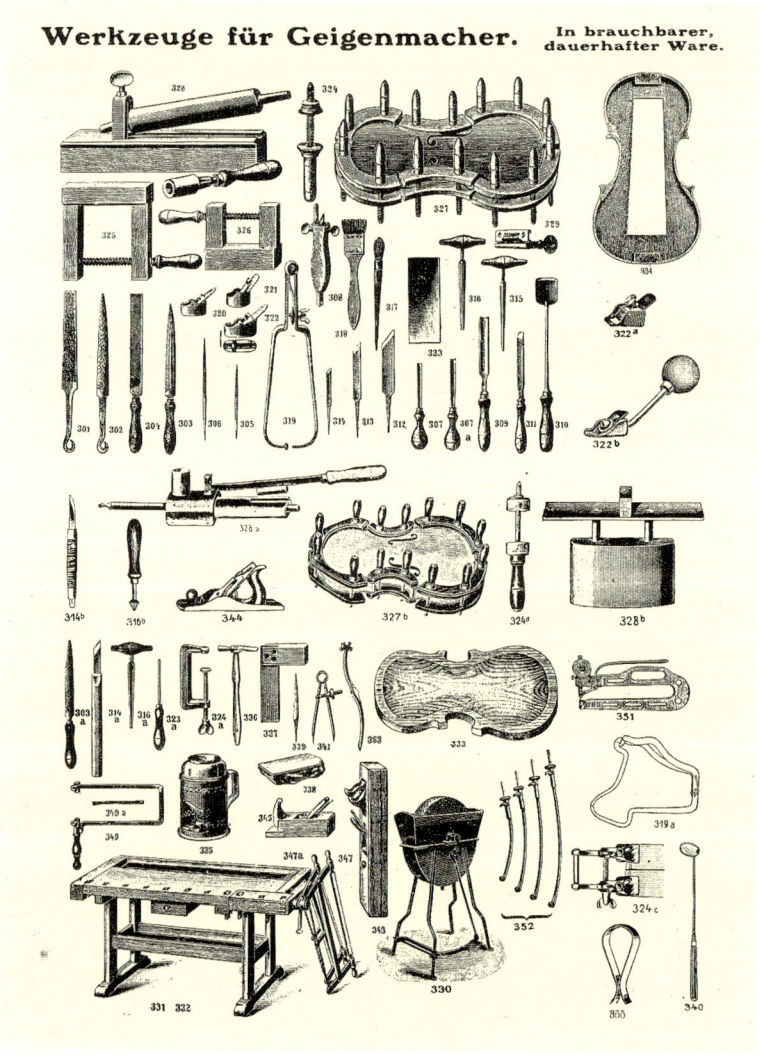

films) made by the 3M company (a glass or stone plate can be used as a flat
base). When using machines, an overheating of the steel must be avoided,
since it would result in the shortening of the tool's lifespan and it quickly
becoming dull again. Wet grinding machines are expensive, but have the
great practical advantage of keeping the blade cooled while sharpening the
tool accurately by means of grinding guides.

Glues

Even today, traditional hide or glutinous glues are used in the craft of
instrument making. They are obtained by boiling animal bones, cartilage
and skins and fishbones. Depending on the raw material, a distinction is
made between bone glue, skin glue, rabbit glue, fish glue and house blister
glue. Purified glutin glue is also known as gelatine and is being used for
food preparation, as well.

Hide glues have excellent properties, but are more complicated to process than yellow glue (PVA), which is why they are no longer used in industry.

In violin making, hide glue is preferred. It dries as hard as glass, and a
well-done glue joint may be of greater strength than its surrounding parts.
Nevertheless, most glued joints can be reopened with astonishing ease, which
is an important prerequisite for successful repairs. Another great advantage
over more modern glues is the fact that hide glue transmits sound waves
very well through the glue joints due to its great hardness.

Hide glue is supplied in dry form as granulate or pearls and is only
prepared immediately before use. Within a few hours of being mixed with
an equal amount of water in a glass, the dry glue completely absorbs the
liquid. The swollen glue is brought to a temperature of 50 to 65° C in a water

dry hide glue pearls

pearls soaked in water

liquid warm
hide glue

bath, while more warm water can be added to achieve the desired viscosity. It is ideal when the warm glue has a consistency of syrup or thin honey. When the glue has cooled down, it can be reheated and used again later, but unfortunately it moulds quickly. If the cooled glue residue dries out quickly enough, it can be used again, but usually it is spoiled after a few days.

Heating the glue at the right temperature is crucial. If the glue is too cold, it neither has the right viscosity, nor the optimal adhesive quality. Temperatures above 65 °C denature the proteins, weakening the adhesive strength of the glue. This is why warm glue is usually prepared in a water bath, for which baby bottle warmers are a practical and inexpensive option. Iron and non-ferrous metals discolour the glue and reduce its adhesive power. Therefore, glue-holding containers should be made of glass, ceramic, stainless steel or aluminium and the glue brushes should not have any ferrous parts. Since hide glue, unlike yellow glue, does not fill joints, a good form closure is decisive for a successful gluing process. The wooden surfaces must therefore be precisely finished and fit without gaps. When gluing, the pieces must be pressed together with a clamp for at least 30 to 60 minutes.

Commercially available wood glues are usually cold yellow glues that can be processed right away. They are also known as dispersion glue or polyvinyl acetate (PVAC). Parts that have already been treated with yellow glue cannot be re-glued with warm glue without further preparation. The yellow glue must first be sanded down thoroughly and washed out with steam and vinegar essence.

Polyurethane glue (PU or PUR glue) is a single component that hardens with the help of moisture. If sprayed with water, it will foam slightly, making it ideal for gap or joint fillings.

Epoxy resin is a two-component glue that is also used, for example, as a fibre composite plastic in the manufacturing of glass fibre or carbon fabric parts. Like PU glue, epoxy resin can only be used for very specific repairs.

Superglue (cyanoacrylate), on the other hand, is a practical remedy in everyday workshop life. It is not suitable for gluing larger surfaces, but a nut attached with two drops of superglue holds reliably and still can be removed again with a light blow of a hammer. It is transparent and very thin, making it ideal for filling cracks or even wormholes in fingerboards (mixed with some ebony dust if necessary). Superglue can be dissolved again with acetone. Special cyanoacrylates also find application in the medical field as a wound closure alternative to stitching.

In a glued or bonded joint, the intention is generally to achieve a balance between adhesion (adherence) and cohesion (internal strength of a material). In instrument-making glues whose cohesion is lower than that of the work pieces are also deliberately used, since an open glue joint is easier to repair than a crack in the wood (cohesion fracture).

Sound improvement from the laboratory

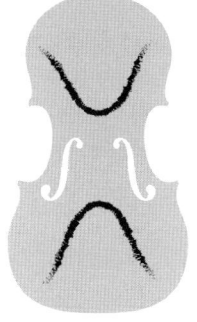

Chladnian sound figures

The German lawyer, physicist and astronomer Ernst Florens Friedrich Chladni (*1756 †1827) discovered that patterns are created on a thin metal or wooden plate sprinkled with sand when stimulated with a violin bow or tuning fork. When resonating, a plate or membrane is divided into regions that vibrate in opposite directions, bounded by lines where no vibration occurs (nodal lines). These patterns make the nodal lines visible. Due to gravity, the sand moves from the strongly vibrating regions to regions that have weaker or no vibrations. This results in different characteristic patterns that depend on the plate's natural frequency, as well as the applied sound frequencies.

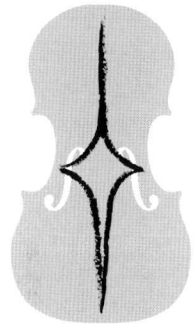

Chladnic sound patterns are used in the construction of string instruments, for example, when stimulating a freely vibrating top (or back) with a loudspeaker connected to a frequency generator. The soundboard is then refined until the shape of the "mode" corresponds to the ideal picture of the respective frequency.

Mode Matching

The term Mode Matching (or Mode Tuning) goes back to the American luthier and physicist Dr. Carleen Hutchins (*1911 †2009). Hutchins was intensively involved with acoustics within the field of violin making. The purpose of mode matching is to determine the different natural resonances of acoustic subsystems (i.e. parts of the instrument), and to match them up with each other as well as possible. She thereby systematized and formulated a process that violin makers have been practicing intuitively and based on experience for centuries. In practice, it translates to the individual shaping of a top, back or neck, while taking into account the special properties of the used wood. Mode Matching can be applied to both the construction of new instruments, and, to a lesser degree, the fine tuning of certain resonances in already existing ones.

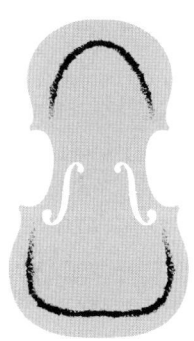

The natural resonance of the air inside the body, the so-called Helmholtz resonance, is designated by Hutchins as A0. The letter A stands for Air, while the number 0 stands for the lowest natural resonance. Higher natural resonance tones (modes) do exist and are designated A1, A2, A3, etc. In practice, however, only the most clearly perceptible, lowest natural resonance A0 plays a role and can be determined by placing a loudspeaker

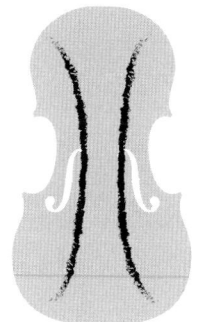

Chladnian sound figures on a violin top

connected to a frequency generator into the bass and slowly increasing the generated sound frequency. The frequency that is noticeably amplified by the bass is Ao.

The second important natural resonance is that of the body Bo. To determine Bo, tap the knuckle of your finger against the overhanging end of the fingerboard, the scroll or the neck. Even though this tapping sound might not be as clear and distinct as on the wooden bars of a marimba, it can be determined with a little practice.

In order to determine the wood resonance W' lay the instrument on its side and sing through the bass side *f* hole, while your hands rest on the upper and lower block. The sung frequency that most clearly stimulates the frame to resonate is the sought-after W' frequency.

The goal of Hutchins' Mode Matching is to keep the delta of Ao and Bo as low as possible by bringing both frequencies as close as possible to each other. This can be achieved by removing mass from the underside of the fingerboard, for example, or by adding extra weight. Other compensating variables include the weight of the tailpiece or the length of the suspension cable.

Vibration dedampening

If a bass is exposed to vibrations for a long time, the acoustic properties of the wood change. Many musicians therefore prefer old basses that have been "tuned in" over decades of use.

G. A. von Reumont applied for a patent in the 1970s for a process that would improve the sound of musical instruments by speeding up their breaking-in period. Vibration dedamping (VED) aims to "acoustically de-attenuate" the instrument by exposing it to strong mechanically generated vibrations in a targeted and controlled manner until the damping level drops.

For a dedampening treatment, the vibration transducer, a DC motor from airplane model making with an imbalance, is attached to the bridge. With the laboratory power supply unit, the power supply is adjusted to achieve and maintain a certain frequency. As the damping decreases, the power consumption of the motor decreases accordingly as indicated by the power supply unit. As soon as the power supply remains constant, the dedamping of this one frequency is completed and treatment can be continued with another frequency.

Users report that basses sound more open, respond more easily and have a longer sustain after the dedampening treatment. Skeptics, however, consider the energy balance to be insufficient as proof of effectiveness, as other factors (measurement inaccuracies, motor wear) could also serve as scientific explanations.

Can a sound improvement be measured at all? Admittedly, there are scientific measuring methods such as frequency curves and modal analysis. These methods can only detect, whether a change occurred, but not if that change necessarily resulted in an improvement.In the subjective evaluation, double-blindfolding is necessary in order to exclude the influence of expectations. For this purpose, neither the testing persons nor the test supervisors must know whether or not a sound-improving measure has been taken on an instrument.

Wolf tones

A wolf tone is a floating sound that can occur when playing a certain note and is also described as howling, flickering, or stuttering sounds. In addition, resonance weaknesses of certain frequency ranges (such as poorly responding, quieter or queasy notes) are referred to as wolves or false wolves. The main cause is the interaction between the body resonance of the instrument and the tone played. This phenomenon can occur with all stringed instruments, but is more common with the cello and double bass than with the violin or viola. Although the soundboards of cello and double bass are thicker than those of violins, they are thinner in relation to their body size. This favours the interaction between the body resonance of vibration and string vibration on the lower string instruments.

The appearance of a wolf tone is not an indication of an instrument of inferior quality. Some people even believe that any good sounding and well responding instrument must almost inevitably have a wolf. The degree to which a wolf becomes a handicap or nuisance very much depends on the player. While some wolves can be "played away", others are so disturbing that instrument-building measures are recommended. In the best case scenario, a simple string change will make a difference. Other remedies include a slight shift of the soundpost, an adjustment of the string's afterlengths, or a differently weighted tailpiece. The adjustable metal endpin rod projecting into the interior of the body can act like a tuning fork and may cause the wolf tone, as well.

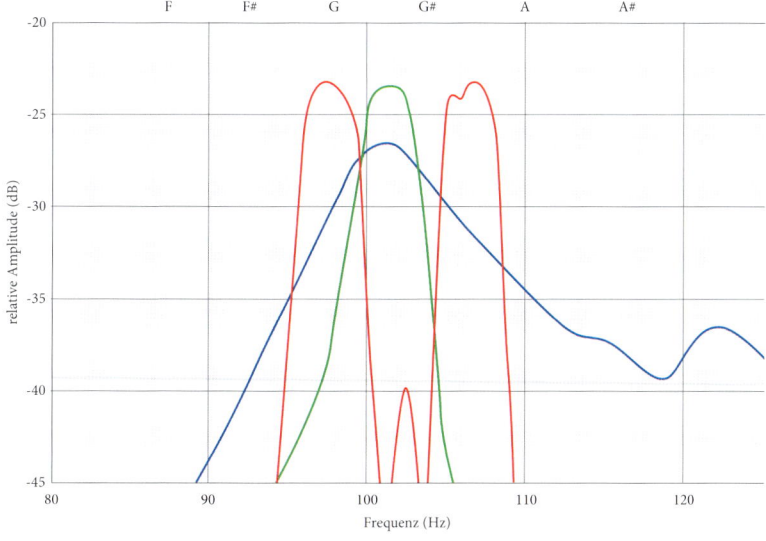

Blue: body resonance

Red: wolf tone

Green: tone after application of wolf terminator

source: Hideo Kamimoto

On the double bass a wolf usually occurs in the range between F2 (87 Hz) and A#2 (117 Hz), and is particularly frequent between G2 (98 Hz) and A2 (110 Hz). The diagram on page 189 shows an example of the resonance behavior of a ¾ bass. The body resonance (blue curve) has its peak between G and G# (around 102 Hz), while a "stuttering" wolf (red curve) "resides" in that same range, featuring two peaks of 9 Hz apart. Finally, the green curve shows the change in resonance behavior after a wolf tone eliminator has been attached. The tone responds more easily and sounds without stuttering.

Simple wolf tone eliminators are weights that are attached to the string's afterlengths. Ideally, they can help to match the natural frequency of the tailpiece with the disturbing natural vibration of the body and thus tame the wolf. Somewhat more complex are wolf tone eliminators (or wolf tone resonators), which are attached to the soundboard as vibration absorbers. Depending on the model, they are glued to the top on the inside or outside or held there with a magnet. The most effective location for the wolf tone eliminator can only be determined by trial and error, but is usually found in the area below the bass side ƒ hole. These vibration absorbers have a moving mass that change the interaction by absorbing the vibration energy of a certain frequency.

Wolf tones are particularly problematic when playing with the bow. With pizzicato the effect is perceived as less disturbing, since the tone fades faster. However, by eliminating the wolf, a positive effect on the finish of a plucked note can be observed, as well. A possible explanation is the reduced absorption of vibrational energy from the string due to the altered interaction between tone and body resonance, which in turn leads to a longer sustain.

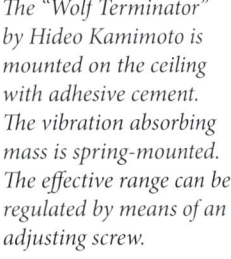

The "Wolf Terminator" by Hideo Kamimoto is mounted on the ceiling with adhesive cement. The vibration absorbing mass is spring-mounted. The effective range can be regulated by means of an adjusting screw.

No. 781—Our Special $8.65 Violin Outfit. We include in this outfit a genuine Stainer model violin, which alone retails at more than our price for the complete outfit. It is reddish-brown in color, shaded and handsomely polished, and has ebony fingerboard and tail piece. The violin bow is of special quality, made of Brazil wood, with ebony frog, pearl slide and full German silver trimmed. The violin case is of selected wood, black varnished, full lined with flannel and complete with nickel plated lock, handle and hook hasps. Strings are of superfine quality. The instruction book, sent free, is the most complete published. Good-sized cake of bow rosin also included; weight, boxed, 10 pounds. Our special price, complete, $8.65. The above is an outfit of remarkable superiority. Many a violin alone has been retailed at double our complete outfit price and was not equal in tone, quality or finish to the one we furnish. Keep in mind our liberal C. O. D. terms.

Our Genuine Gaspar Da Salo Model Violin and Complete Outfit for $16.50.

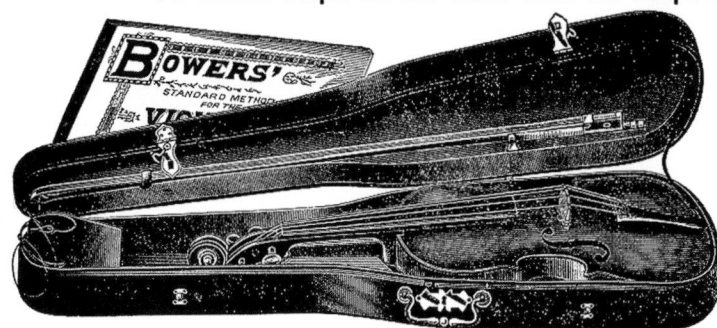

No. 783. **A most amazing offer.** The violin is a beautiful model, with name carved in scroll, and very fancy inlaying in back. The instrument is one that will attract the interest of professionals, on account of its beautiful full, round tones, as well as the richness of the finish and desirability of model. Full ebony trimmed. Reddish-brown color. We include a violin bow of decided excellence, it being made of Brazil wood. Round stick, with rounded ebony frog, German silver lined, fancy German silver button, pearl eye and pearl slide. The fine wood violin case is exposition shape, black varnished, full lined with flannel, with handle, lock and clasps. The full set of strings is of the most select superfine quality. The very best "Reform Rosin," on metal spools, in pasteboard box. Instruction book given is the best and most complete ever published. This complete outfit would retail at $30.00 or more. The violin alone is one that sells at $25.00 in the few retail stores that handle goods of such high grade; weight, boxed, about 12 pounds. Our special price, $16.50.

DOUBLE BASS VIOLS.

We quote below a complete line of double bass viols, one-quarter, one-half and three-quarter size. Prices include complete instruction book and bow of superior quality. Weight, boxed, averages about 125 pounds.

ONE-QUARTER SIZE.

No. 784—Double Bass Viol. One-quarter size, 4 strings, dark red shaded, finely polished, special quality, patent head. Our special price, $19.95.

ONE-HALF SIZES.

No. 785—Double Bass Viol. One-half size, 3 strings, dark red shaded, handsomely polished, very excellent quality, patent head. Our special price, $18.35.

No. 786—Double Bass Viol. Same as No. 785, above, with 4 strings. Our special price, $19.40.

No. 787—Double Bass Viol. 3 strings, dark red shaded, highly polished, finely decorated, inlaid edges, very fine quality, patent head. Our special price, $29.90.

No. 788—Double Bass Viol. Dark red shaded, very finely polished, inlaid edges, swelled back, very superior quality. This instrument possesses a tone of remarkable purity and power. A bass viol far superior to anything found in an ordinary retail store. Patent head, 4 strings. Our special price, $44.95.

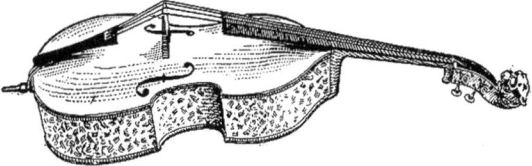

THREE-QUARTER SIZES.

No. 789—Double Bass Viol. Three-quarter size, dark red, shaded, polished, very excellent quality, and possesses a tone of decided quality. Patent head. Our special price, $22.50.

No. 790—Double Bass Viol. Same, with 4 strings, $24.00.

No. 791—Double Bass Viol. 4 strings, dark red, shaded, finely polished, inlaid edges, superior quality in make and finish, patent head, rich and mellow tone. Our special price, $34.95.

No. 792—Double Bass Viol. 4 strings, patent head, dark red color, shaded, beautifully polished, inlaid edges, swelled back. The tone of this instrument is exceptionally fine and the finish is superb. Our special price, $45.00.

VIOLONCELLOS.

The following violoncellos are with peg head. We also quote a line with patent head. Instruction book included, free. Customers will find a very complete list of violoncello bows and other furnishings further along in the catalogue quoted at from one-half to one-third dealers' prices. Sent C. O. D., subject to examination. Weight of violoncellos, boxed, about 45 pounds.

No. 793. Reddish-brown color, very good quality, peg head. Our special price, $7.65.

No. 794. Reddish-brown color, superior quality, rich tone and fine finish, peg head. Our special price, $8.35.

No. 795. Light red color, very good quality, inlaid edges, excellent finish and superior tone, peg head. Our special price, $10.95.

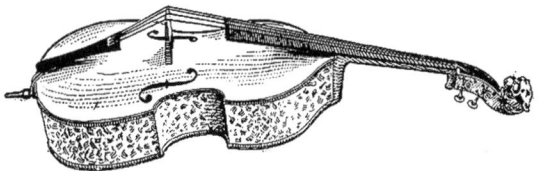

Violoncellos with Patent Head.

No. 796. Reddish brown color, very excellent finish and good quality, patent head. Our special price, $7.90.

No. 797. Medium brown color, finely polished and finished, quality is excellent and tone is especially good for a low priced instrument, patent head. Our special price, $9.35.

No. 798. Reddish-brown color, inlaid edges, brass plates. This instrument is especially excellent both in tone and quality. Made by the same factory that manufactures all our fine instruments. This one fact is sufficient guarantee of genuine high grade of material and workmanship. Weight, boxed, 43 pounds. Our special price, $11.55.

No. 799. Dark brown color, superior model, decorated with fancy inlaid edges, brass plates, patent head. The tone is rich and resonant. Our special price, $15.20.
☞ We send any violoncello C. O. D., subject to examination, on receipt of $2 with order as guarantee of good faith.

IF ANY MUSICAL INSTRUMENT DOES NOT MEET YOUR APPROVAL AFTER 5 DAYS' FAIR AND HONEST TRIAL, IT CAN BE RETURNED TO US PREPAID, AND ENTIRE AMOUNT REFUNDED.

The acquisition of a double bass

Around 1900, the extensive assortment of the Chicago mail order company Sears, Roebuck & Co. included not only clothing, household goods, furniture and tools, but also string instruments and accessories

The acquisition of a double bass

Many people who are interested in buying a double bass already play another instrument, such as guitar or electric bass. The entry into the world of the double bass is usually much more expensive, as everything is one size bigger—including the price. Even a simple double bass costs the multiple amount of a comparable electric bass or guitar. Maintenance expenses, i. e. strings and repairs, are also significantly higher.

In addition to monetary considerations, the double bass novice faces several other hurdles. General music stores and violin shops usually only have a small number of instruments in stock, and specialized dealers with large inventories of basses to choose from are limited. It should be considered that non-specialized dealers and mail order companies usually do not have the expertise to provide a proper set up, resulting in more or less unplayable instruments. As a result, follow up costs for decent strings and a professional set up need to be added to the purchase price.

Even among violin makers the double bass has a different status than other members of the string instrument family. Basses need more space, their production requires more physical strength and material, and yet their prices are lower than those of violins, violas and cellos—which makes them less attractive to make and market. Still, there are a good number of luthiers, who take advantage of this niche and specialize on the construction, restoration, furnishing and trading of double basses.

In advertisements and at Internet auctions, so-called cheap instruments are being offered now and then, but many of them are overpriced or in need of repair. Some people manage to find a bargain here, but without experience and expertise there is a high likelyhood of purchasing junk. Anyone who has the opportunity to do so should definitely seek the help and advice of double bass teachers or more experienced professionals.

The double bass virtuoso Serge Koussevitzky owned valuable double basses by Maggini, Guarneri and the Amati from Dragonetti's possession. For his performances, however, he mostly used a double bass from the Glässel & Herbig factory (Markneukirchen/ Germany).

Good advice from an instrument catalogue from Mirecourt (1920s):
"Our double basses are available with either new or old-imitation varnish, but we recommend our customers to option for the old-imitation varnish. A new varnish is too sensitive for instruments exposed to such strong impacts."

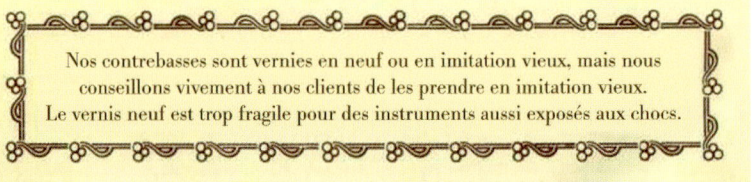

Nos contrebasses sont vernies en neuf ou en imitation vieux, mais nous conseillons vivement à nos clients de les prendre en imitation vieux. Le vernis neuf est trop fragile pour des instruments aussi exposés aux chocs.

Old or new bass?

Old instruments possess a unique fascination. Basses which bear the maker's label and are of historically interesting origin achieve high collector's prices, especially old Italian basses, but also French, English and German instruments with history are in great demand. Although the age of the used tonewood is an important qualifying factor, old basses are not necessarily better than new ones. Bass makers today are able to build instruments as fine as the masters of past centuries. More important than age alone is the skill, care and experience of the bass maker and the quality of the tonewoods used.

For most musicians and instrument makers there is no question that an instrument sounds better when it has been played a lot. It is the prevailing doctrine, that the wood and the instrument as such must settle in first, before it can exploit its full tonal potential. Surprisingly, there is little scientific evidence for this positive effect. The material wood is subject to measurable changes in its acoustic properties due to aging: the speed of sound increases and damping decreases. In addition, old wood reacts less sensitively to fluctuations in humidity. It can also be observed that acoustic properties change when wood is continuously exposed to vibrations—as is the case with a musical instrument that is being played a lot. But do these physically measurable changes necessarily lead to better sound characteristics? The human factor might also play a role in the breaking-in effect. Do old basses sound so fantastic because they have been played a lot—or were they played (and cared for) a lot because they sound so good, while not so good sounding ones have been sorted out? And surely familiarity contributes to the breaking in effect, as well: the musician adapts to the characteristics of an instrument, which allows him to bring out its strengths and therefore improve its sound.

In 2010, a study in Indianapolis investigated whether old violins really sound better than new ones. In a double blind test, participants of a violin competition compared three old violins (two Stradivari and one Guaneri del Gesù) with three contemporary violins. Neither the musicians nor the audience members were able to distinguish the sound of new versus old violins. Even more: the sound of one of the new violins was preferred by the majority, while a Stradivarius came in last!

At the Sorbonne University in Paris, the test was repeated in 2014 on a larger scale to verify the results from Indianapolis. For this purpose, the number of instruments was increased to six old (five of which were Stradivarius) and new instruments, and tested both in a rehearsal room familiar to the musicians, as well as in an unfamiliar concert hall. When asked the hypothetical question of which instrument the musicians would choose for a solo tour, one of the new violins received the most votes, while one of the Stradivarius violins received the least.

A label inside the stringed instrument provides information about the maker— the master's "business card". But old labels are not reliable: not only the models but also the notes of old masters have often been imitated. This did not necessarily happen with fraudulent intent, but to imitate a model as faithfully as possible down to the last detail.
The illustration shows a catalogue from 1915, which illustrates the offered violin models, using their imitated labels.

How is the condition of the bass?

Open glue joints at the transition from rib to back and top are easy to detect by lightly tapping along the edges with the knuckle of a finger. Tapping the wood over an open seem will result in a "clacking" sound, yet these kind of damages are easy to repair.

It is a different story entirely with cracks, and almost every older bass has them. If repaired professionally, cracks are usually unproblematic, but if they have not, they might depreciate the value of an instrument considerably. Especially concerning are cracks anywhere near the sound post: repairing them with a sound post patch is very costly and reduces the value.

Some cracks can be repaired from the outside through the *f* holes. Occasionally though, either the top or the back will have to be removed—a routine procedure for the expert, as long as no white glue or epoxy had been used during the making or previous repairs, yet instrument makers traditionally use organic hide glue, which can be dissolved again under the influence of heat and moisture.

More serious is a warped or crooked neck. A warped neck can be recognized by looking from behind the scroll down along the fingerboard and the strings towards the bridge. On older, valuable instruments, a neck replacement is usually carried out as a neck graft, whereby the original pegbox and scroll are kept and glued to a new neck. This way the original, historical condition and character of the instrument is largely preserved. However, a neck graft is only worthwhile for expensive basses.

How is the playability?

If a bass is set up poorly or even unplayable, its sound potential can only be assessed to a limited extent. Unfortunately, this applies equally to old and new basses. A poorly set up fingerboard usually will cause the

With this bass, the top has sunk in the area of the lower bass bar. Probably the bass bar was glued in with too much tension and pulled the top inwards at the ends. There is no acute need for repair here—but in the long term this can lead to tension cracks in the top.

strings to rattle or buzz. The fingerboard will need to be redressed, or even replaced entirely, should it be too thin or of inferior wood quality. A new fingerboard will most likely require a new bridge as well. The bridge should also be replaced if it is bending upwards towards the fretboard: it could tip over under the tension of the strings and thereby cause severe damage to the soundboard.

What size and scale length has the bass?

The vibrating string length between the upper saddle and the bridge is called the scale length. Today, ¾ size basses with a vibrating string length between 104 and 106 cm are most common, but up to 108 cm is still considered playable for most average sized players. Older basses sometimes have a scale length of 110 cm or more, which makes them harder to play and sell, no matter how good they sound. Therefore, beginners should start out with a standard scale length instrument.

A large bass usually has more volume and assertiveness than a smaller bass—that's why ⁴⁄₄ size basses are more common in orchestras. Soloists usually prefer smaller instruments with sloped shoulders that allow easy access to the thumb position. ¾ size basses are easier to amplify than larger models, since they are less susceptible to feedback and rumbling.

Depending on the position of the neck-body transition, we speak of a D or E♭ neck. If the middle finger of the left hand grips a D on the G-string, opposite to the thumb that is "locked in" at the base of the neck, we are dealing with a D scale; if it is an E♭, we are dealing with an E♭ neck, which is often found on older German basses. The D neck is more common, though, so being familiar with this would be advantageous when playing rentals.

Bad surprise: Only after opening the bass and removing some old cleats, it became apparent that the lower part of the top and the bass bar are badly affected by worm damage. This damage was not visible from the outside of the bass.

How does the bass sound?

For most musicians the sound should, of course, be the main focus when assessing an instrument in addition to quality of materials, workmanship and design. Does the bass have a balanced sound on all strings and in all registers? In addition to a round, powerful tone, the response and (especially in jazz) the duration of the sound (sustain) are also important. Since the sound spreads more forward than upward, the perception as a player is different from that of a listener who is standing a few steps away. Therefore, when evaluating a bass, it helps to have a colleague play it and compare the different characteristics. The room acoustics also play a significant role: playing into a corner will reflect a lot more sound to your ears than when standing in the middle of the room.

The back of this Hungarian bass seems at first sight to be made of well flamed maple. On closer inspection, however, it can be seen that the flames were merely painted on before being varnished.

Which strings are on the bass?

To judge the sound it is helpful to know which type of strings are on an instrument, since they are one of the main sound-determining factors. If you are not familiar with them and their properties, it is much harder to distinguish the sound of the strings (changeable) versus the sound of the bass (only adjustable to an extent). The strings must suit the instrument and its intended use. Is the bass equipped with gut or steel strings, thin or thick gauge? Is a thin or thick gauge strung? Do the strings bow well, or do they have a long enough sustain when played pizzicato? If you are looking for a bass to play jazz, it is difficult to judge an instrument that is equipped with typical orchestral strings and vice versa. The expert can identify most string brands by the color of the yarn winding in the pegbox and on the tailpiece, and use this in his assessment.

The Pöllmann company— today a renowned name in double bass making—was known at the beginning of the 20th century as a full-range music dealer with an extensive catalogue. Naturally, double basses were already part of their assortment at that time.

Max Pöllmann, Markneukirchen i. S.   19

Kontrabässe.

Erlaube mir zu bemerken, daß meine Kontrabässe aus **nur sehr gut getrocknetem Tonholz** gefertigt sind, auf das solideste gearbeitet werden und eine **außergewöhnliche, starke Tonfülle** besitzen. Bitte daher, selbige nicht gleich bei Wahl mit manch anderem Fabrikat in Vergleich zu nehmen.

		per Stück Mark					
		3 saitig			4 saitig		
No.	Größe:	¹/₂	³/₄	⁴/₄	¹/₂	³/₄	⁴/₄
235	Mit ☐ Eisen-Mechanik, rotbraun lackiert	32.—	34.—	36.—	34.—	37.—	40.—
236	Eisen-Mechanik, mit ☐ Messingplatten, Holz-adern-Einlage	36.—	39.—	42.—	38.—	42.—	46.—
237	Eisen-Mechanik, mit ☐ Messingplatten, Holzadern-Einlage mit **extra Randbereiflung** (Karnies)	39.—	42.—	45.—	41.—	45.—	50.—
238	Mit **Ebenholz-Griffbrett,** ☐ Messing-Mechanik, stark im Ton	46.—	49.—	53.—	50.—	55.—	60.—
239	Mit **langer Messing-Mechanik,** Ebenholz-Griffbrett, extra Randbereiflung (Karnies)	58.—	62.—	66.—	62.—	66.—	70.—
240	Mit feiner **Tiroler-Mechanik, Ebenholz-Garnitur,** fein geflammt, mit Karnies, kräftiger Ton	62.—	66.—	70.—	66.—	70.—	75.—
241	**Orchester-Baß** mit Ebenholz-Garnitur, feine Arbeit, feine **französische Mechanik**	68.—	73.—	78.—	72.—	76.—	80.—
242	**Orchester-Baß mit gewölbtem Boden,** volle Ebenholz-Garnitur, fein geflammt, vorzüglicher Ton, Mechanik mit ganzen Messingplatten	—	86.—	90.—	88.—	94.—	100.—
243	**Feiner Konzert-Baß,** fein gewölbter Boden, vorzüglich in Ton, Holz und Arbeit, mit ff. französischer Mechanik	—	110.—	115.—	—	115.—	125.—
244	**Hochfeiner Konzert-Baß** mit hochfeiner Neusilber-Mechanik, großer, edler Ton	—	125.—	130.—	—	130.—	135.—
245	**Künstler-Baß,** höchste Vollendung	—	150.—	170.—	—	175.—	200.—

Alle Orchester- und Konzert-Bässe werden auf Wunsch mit kunstvollem, geschnitztem **Löwenkopf** am Hals geliefert und erhöht sich der Preis um Mk. 6.— bis 10.—.

Bestandteile für Kontrabaß.

No.		per Satz Mark
246	**Mechaniken,** solide Arbeit, von Eisen ☐	3.50
„	von Messing ☐	4.50
„	lange, starke Platten	7.—
„	ff. Tiroler, von Messing	11.50
„	feinste Tiroler, von prima Neusilber	14.—

No.		per Stück Mark
247	**Stege,** ohne Herz	.60
„	besser, mit Herz	1.—, 1.25
„	feinste Arbeit	1.50, 2.—
248	**Saitenhalter,** von Birnbaum, einfach	1.—
„	besser	1.50
„	Ebenholz, einfach	3.75
„	feinste Ausführung	6.50
249	**Dämpfer,** von Ebenholz, einfach	1.25
„	besser	1.75
250	**Stachel,** einfach	.75
„	besser	1.—, 1.50
251	**Hälse,** einfach	6.—
„	besser	8.—, 15.—
„	feinste	8.—, 15.—
252	**Griffbretter,** von Ebenholz	7.—, 8.—, 10.—

—— **Baßsaiten** siehe unter Saiten. ——

Varnish

Varnishes that are being used in traditional violin making commonly are based on oil or alcohol and are applied in several layers by hand. After each layer has been applied, the varnish must always dry and get sanded, which makes the varnishing process very complex and time-consuming. However, this is the only way to achieve these wonderfully three-dimensional, "deep" textures in varnished wood.

In mass production, lacquers that are easier to process and quick-drying are used today. Until a few decades ago, these were mainly nitrocellulose lacquers, which could be applied very thinly and were therefore very suitable for musical instruments. Due to the high solvent content, however, nitrocellulose varnishes pose health risks for the maker. Today, products with a less questionable health factor such as Desmodur, DD nitro component coatings and pulyurethane (PU) coatings are being used and are applied by spray gun. High-quality instruments are only varnished with traditional natural resin varnishes based on spirit or oil. Although they are more sensitive than industrial lacquers, their great advantage is that small flaws are easier to retouch.

The varnish colour of old basses does not always correspond to the original condition. Some varnish components oxidize and make the varnish darker. With this now blonde Framus bass from 1954 (see also page 237) it is the other way around: sunlight has made the pigments lighter; the original reddish-brown colour is only preserved underneath the plate of the gears.

To produce spirit varnish, shellac flakes are dissolved in alcohol and mixed with various other resins (e.g. copal, gum elemi), oils, turpentines and plasticizers, depending on the recipe. Spirit varnish has a yellowish to reddish hue. For other colours natural or synthetic dyes are added to the varnish.

Shellac

Copal

Gum Elemi

Prices yesterday and today

Over the last decades our favorite instrument, the double bass, has undoubtedly gained in popularity. Never has there been so many double bass lessons taught at music schools as today. But a double bass is still a comparatively expensive acquisition. What effect does increased demand have on prices?

A glance at old catalogues reveals some interesting facts: in the GEWA catalogue from 1960, an entry-level plywood bass with hardwood fingerboard cost 494 DM, and a well flamed, solid bass with ebony fingerboard 980 DM. Converted into Euro that would be about 250 € and 500 € respectively. Sounds cheap—but were these really bargain prices? Probably not. In 1960, the gross annual income in the FRG was 3,144 €, increasing about 10 times to 31,089 € in 2013. Calculated accordingly, the plywood bass was around 2,500 €, and the fully solid bass was 5.000 €. So plywood basses have effectively become much cheaper since 1960, whereas a well flamed, fully carved bass made in Germany is hardly available for 5,000 € today. However, this is also due to the fact that German bass makers have left the lower-priced category to imports from Eastern Europe and China, who can offer this type of instruments for as little as 2,000 €. The price of a GEWA master bass in 1960 was 1,580 DM—that would be about 8,000 € according to today's purchasing power, which is what you will have to pay for a good master bass today. For comparison here are some other prices in Germany from 1960:

Dressing the fingerboard and a new bridge, plus a glued crack all for 15 Marks. A loaf of bread still cost 0.31 Reichsmark in 1935. Today's workshop visits have thus become considerably more expensive compared to the cost of living.

a newspaper copy	*10 Pfennig*
1 liter of gas fuel	*60 Pfennig*
250 grams of butter	*1.62 DM*
Volkswagen 1200 (Beetle) car	*3,790 DM*
a beer at the jazz club	*1 DM*

Even more difficult to estimate and convert are the prices found in catalogues from the 1920s as living conditions and expenses have changed so much since then. A pricelist of Wunderlich from Markneukirchen (see page 202) lists the following prices:

double bass, plain, pearwood mounted	*135 Goldmark*
double bass, round back, ebony mounted	*200 Goldmark*
double bass, A-grade woods,	
superb workmanship, best ebony	*400 to 750 Goldmark*
artist bass bow	*30 to 100 Goldmark*
Tyrolean machine head, brass	*13 Goldmark*
doube bass soft case, best canvas	*20 Goldmark*
rosin	*0.25 to 1 Goldmark*

These above prices refer to 4-string (E-A-D-G) in ¾ size. The 3-strings (in fifths tuning G-D-A), which were just as popular at that time, were five percent cheaper. It is also noticeable that only more expensive basses were equipped with ebony fingerboards—for entry-level instruments a pearwood fingerboard was standard. If you calculate in Euro instead of Goldmark and add a zero to the prices, you get amazingly close to today's prices. The price structure has changed very little in 100 years, apart from the fact that today's simple beginner's basses are made of plywood and no longer solid, as they were decades ago. An average monthly salary at the end of the 1920s was around 90 Reichsmark—so for a simple bass an average earner had to work for about two months.

Double bass assortment of the Schuster company: The basses were offered in different sizes and shapes and as four- and three-string models.
The removable neck was also available for an extra charge—safe double bass transport was an issue long before the arrival of aviation.

Not only the prices have changed, but also products and equipment. Whereas 100 years ago there was no alternative to gut strings (E/A wound, D/G plain), today there is a wide variety of string types and materials for core and wrapping available. Steel strings did not become popular until after World War II and were initially significantly more expensive than gut strings. In 1960 a set of Thomastik Spirocore cost 63.30 DM or about 30 €. But based on the average annual income of the time that would be 300 € today. Adjusted for VAT, Spirocore strings today are only half as expensive as in 1960.

61

Baßbogen-Bestandteile.

Reichsmark

Nr.		Stück
302	**Frösche**, Ebenholz, Perlmutterschieber, Neusilberbahn, schwarze Schraube . . . . Stück	8.50
305	„ „ „ Neusilberschraube . . . . „	10.—
309	„ „ „ volle Neusilberausstattung . . . . „	12.—
321	**Schrauben**, runder Ebenholzknopf . . . . Stück 1.20 Dutzend	13.80
324	„ eckiger Ebenholz- und Neusilberknopf . . . . „ 2.20 „	25.20
330	**Muttern** allein . . . . „	3.60
328	**Platten**, Elfenbein, schwarzes Holz unterlegt . . . . „	18.—
333	**Haare**, schwarz, beste Sorte . . . . 1 Bezug —.60 „	6.—
336	„ weiß . . . . 1 „ 1.30 „	15.—

Baß-Saitenhalter.

Bei Bestellung wolle man angeben, ob dieselben mit 3 oder 4 Löchern gewünscht werden.

361	Birnbaum, schwarz gebeizt, Ebenholzsattel, Perlmutterauge . . . . Stück	4.80
366	Ebenholz, gut . . . . „	8.40

Baß-Henkelsaiten.

375	Darm, rot, sehr stark . . . . 1 Länge	1.50

Baß-Mechaniken.

Geschmiedete, gute Arbeit.

Nr.		Für 3saitige Bässe.	Für 4saitige Bässe.
491	Eisen, ¼ Platten, eiserne Griffe, Hartholzwirbel . Satz	7.50	9.50
493	Messing, ¼ Platten, belegte Griffe, „ „	9.50	12.—
493½	„ „ ganze Platten, belegte Griffe, Ebenholzwirbel . . . . „	15.50	18.50
0497	„ „ ganze Platten, Messingwirbel . . . . „	13.50	17.50
494	„ „ ¼ Platten, Messingwirbel, fein . . . . . „	16.—	21.—

Beste Arbeit. Stempel „Gebrüder Schuster".

497	Ganze Platten, Messing . . . . Satz	18.—	21.—
498	„ „ Neusilber . . . . „	25.—	31.—
500	¼ Platten, Neusilber . . . . „	26.—	34.—

Nr. 494, 500.

Baß-Stege.

532	„Dresden", ohne Herz . . . . Stück	1.70
534	„Aubert", mit Herz, gut . . . . „	2.20
540	„Bausch", „ „ ausgesuchtes Holz . . . . „	3.—
542	„Gebrüder Schuster", mit Herz, bestes, ausgesuchtes Holz . . . . . . „	4.50

Baß-Dämpfer.

543	Ebenholz, gut . . . . Stück	2.40
544	„ fein, geschweifte, massive Form . . . . „	3.80

Baß-Stachel.

Nr. 551, 554.

551	Ahorn, etwa 20 cm lang . . . . Stück	1.80
554	Ebenholz, etwa 23 cm lang . . . . „	6.—
558	„ verstellbarer Eisenstachel, etwa 25 cm lang . . . . „	3.50
559	Hartholz, mit Ringzwinge innen, Flügelschraube, verstellbarer Stab . . . . „	10.—

Baß-Griffbretter.

631	Birnbaum, schwarz . . . . Stück	5.50
632	Ebenholz, „Makassar", gut . . . . „	17.—
636	„ „Madagaskar", fein . . . . „	28.—
638	„ „ sehr fein . . . . „	42.—

Baß-Sattel.

639	Ebenholz, für Griffbrett, fertig geformt . . . . Dutzend	2.40
641	„ „ Saitenhalter „ „ . . . . „	3.60

Baß-Hälse.

642	Fertig geschnitten, ohne Wirbellöcher, Buchenholz . . . . Stück	16.—
644	„ „ „ „ Ahorn . . . . „	20.—
646	„ „ „ „ geflammt . . . . „	27.—
648	„ „ „ „ „ fein . . . . „	40.—

Catalogue from C. A.
Wunderlich, Siebenbrunn
near Markneukirchen/
Germany (1926)
"The cheap is usually
the most expensive! (…)
Musical instruments remain
confidential items. They
are sometimes offered at
ridiculously low prices. But
I can assess the quality of
these goods, when these
instruments are sent to me
often still unused with the
request for setup. (…)
Every day I receive letters of
appreciation. Ask in the best
musical circles, they will
confirm that my goods are
of the best quality."

Das Billige ist meist das Teuerste!

Hiermit überreiche ich Ihnen meine Preisliste mit der Bitte, daraus zu wählen. Ich habe wieder die kleine Form gewählt, da sie recht handlich und bequem ist.

Musikinstrumente bleiben Vertrauensartikel.

Spottbillig werden sie mitunter angeboten. Um was für Ware es sich aber bei den billigen Angeboten meist handelt, das sehe ich an den Instrumenten, die mir — oftmals noch unbenutzt — mit der Bitte um Aenderung oder Umstimmung eingesandt werden.

Auch ich kann billig liefern. Ich muß mich dann in der Qualität nach dem Preise richten. Müssen Sie aus irgend welchen Gründen billige Ware kaufen, so wenden Sie sich vertrauensvoll an mich und geben Sie an, wieviel Sie ungefähr anlegen können. Ich werde Sie wohl immer zufrieden stellen können. Die in dieser Liste verzeichneten Artikel stellen Qualitätsware dar. In allen Erdteilen sind meine Waren seit Jahrzehnten eingeführt, sie erfreuen sich überall des besten Rufes. Fragen Sie in besten Musikerkreisen, man wird Ihnen bestätigen, daß meine Waren von bester Güte sind.

Nach wie vor bin ich bemüht, die Instrumente nach Möglichkeit zu vervollkommnen. Dazu aber müssen auch Sie mir helfen. Geben Sie mir Anregung, wo Verbesserungen notwendig sind. Ich lasse jede Idee nachprüfen.

Erteilen Sie mir Ihre werten Bestellungen. Ich werde sie bestens erledigen. Sollten Sie einen Artikel wünschen, der in der Liste nicht enthalten ist, so verlangen Sie bitte Sonderangebot.

In Erwartung Ihrer geschätzten Aufträge empfehle ich mich Ihnen

hochachtungsvoll
C. A. Wunderlich.

Achten Sie bitte genau auf meine Firma
C. A. Wunderlich, Siebenbrunn (Vogtl.)
Es gibt ähnlich lautende Namen.

Sendungen an mich durch „Eilboten" bestellen sind unnötig, da ich täglich mehrere Male …

Versand-Be…

Die Preise verstehen s… (4.20 Goldmark = 1 U.S.A… in Reichsmark zu erfolgen. Berliner Dollar-Mittelkurs am… maßgebend.

Aufträge werden nur u… möglichkeit angenommen.

Versand gegen Nach… sendung des Betrages. Wird… bis zu 60 Tagen gewünscht,… von Referenzen und Klarleg…

Bei Sicherstellung und… liefere ich in zahlungsfähige Pe… wenn die Hälfte oder mindes… preises sofort angezahlt und c… einanderfolgenden Monatsra… samtbetrag muß also in 3 bzw… Die gelieferte Ware bleibt mei… ständig bezahlt ist.

Messingblasinstrumente „Spezial" auf Teilzahlung.

Bei Beträgen unter Mk. 4… geschlossen. Die Monatsraten d… betragen. Wird Teilzahlung ver… zunächst über seine finanziellen … entsprechende Auskunft zu geb… vertrag zu unterschreiben, für c… Verlangen gern zusende. Auf … eingegangenen Verpflichtungen m… geachtet werden.

Erfüllungsort für Zahlung … Teile ist Siebenbrunn (Vogtl.) … ohne Rücksicht auf die Höhe des C… Adorf i. V. zuständig.

Rücksendung von Waren bed…

Verpackung zum Selbstkost… Porto, Fracht pp. ist vom Empfänger… nehme ich zu ²/₃ des be…schneten sie mit anrechnen …

Kontra-Bässe, ohne Bogen

			Ia Qualität	Ia Qualität

Die Preise verstehen sich für ³/₄ Bässe als die gangbarste Größe.

3 saitige sind 5% billiger, 5 saitige 20—25% teuerer als 4 saitige. ½ Bässe sind 5% billiger, ⁴/₄ Bässe 5% teuerer.

		4 saitig Gm.
No.		
672	Gewöhnlich, eingelegt. mit ¼ Messingplatten · 135.—
673	„ ¼ besser 160.—
675	„ wie No. 673, mit ⁴/₄ Messingplatten 170.—
676	Besser eingelegt, mit ⁴/₄ Messingplatten, Karnis, mit Birnbaum-Garnitur · 175.—
677	Besser, feine Schrauben, schön geflammtes Holz, Ebenholz-Garnitur · 200.—
	bessere Qualität, Tyroler Schrauben · 230.—
678	Gewölbt, sonst wie No. 677 · 265.—
679	„ feinstes Holz, nach Form einer Violine, Tyroler Schrauben · 300.—
680	„ feinstes Holz, Pariser Mechanik, beste Ebenholz-Garnitur · 335.—
681	allerfeinstes Holz, beste Neusilber-Mechanik, tadellose Arbeit das Stück von Gm. 400.— bis 750.—
682	

Mit Karnis kostet das Stück Gm. 10.— mehr.

Mit abschraubbarem Hals kostet jeder 5% mehr.

Auf Wunsch meiner w. Abnehmer habe ich für Dilettanten-Orchester pp. eine **billige** Sorte Bässe noch eingeführt. Ausführung genau wie vorstehend beschrieben, nur ist die Arbeit nicht so sorgfältig und der Ton nicht ganz so groß. Diese II. Qualität kostet

No.	672	673	675	676	677	678
Gm.	75.—	90.—	100.—	115.—	135.—	160.—

Schulen für alle Instrumente Preis 2.— bis 5.— Gm.

Künstler-Bässe

⁵/₈ Größe, sehr gut im Ton, da nur von bestem Tonholz auf das sorgfältigste gearbeitet. Für Baß-Virtuosen kleiner Statur, sowie für Ensemble-Musik geeignet.

Sehr leicht!	Sehr leicht!
No.	Gm.
6677 Flacher Boden · 160.—
6678 Gewölbter Boden, Ebenholz-Garnitur · 250.—
6679 Gewölbter Boden, Ebenholz-Garnitur, ff. · 325.—
6682 Gewölbter Boden, beste Arbeit, ganz vorzüglich im Ton · bis 750.—

Alte u. gespielte Streichbässe sind stets am Lager.

	Gm.				
Baß-Bogen ·	5.—	7.—	12.—	15.—	20.— 25.—
Künstler-Baßbogen, lang Gm. 30.—	50.—	75.—	100.—		
Baß-Stege · Stück	2.50	4.—	5.—	10.—	
Baß-Bogen-Bezüge, schwarz · · ·			.30	weiß 1.10	
Baß-Dämpfer, Ebenholz · · ·			2.— und 3.—		
Baß-Kolofon · · Stück .25	.40	.60	1.—		

Kontrabaß-Mechaniken, 4 saitig

No.	der Satz Gm.
727 Von Eisen, gewöhnlich · 5.—
798 Mit 4teiligen Messingplatten · 7.—
729 Mit langen Messingplatten, platt. Griffe · 9.—
730 Ganz von Messing (Tyroler) · 13.—

Baß-Ueberzüge

	Gm.
(sackartig) bestes Segeltuch · 20.—
gefüttert · 30.—
nach Form mit Ledereinfassung · 45.—
gefüttert · 60.—

Baß-Holzfutterale

schwarz lack., halb gefütt., mit angesetztem Hals " 85.—
mit besserem Beschlag " 100.—
ganz gefüttert, mit Springer oder Anleger " 150.—

sowie billigere und bessere Sorten.

Schulen für alle Instrumente 2.— bis 5.— Gm.

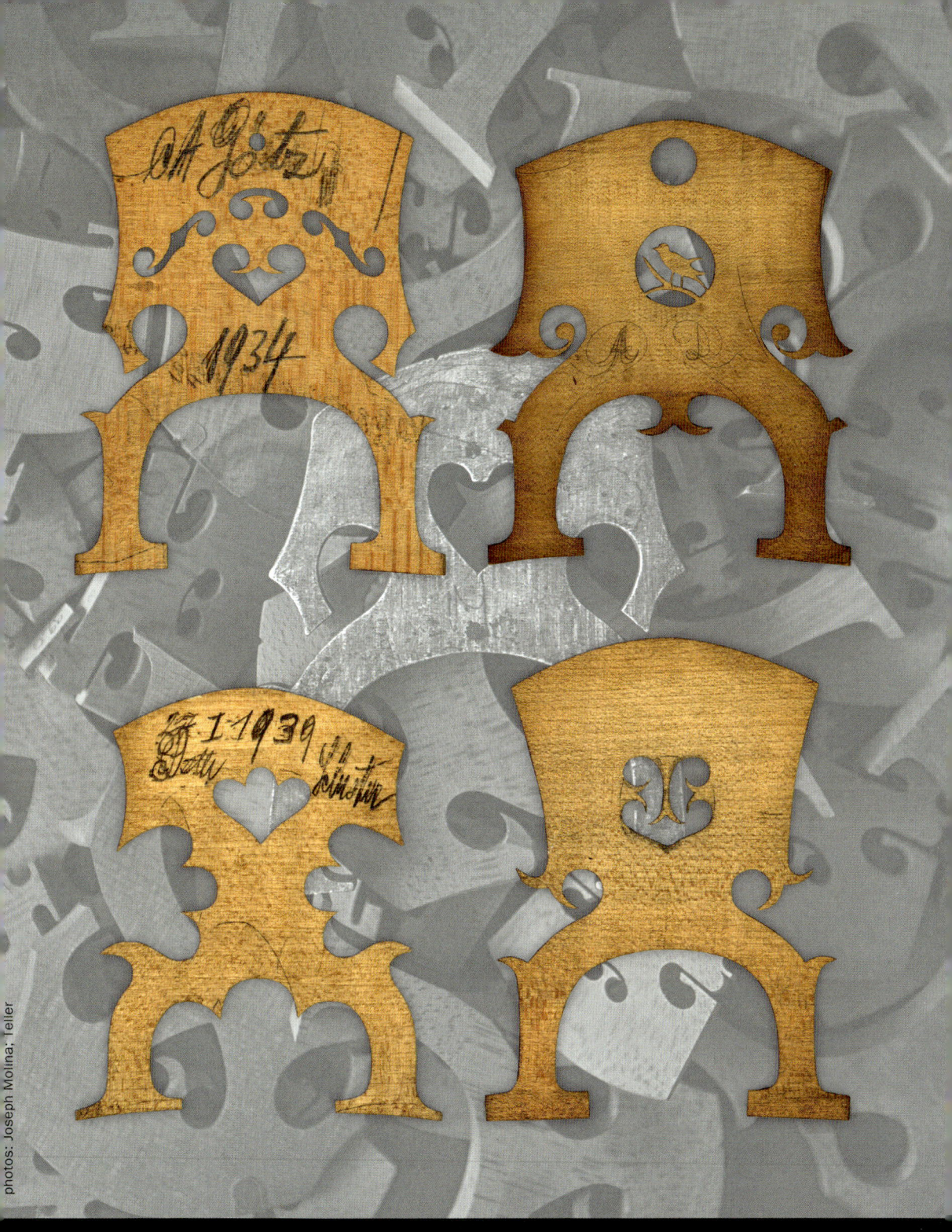

Instrument Portraits

Templates for double bass bridges (Teller company). The shapes of the templates were transferred to the bridge wood, then the holes were drilled and the shape was sawn out with a scroll saw.

Gasparo da Salò

*Gasparo da Saló
around 1570
(Museum of the
city of Salò)*

Gasparo da Salò (actually Gasparo Bertolotti; * May, 20 1540 in Salò; † April, 14 1609 in Brescia) was an Italian violin maker and bassist, who was considered the "Stradivarius of the double bass" after founding the Brescian school of violin making. Just as his Cremonese contemporary Andrea Amati is regarded as the creator of the modern violin, Gasparo da Salò is considered the forefather of the double bass as we know it today, even though the name contrabasso only became customary after his death.

Apart from double basses, most other preserved instruments of his are violas. Gasparo grew up in Salò, a town on Lake Garda, before he moved to Brescia as a young man. Compared to the Cremonese masters, the instruments from Brescia are somewhat less precisely crafted. However, Gasparo's basses and violas are considered to have an excellent sound.

The bass pictured here today is displayed at the museum of the city of Salò. Typical for Gasparo are the ƒ holes: very wide apart, with narrow ƒ keys (the top parts pointing to the upper and lower hole of the ƒ) and rather small holes. The purfling is done in a double line. The arch of the top is not very pronounced and does not show any fluting towards the edge – instead it runs out flat.

photos: Fotostudio Rapuzzi per cortesia del MU.S.A.

Gasparo da Salò

This bass by Gasparo da Salò is played today by the Swedish bassist Dan Styffe (Oslo Philharmonic Orchestra). Giovanni Bottesini described it as the best instrument he had ever played.

Its history can be traced back with amazing accuracy. The violin dealer David Laurie from Glasgow (Scotland) discovered the bass in 1868 in a monastery in Padua (Italy), for which it was originally commissioned. In 1876 it was sold to the bassist James Scott Marshall from Glasgow and remained in Scotland until after the Second World War. Then it changed hands to Canadian jazz bassist Jack Fallon, who worked in London, before it was finally purchased by the Norwegian foundation Dextra Musica.

The varnish of this bass is very dark, which might not necessarily have been Gasparo's intention; it is more likely, that this fantastic patina was caused by the centuries-long oxidization of wood and varnish. The neck and scroll pictured here are probably not original, as is common with many instruments of this age.

Gasparo da Salò

Giovanni Paolo Maggini

Giovanni Paolo Maggini (*1580 †1631) is from Botticino Sera, near the city of Brescia. He was apprenticed there by Gasparo Betolotti da Salò, before becoming independent in 1607. He is strongly influenced by da Sálo, but his later instruments also show characteristics of the Cremonese school.

His death (he died at the age of 50 of the plague) marked the end of the Brescian school of violin making, of which he is considered the most important representative.

About a dozen of Maggini's low string instruments have survived, which were originally built as viola da gambas (with 5 or 6 strings and partly fretted fingerboards) and were only later converted into cellos or double basses in the modern sense of the word.

This very well preserved instrument belonged to Alphonse-Joseph Delmas (*1891 †1958), a French double bassist and instructor. In 2010 it achieved a sales price of of $186,000 at an auction. The scroll is considered to be original and has a distinctive "tip" in the middle of the pegbox. In order to increase the scale length (playable string length), the top block was lengthened—the pictures show that this was done by adding about 5 cm to the ribs and by doubling the bottom plate.

Giovanni Paolo
Maggini, ca. 1620

Hans Christoph Zäncker

Visitors of the Museum of Musical Instruments in the German capitol Berlin will immediately notice this mighty double bass by Hans Christoph Zäncker in the exhibition area. Not much is known about Zäncker—he lived and worked in the late 17th century in "Hermsdorf unter dem Kynaste", a town in the Riesengebirge (Krkonose Mountains, today part of Poland). There is no record of the existence of any other of Zäncker's instruments today.

This double bass has been in the possession of the museum for about 100 years and is largely in its original condition. While many instruments of this period have been modernized and adapted to contemporary requirements in past centuries, this bass has remained largely untouched. Only the wooden pegs were replaced with iron gears in the 18th or 19th century, and the scroll, which seems too small in relation to the bass, is not original either.

The bass with a total length of 200 cm has a body length of 112 cm and a scale length of 111.5 cm, which corresponds to a large ¼ size. The top is made of spruce or fir, sides and back of poplar. The neck, the decorated fingerboard, nut and tailpiece are made of maple. The bass has no top block; instead, the poplar ribs were inserted into slots in the neck heel and wedged there. The poplar back also has a groove into which the ribs were inserted. No linings were used—a typical way of building for the era.

The bridge of only 13 cm hight and the two low gut strings are possibly original and therefore as old as the instrument. The two original gut strings are tightly spun and neither wound nor bleached. Their diameters of 7 mm (E string) and 4.2 mm (A string) are enormous, just like the size of the imposing neck. In general, this bass must not have been easy to play: the wide shoulders of the upper bow, but also the flat neck angle and small neck projection indicate that virtuoso playing in the upper register or thumb position was still unusual. The fingerboard is only 82 cm long, which results in the range ending at F♯.

Hans Christoph Zäncker,
17th century

Peeter Borlon

Peeter Borlon, 1647

This early double bass was built in 1647 by Peeter Borlon as "doksaalcontrabas" for the cathedral in Antwerp/Belgium. Borlon came from a respected family of musicians and was dean of the minstrels' guild in his home town. As an instrument maker, he achieved the status of supplier of the court.

Before the double bass became an orchestral instrument at the beginning of the 18th century, they were mainly used in churches to accompany Gregorian chant. This instrument, too, which was originally built as a six-string viol and only later converted to a three-string double bass, initially served clerical purposes.

The back of the bass was subsequently provided with a Latin inscription, which can be interpreted as a reference to its history:

AntVerpIæ In sanCtæ MarIæ VIrgInIs / Uno aLteroqUe æVo / JehoVæ LaUDes CantaVI

(In Antwerp, in the Cathedral of the Blessed Virgin Mary, I have sung praises to Jehovah in one life and in another.)

The CamelCaps (capitalized letters) can also be read as Roman numerals (V/U, I, C, L, D). When added together they give the year 1847, which may have been the year the instrument was converted from a six-stringed viol ("in one life") to a three-stringed double bass ("in another life").

photo: Bart Huysmans, Michel Wuyts; translation of the inscription: Christoph Schöpsdau

Johann Joseph Stadlmann

This double bass in gamba form was made between 1720 and 1729 in the workshop of Johann Joseph Stadlmann in Vienna and is now on display at the Museum of Musical Instruments in Berlin (Cat. No. 5193).

Stadlmann was one of the most important bass makers of the Viennese School. His son Johann Joseph and grandson Michael Ignaz were also respected instrument makers and bore the title court lute maker. Typical for Viennese instruments is the gamba shape and a flat back, as well as an elongated pegbox with a small scroll. Many instruments have been converted to four strings over time, but were originally designed to have five. This bass also has frets made of gut strings strung around the neck.

Other important bass makers from Vienna were: Anton Posch, Martin Stoss, Johannes Leidolff, Mathias Thir, Sebastian Dalinger, Johann Hinle.

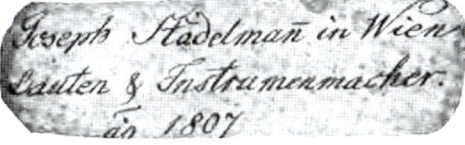

Matteo Gofriller

Although Venice's significance was already on the decline in the 18th century, it was still an important economic and cultural centre. Numerous theatres and the public opera house led to a great demand for musical instruments. Martin Kaiser (*1642 †1695) from Füssen was one of the first instrument makers to settle in Venice.

Matteo Gofriller (*1659 †1742) moved to Venice from Brixen (today South Tyrol, Italy) in 1685, where he probably learned his trade from Matthias Alban (Bozen, South Tyrol) and Martin Kaiser. In 1686 he married one of Martin Kaiser's daughters, became a Venetian citizen and started running his father-in-law's workshop in 1690. The Gofriller couple had 12 children, of which son Francesco became a violin maker, as well. Together with his contemporary Domenico Montagnana (*1686 †1750) he is considered the leading representative of the Venetian violin making school. While his contemporaries mainly built violins, Gofriller focused on low string instruments and is best known for his cellos. Even in retirement he continued to work,

but did not always stick labels in his instruments. This may have contributed to the fact that many of his later instruments were wrongly attributed to other violin makers, especially the Guarneri family, Carlo Bergonzi, and Antonio Stradivari. Among the noticeable musicians who played one of Gofriller's instruments was Pablo Casals, even though his cello was long considered the work of Carlo Bergonzi. Gofriller and his contemporaries built cello models, that were quite large and wide. Like many other instruments, Casal's cello was later scaled down to the dimensions of the slimmer and smaller Stradivarius model in order to adapt to changing requirements.

The double bass pictured here has been in the collection of the Musée de Philharmonie des Paris since 1875. Inside is a fake handwritten Amati note. The back and sides are attributed to Gofriller, while the top was reworked by Domenico Busan.

Remarkable is the tailpiece: it is much too wide and spreads the strings' afterlength dramatically.

photos: Jean-Marc Angles

Matteo Gofriller,
ca. 1700

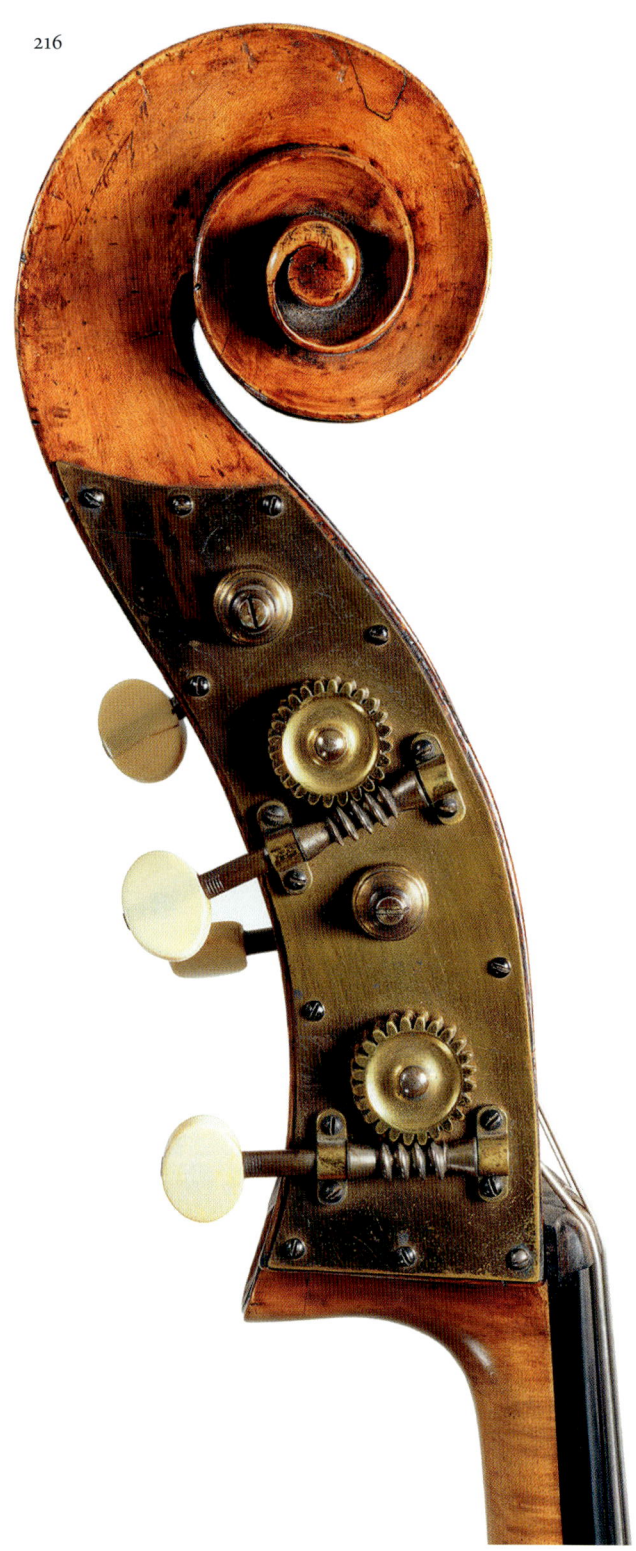

Domenico Montagnana

Domenico Montagnana (*1686 † 1750) came to Venice at the age of 15, where he was apprenticed to Matteo Sellas and Matteo Gofriller. In 1712 he opened his own workshop.

His early instruments are still strongly influenced by Jakob SStainer, while his later models were built wider and with flatter arching. Since there are hardly any expenses for the purchase of bass machines in his books, it is assumed that he built only very few basses. Today his name stands above all for excellent cellos.

This bass has a vaulted, two-piece back made of flamed maple, while the spruce top consists of four parts. The varnish is of red-brown colour on a golden ground. Although there are five bulging peg-holes in the pegbox, Towry Piper assumes in his 1911 article in *The Strad* magazine that Montagnana did not make the instrument as a five-string violone, but as a three-string bass.

In 1999 this bass was sold at an auction by Sotheby's for £ 155,000. In 2015 it was sold again and made available to the Dutch bassist Niek de Groot as a lifetime loan.

Domenico Montagnana,
1747

Domenico Busan

Domenico Busan (*ca. 1720 in Treviso; †1783 in Venice) came to Venice around 1744 and began working as a violin maker and musician. Today he is best known for his double basses, but he also made violins and cellos.

This instrument has the reddish-brown varnish typical of Domenico Busan. The back is decorated with relief-like ornaments at the upper and lower end, as can be found on instruments made by his Venetian colleagues Gofriller and Montagnana. Today, the instrument is owned by the Conservatorio di Musica in Venice.

photos: Sergio Scaramelli

Domenico Busan,
1781

Giovanni Battista Ceruti

Giovanni Battista Ceruti (*1756 †1817) was one of the most important Cremonese violin makers of his time. He was born in Sesto, a small town north of Cremona, and initially worked as a weaver. In 1785 (i.e. at the age of almost 30), he moved to Cremona and became a violin maker. Cremonese violin making was struggling at the time, suffering from growing competition from Germany and declining demand from the courts of nobility, which almost led to the disappearance of violin making from its former center. After the death of Lorenzo Storioni in 1802 Ceruti was the only remaining violin maker in Cremona.

The bass pictured here is the only surviving one attributed to Ceruti. He probably used a similar bass by Giovanni Paolo Maggini from Brescia as a model. Back, rib and neck are made of walnut, instead of maple, while the top is made of spruce (Ceruti had to add some wood on both sides in the lower bout). It was not untypical for Italian basses to be built with types of wood other than maple: walnut and poplar can be found on several instruments. The red-brown varnish is largely original. The bass has a well preserved label ("Jo: Baptista Ceruti Cremonensis, fecit Cremona 1800") and two brand stamps with the initials "GBG". In the violin making museum in Cremona there are stencils and drawings on display, which Ceruti used in the making of this bass.

The bass is currently played by Håkon Thelin (Oslo Sinfonietta).

photos: Dextra Musica, Oslo/Norwegen

Giovanni Baptisti
Ceruti, 1800

Giuseppe Baldantoni

Giuseppe Baldantoni (*1784 † 1873 in Ancona/Italy) was first trained as a mechanic in his father's workshop. At the suggestion of his violin teacher he began violin making as an autodidact around 1820. He built over 200 instruments, including numerous double basses. The study of the first book on Italian string instrument making, Antonio Bagatella's (*1755 †1829) "On the construction of violins, violas, cellos and and violons" (published in 1806) had a great influence on his work and encouraged him, to build double basses in the shape of a guitar. Typical for his double basses is also the pegbox with its round bottom. After his death in 1873 his sons continued his workshop.

The neck of this double bass can be removed for transport purposes: a concealed iron latch holds the neck base in the neck block, where it is secured by a screw through the back—due to his background as a mechanic, the construction and implementation of this design was certainly no problem for Baldantoni.

The original neck angle was adjusted to today's requirements during a restoration in 1951—the picture shows the wooden wedges inserted for this purpose.

photos: Sergio Scaramelli

Giuseppe Baldantoni, 1850

Frederick Lott Jr.,
ca 1840

English bass building reached its heyday in the first half of the 19th century and was very much in the tradition of the Italian masters.

English basses are often somewhat larger than their Italian models (110-116 cm body size), and have slightly thicker tops. Flat maple backs dominated, and elaborately and precisely worked brass machine heads, such as the ones made by William Baker, were typical, too.

Well-known bass makers of the English school are Vincenzo Panormo and his son George, John Frederick Lott, Bernhard Fendt and his son Bernard Simon Fendt, William Tarr, James Cole, Thomas Kennedy and William Calow.

Bernard Simon Fendt (*1800 †1852) was the oldest of four brothers of violin makers, whose German-born father Bernhard Fendt (*1764 †1834) worked for Thomas Dodd (*1764 †1834) from 1798— 1809.

Dodd was originally trained as a bow maker, but started making and, above all, trading in violins towards the end of the 18th century. In Bernhard Fendt and John Frederick Lott he employed two of the most important English bass makers in his workshop. Bernhard Simon Fendt learned his trade at one of Dodd's competitors, after he and his father started working at John Betts' workshop. After working for Betts' successors from 1832 on for a while, he founded the company Purdy & Fendt together with George Purdy. His violins are mainly Amati and Stradivari copies, and his basses are inspired by the work of Gasparo da Salò. In 1851 he won the first prize at an exhibition in London for an instrument quartet after Guarneri.

The bass pictured here was put up for auction in 2010—previously it had been in the possession of the Royal Artillery Band since 1858. The experts at Brompton's auction house attribute the bass to Bernard Simon Fendt. The buyer, however, a dealer from London, recognized the bass as an instrument from the workshop of John Frederick Lott Jr. It is pictured here as a five-string, with one peg used twice—a fifth mechanism was added to the inside of the pegbox.

Since the neck and scroll were the result of an earlier repair, they were rebuilt in Lott's style in the course of the restoration, reestablishing the bass to a four string instrument.

John Frederick Lott,
ca. 1820

John Frederick Lott (*1775 †1853) originally was a chair maker of German descent, who came to violin making through his friendship with Bernhard Fendt, also from Germany. His two sons George Frederick (*1800 †1868) and John Frederick L. junior (*1804 †1871) became violin makers, as well.

Lott's double basses are considered "equal to the Italian ones", and Raymond Elgar describes him in "Introduction to the Double Bass" as "the king of the English Double Bass makers".

Lott and Fendt worked together at the workshop of bow maker and dealer Thomas Dodd, building violins, cellos and basses after Italian models. During this time, the trade with Italian instruments flourished, as well: in order to avoid import taxes, the London dealers had the instruments dismantled in Italy before importing and reassembling them in their workshops, supplementing them with parts from their own production. Around 1820, when Dodd began to specialize more and more in the increasingly fashionable keyboard instruments, Lott left Dodd's workshop.

The fingerboard extension including the mechanics was installed later and is not original.

The London music dealer Hawkes had a double bass in his catalogue at the beginning of the 20th century, which was based on a model by Vincenzo Panormo and sold in fairly large numbers. British military bands in particular appreciated the model's robust characteristics.

Vincenzo Trusiano Panormo (*1734† 1813) was born in Monreale near Palermo (lat.: Panormo; hence the name addition) in Sicily. He learned his craft in Naples and then emigrated to France, where he worked in Marseille and Paris. In 1789 he moved to Dublin and two years later finally settled in London, where he became the workshop manager for John Betts. The bowmaker and violin maker John Betts (*1752 † 1823) imported instruments from Italy on a large scale and made a name for himself particularly as a connoisseur and expert. As such he played a major role in establishing Stradivari's reputation as the epicenter of violin making. In addition to Panormo, who is considered one of the best English violin makers of his time, a number of other outstanding violin makers worked in Betts workshop, including bass maker Bernhard Simon Fendt. Panormo built about 20 double basses, some of them commissioned by the double bass virtuoso Domenico Dragonetti. His most famous model, which served as a model for

Engraving on the tuning gears of a bass by Vinzenzo Panormo

Hawkes, is a large instrument with deep ribs, broad shoulders and wide upper bows. To improve playability, the back has a pronounced sloping (bend) back.

Hawkes offered the bass in three different versions: Professor, Concert and Panormo. The entry model was the Professor: it was often equipped with karnies (hoops also on the outside of the frame) and had a flat bottom, while the Concert and Panormo had a curved bottom. In 1924 the price of the three models was £ 22 for the Professor, £ 26 for the Concert and £ 36 for the Panormo. As a three-string version—which was still common at the time—the models were already available for £ 20, £ 24 and £ 32.

Hawkes commissioned his basses from various workshops, which explains, why there is only speculation as to which bass makers built the instruments. The most expensive Panormo models were built in England by a builder only known by the name of Green. Only the best wood was used for the English Panormo models, and the mechanics, varnishing and entire workmanship were of very high quality. However, the majority of the Hawkes basses were built in workshops in France (Mirecourt) and Germany (Markneukirchen)— nevertheless, they were attributed to the English school.

photos: Brompton's Auctioneers

Hawkes and Son,
London around 1920

*Jérôme Thibouville
Lamy (J.T.L)
around 1890*

French violin making flourished in the years 1800-1880, during the lifetime of Jean-Baptiste Vuillaume (*1798 †1875). Vuillaume was of outstanding importance for the violin making of his time. He studied the instruments of old Italian masters very carefully and produced copies of outstanding quality. He was born into a family of violin makers in Mirecourt, the French centre of violin making: his father and grandfather (who was trained by Stradivari), as well as his brothers were all violin makers. Vuillame was also an excellent bow maker, and Hermann Richard Pfretzschner from Markneukirchen worked at his Paris workshop at times, bringing back important impulses with him to Germany.

In addition to numerous craftsmen's workshops, there were several larger manufacturers in Mirecourt: Gand-Bernandel, Laberte-Humberte, Couesnon and Thibouville Lamy, whose instrument is pictured here.

Jérôme Thibouville Lamy (J.T.L) employed up to 1000 workers in its prime, making up to 150,000 mainly stringed instruments per year. At the beginning of the Second World War, the instrument making in Mirecourt practically came to a standstill. Many of the bombed-out workshops and factories were not rebuilt, leading to the relocation of some manufacturers to England. Jérôme Thibouville Lamy still exists as a company in London today, but is now purely a trading company without own production.

Characteristic for French basses are elegantly carved snails and *f* holes; the models typically have very playable proportions and slim shoulders. The sides and back are usually made of maple, often very nicely flamed. Also typical are very high quality brass single machine heads.

Important bass makers from Mirecourt were Jean-Baptiste Vuillaume, Auguste Bernandel, his son Gustave, Charles Nicolas Gand (Gustave Bernandel married Gand's daughter and founded the Gand-Bernandel manufactory), François Jacques Barbe, Paul Claudot, Georges Chanot, Honoré Derazey, Gabriel Xavier Jacquet, Joseph Pierre Hel.

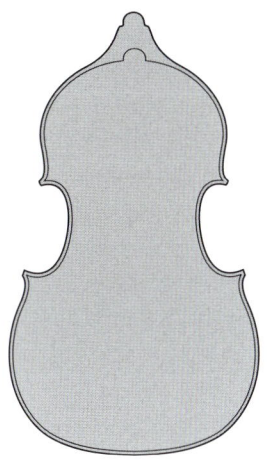

On the tops and backs of some French basses, the purfling was made in the shape of a violin for aesthetic reasons.

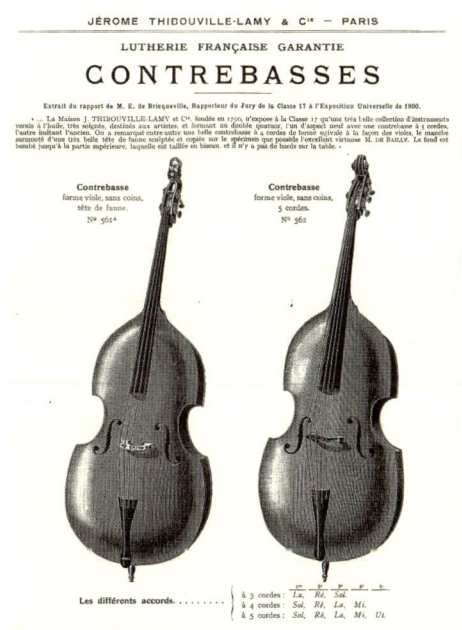

The "Karr-Koussevitzky" bass

Gary Karr in front of a portrait of Serge Koussevitzky.

Antonio (1560-1649) and Girolamo (1562-1630) learned the craft of violin making from their father Andrea Amati (1525-1611). The Amati brothers were the most respected violin makers of their time; Girolamo's son Nicolò also became a violin maker and was the teacher of Antonio Stradivari.

When the American double bassist Gary Karr made his concert debut in New York in 1962, Olga Koussevitzky was one of the guests. Serge Koussevitzky's widow was so impressed by the young virtuoso that she decided to pass on her husband's Amati double bass to him.

Gary Karr played this historic Amati bass for the more than 40 years of his career and recorded all of his albums with it. In 2004 he donated the bass to the International Society of Bassists (ISB), which he had founded. On this occasion the bass was examined in detail over two days by luthiers and double bass experts David Gage, Don Robertson, Steven Reiley and Dustin Williams. Koussevitzky had bought the bass in 1901 for $3000 from a French dealer. Nothing is known about previous owners. At that time the bass was considered to have been made in 1611 at the Cremonese workshop of Antonio and Girolamo Amati—the only known bass from this workshop to which 117 violins, violas and cellos have been attributed.

A recent examination of the bass revealed that the top, lower and middle bows are very similar in varnish and wood aging, but the back and upper bow differ. In the area of the middle bow the top has the original three-layer purfling, while above and below the middle bow a four-layer purfling was used. This change in the purfling is a clear in-

dication that the bass originally had a wider shape and was subsequently converted to its slender form. As part of this conversion the bottom as well as the top and bottom blocks were replaced. The execution of the conversion led the team of experts to conclude that it was a French work from around 1850—at that time instruments were more frequently converted in this way to adapt them to changing requirements. According to the experts, however, the bass in its original form is not an Amati from the 17th century, but was probably built in France around 1800.

To verify this thesis, the bass was subjected to a dendrochronological examination at the end of the investigation. This scientific age determinating method using the annual rings of the spruce top was carried out by Dr. Henri Grissino-Mayer at the University of Tennessee in Knoxville. He came to the conclusion that the wood, that had been used for the top, must have been felled in the Tyrolean Alps around 1775–1790, making it impossible for the bass to have been made during Amati's lifetime.

But this does not lower the instrument's idealistic value: "Whether the bass is an Amati or not is irrelevant to us," says Madeleine Crouch, managing director of the ISB. "What makes this bass so special for us is the fact, that Gary Karr played it for 40 years".

233

The neck and pegbox of the bass are recent—but these works are documented and were commissioned by Gary Karr.

Gary Karr on a CD cover with his Amati (left) and Bottesini's Testore bass (right)

photos: ISB

Bass making in Mittenwald

Germany, with its traditional instrument-making centres around the towns of Mittenwald and Markneukirchen and, after the Second World War, the region around Bubenreuth (Franconia) and Nauheim (Hesse), at times supplied 90 percent of the world market with instruments. The variety of schools, models and typical features of the individual workshops is correspondingly large.

The German post honoured Matthias Klotz with a special stamp in 1993.

This bass in busseto form was made by publisher Neuner & Hornsteiner and is based on a model by Matthias Klotz. Klotz lived from 1653 to 1743 and is considered the founder of violin making in Mittenwald. He learned the trade in Füssen and Padua (Italy), and trained numerous violin makers including his sons in Mittenwald.

The origins of the Neuner & Hornsteiner company can be traced back to the year 1750. At the end of the 19th century Neuner & Hornsteiner employed up to 180 violin makers and produced about 15,000 instruments per year, making them one of the largest manufacturers of stringed instruments in Mittenwald next to J.A. Baader & Co and Jais. They operated their own sawmill and had parts or whole instruments delivered by numerous workers.

Ludwig Neuner is considered the most important violin maker of his family. He was a cellist and learned the craft of violin making in Munich, Berlin, and from 1840, on with J.B. Vuillaume in Paris. From there he brought back copies of important master instruments by Stradivari, Guaneri and Amati, which served as models for Mittenwald violins. In 1925 the company celebrated its 175th anniversary, but it was not a happy one: many qualified violin makers had died in the war and demand and sales had collapsed in the resulting global economic crises. In 1930 Neuner & Hornsteiner ceased operations.

photos: David Gage

The bass pictured here was built in 1943 at the workshop of Alfred Meyer in Markneukirchen in the Saxon Vogtland. In 1904, Gustaf Alfred Meyer founded his workshop, which was taken over by his son Kurt Alfred in 1932. It still exists in its original location and has been run by Günther and Marco Focke since 1987.

Among the renowned builders of the so called "Musikwinkel" region is Emanuel Wilfer sen., who founded a workshop in Schönbach in 1905. His sons also became bass builders: Emanuel Wilfer jr. continued his father's workshop, while Wenzel Bruno Wilfer founded his own workshop. Many basses built in these two Wilfer workshops ended up being sold as the instruments of John Juzek, an American luthier and dealer originally from Prague. After the Second World War, the Wilfer brothers resettled with their workshops in Bubenreuth and Möhrendorf.

Emanuel Wilfer's workshop was continued by his sons Werner Josef and Rudolph Wilfer and today is under the management of Roland Wilfer.

In 1888 Hermann Alexander Pöllmann founded a music shop and workshop for double bass construction in Siebenbrunn near Markneukirchen. His son Erich Max Pöllmann joined the business in 1911, but founded his own workshop in 1920 in Jügelsburg near Adorf in the house of his father-in-law, the violin maker August Ernst Voigt. In 1940 E. M. Pöllmann returned to Markneukirchen and passed his master craftsman's examination in 1944. In 1952 his nephew Günter Krahmer began training in his workshop. After he had passed his master's certificate in 1959, he left the former GDR and moved to Mittenwald. There he founded his own workshop, which has been run for many years by his sons Michael and Ralph under the name Pöllmann.

Josef Rubner founded his workshop in Markneukirchen at the beginning of the 20th century. In the mid-1930s his son Otto Rubner joined the workshop, managing until 1960. After the Second World War he was expropriated and his workshop was affiliated to the state-owned company Musima, which from then on used the name Rubner for basses of various quality levels. Since the German reunification and the dissolution of Musima, Gewa has continued to use the name Rubner.

Gustaf Alfred and Kurt Alfred Meyer at their workshop, 1938

Alfred Meyer, 1943

The upper ribs were inserted into the side of the neck heel, since there is no neck block. The neck angle, which was too flat for today's needs, was raised with a wedge under the finger board.

Basses without a neck block are often attributed to the region of Tyrol, as well. However, there were only a few individual instrument makers there and no factories or manufactories that produced instruments in large numbers. Until the end of the 19th century, better Bohemian instruments were labeled as "Tyroean violin/bass" in the dealers' catalogues, which might be the origin of this mistake.

This instrument has characteristics that are typical for Bohemian basses, but are not immediately recognisable from the outside. The bass bar was "left standing" when the top was carved, instead of glued on later. The beech wood neck is not inserted into a neck block (top block), but is directly connected to the ribs, back and top as it is common with a Spanish concert guitar. In America these basses are therefore nicknamed "blockless wonder". The neck base is continued under the top and back and additionally secured with wooden dowels; the rib was inserted into a slot in the neck base on both sides—hence the characteristic "hump". This construction method makes it difficult to adjust the neck angle, which is too flat for today's requirements. Therefore in this case, a wedge was glued under the fingerboard in order to correct the angle.

A plywood bass from Framus with rare wedge shape: The body tapers strongly from the lower to the upper bout.

Bass making at Bubenreuth

After the war, many violin makers expelled from the Bohemian town of Schönbach worked for the newly founded company Framus. After its foundation in 1945, Framus initially started with the handcrafted production of string instruments, and was very innovative at it. In the 1950s, in addition to the electric double bass ("Triumph"), the Bubenreuth company launched a bass model with cutaway: the Framus "Jazz Bass". The shape, inspired by jazz guitars, is intended to make playing in high registers (thumb position) easier. This bass from 1954 is fully carved, while from 1955 onwards, Framus increasingly used plywood. The models with cutaway were produced until the end of the 1960s, before the double bass production was completely stopped due to the insolvency of the Framus company. Today, the name Framus is owned by the Warwick company, even though it no longer makes string instruments.

Acknowledgements

(in order of the year of publication)

Friedrich Warnecke: *Ad Infinitum – Der Kontrabaß. Seine Geschichte und seine Zukunft, Probleme und deren Lösung zur Hebung des Kontrabaßspiels,* Hamburg 1909

Willibald Leo Freiherr von Lüttgendorf: *Die Geigen- und Lautenmacher vom Mittelalter bis zur Gegenwart,* 3. Auflage, Frankfurt 1922

Hans Rödig: *Geigenbau in neuer Sicht,* Verlag Das Musikinstrument, Frankfurt 1962

Raymond Elgar: *Introduction to the Double Bass,* St. Leonards on Sea/UK, 1960; *More about the Double Bass,* 1963; *Looking at the Double Bass,* 1967

Adolf Meier: *Konzertante Musik für Kontrabass in der Wiener Klassik,* Musikverlag Emil Katzbichler, München 1969

Dizzy Gillespie/Al Fraser: *To be or not to bop,* Doubleday, New York, 1979

Alfred Planyavsky: *Geschichte des Kontrabasses,* Verlag Hans Schneider, Tutzing 1984

Hermann Moeck (Publ.): *Fünf Jahrhunderte Deutscher Instrumentenbau,* Moeck Verlag, Celle 1987

Duane Rosengard: *Contrabassi Cremonesi,* Cremona/Italy 1992

Prof. Gerhard von Reumont: *Theorie und Praxis des Vibrationsentdämpfens zur Resonanzverbesserung von Musikinstrumenten,* Siegburg 1996

Bettina Wackernagel: *Europäische Zupf- und Streichinstrumente, Hackbretter und Äolsharfen,* Katalog der Musikinstrumentensammlung des Deutschen Museums München, Verlag Erwin Bochinsky, Frankfurt am Main 1997

Greg Hopkins/Bill Moore: *Ampeg – The Story behind the Sound,* Hal Leonhard, Milwaukee/U.S.A. 1999

Paul Brun: *A New History of the Double Bass,* Paul Brun Productions, Villeneuve d'Ascq/France 2000

John Goldsby: *The Jazz Bass Book, Technique and Tradition,* Backbeat Books, San Francisco/U.S.A. 2002

Martin Kanzler: *Jazz-Lexikon,* Rowohlt Taschenbuch Verlag, Reineck bei Hamburg 2002

Chuck Traeger: *The Setup and repair of the Double Bass for optimum sound,* New York/U.S.A. 2004

Monika Lustig (Hrg.): *Geschichte, Bauweise und Spieltechnik der tiefen Streichinstrumente,* Dößel 2004

Kurt Kauert: *Vogtländisch-westböhmischer Geigenbau in fünf Jahrhunderten,* Dresden 2006

Christian Hoyer: *Framus – Built in the Heart of Bavaria. Die Geschichte eines deutschen Musikinstrumentenherstellers 1946–1977,* Edition Framus, 2007

Gregor Wiedert: *Klangverbesserung von Musikinstrumenten durch Einspielen: Fakt oder Fiktion?,* 2017

Peter Dowdall: *Technology and the Stylistic Evolution of the Jazz Bass,* Routledge, New York/U.S.A. 2017

Klaus Trumpf (Publ.): *Sperger Forum,* Mitteilungsblatt für die internationale Johann-Mathias-Sperger-Gesellschaft

Many thanks to Stefan Lob for the provided scans of pre-war instrument catalogues.

About the author

Jonas Lohse (*1970) lives and works as a double bassist, bass luthier and graphic designer near Frankfurt am Main.
He started out learning to play the guitar and the trombone as a child, before discovering jazz and the double bass as a teenager.
He runs a double bass shop, selling old and new instruments, and providing repairs and setups.

At www.kontrabassblog.de and www.double bassguide.com, he blogs about all things jazz and double bass. For questions and suggestions about this book, you can contact Jonas Lohse at mail@jonaslohse.de.

Double Bass Fingerboard Chart & Cheat Sheet

This fold-out fingering chart in A4 format offers not only an overview of the position of the notes on the double bass fingerboard but also other practical tables: a glossary of important double bass terms in the four languages English, German, French and Italian, an overview of the structure of the chords and nomenclature of the chord symbol notation, a table of tone frequencies in Hertz, and an overview of double bass measurements and sizes (⅛ to ¼).

DIN A4, 6 pages, English, ISMN 979-0-000-00221-0

Fingerboard Chart Poster

This double bass fingering chart shows the positions of the notes on the finger-board, their notation and the positions (Simandl) in 1 : 1 size. The poster also features an overview of the history of the double bass from the 16th to the 20th century.

size 42 cm × 119 cm, English; available at www.kontrabass-atelier.de